Cross-Country Flying

3rd Edition

Other Books in the TAB PRACTICAL FLYING SERIES

Cross-Country Flying

3rd Edition

R. Randall Padfield
Prior editions by Paul Garrison & Norval Kennedy

Distributed by:
Airlife Publishing Ltd.
101 Longden Road, Shrewsbury SY3 9EB, England

All of the TCA charts used in Chapter 9 are from Flight Guide Airport and Frequency Manual available in three volumes: Vol. 1-11 western states, Vol. 2-15 central states, and Vol. 3-22 eastern states. Flight Guide may be obtained from your local airport dealer or Airguide Publications, P.O. Box 1288, Long Beach, CA (213)437-3210. The charts are copyrighted.

THIRD EDITION
FIRST PRINTING

© 1991 by **TAB Books**.
Earlier editions © 1980, 1987 by TAB Books.
TAB Books is a division of McGraw-Hill, Inc.

Library of Congress Cataloging-in-Publication Data

Padfield, R. Randall.
    Cross-country flying / by R. Randall Padfield.—3rd ed.
        p.   cm.
    Rev. ed. of: Cross-country flying / by Paul Garrison. 2nd ed. 1987.
    Includes index.
    ISBN 0-8306-7640-6   ISBN 0-8306-3640-4 (pbk.)
    1. Cross-country flying.   I. Garrison, Paul. Cross-country flying.   II. Title.
TL711.L7G36   1991
629.132'52—dc20   91-9136
                                                    CIP

TAB Books offers software for sale. For information and a catalog, please contact TAB Software Department, Blue Ridge Summit, PA 17294-0850.

Acquisitions Editor: Jeff Worsinger
Book Editor: Tracey L. May
Production: Katherine G. Brown
Series Design: Jaclyn J. Boone
Cover Photograph: Douglas Robson

Contents

Preface

THERE ARE ALL KINDS OF FLYING—SPORTS FLYING, AEROBATICS, SOARING, ballooning, even hang gliding—but to most of us cross-country flying in a powered aircraft is what flying is all about.

Manufacturers of airplanes like to claim in their colorful advertising that anyone can learn to fly. They also like to say that it's comfortable, convenient, safe, and economical. To some degree all of this is true, but then to some degree it is not. True, everyone with a reasonable degree of intelligence can learn to operate an airplane, to take off at the right speed, to fly more or less straight and level, and eventually to put it back on the ground without breaking or bending anything.

But to use an airplane the way it is meant to be used (and the way it has to be used if its rather considerable investment is to be justified), is another story altogether. It involves being able to read a variety of charts, to navigate by means of pilotage or radio aids or both, to understand weather, and to correctly interpret weather reports and forecasts. It requires that the pilot be able to interpret the information provided by his engine, air-data, and navigation instruments, and to translate this information into the correct action at the right time. It may necessitate learning to fly by instruments alone and to operate efficiently within the air traffic control system. And last, but certainly not least, he must be emotionally able to deal with minor, and occasionally major, emergencies without giving in to panic.

Flying, in general, and cross-country flying, in particular, are different from any other more or less normal human pursuit. It has been described with a fair degree of validity as hours of boredom punctuated by moments of stark terror. Whatever it is that we might be doing on the ground, if the occasion demands it we can always stop doing it in order to pause and think out what to do next. Not so in the air. If an unforeseen situation develops, we can't pause to figure out what to do. We've got to keep on flying. And, while modern light aircraft are easier to fly and more forgiving than their predecessors some 30 years ago, they are also faster and in many ways more complicated, requiring that the pilot think ahead to always stay ahead of the airplane itself, the weather, and any situation that might develop.

Those of us who do fly profess to love it, though this, too, is not always the whole truth. For many it is a love-hate relationship, a challenge like no other. And to a large degree it is the challenge part that keeps drawing us to the airport and into the air. In our modern, structured lives few of us ever have an opportunity to pit ourselves alone against an adversary. Most everything we do we do in concert with others. We tend to take the credit when we succeed but just as likely are prone to want to share the blame when we do not.

Not so in the cockpit of a light aircraft. Here we are alone. Granted, we are in control of a machine that has been designed by knowledgeable engineers to perform satisfactorily under virtually all foreseeable circumstances. It has been certificated by an agency of the government to be airworthy, and it has always been maintained by licensed mechanics who put their reputations and livelihoods on the line whenever they sign their names to certify that whatever maintenance work has been done was done in accordance with carefully prepared rules and regulations. In other words, as long as we do our part and do it right, the airplane can be expected to do its part. No wonder, therefore, that the vast majority of accidents and incidents are the result of pilot errors. True, unforeseen mechanical malfunctions do happen. Radios quit working when we need them most, and engines have been known to cease functioning unexpectedly for reasons other than fuel exhaustion; but such instances are so rare these days that little concern is warranted.

With this in mind, the frequently voiced claim that flying is safer than, say, driving must be tempered with one major precondition. The pilot must be as good as his airplane. And not everyone is psychologically equipped to be a good pilot. The inveterate gambler and the excessively macho are likely to press their luck and take unwarranted chances, while the overly timid may tend to relinquish control of the airplane to the machine. The saying that there are old pilots and bold pilots but no old bold pilots is not too far from right. Flying, in general, and cross-country flying, in particular, demand constant attention to a long list of details, a clear head, and a calm disposition. But to those who have mastered the art (and flying is, in fact, an art as much as a skill), it is a delight that can be compared to little else in life.

Flying is like a powerful drug. It effectively removes us from the daily drudgery of life on the ground. It is habit forming. Once hooked, pilots will do most anything to continue to fly. They have been known to sacrifice families and careers, to invent all manner of rationalization in order to justify their avocation. And still, when asked what it is that causes this fascination, infatuation, yes, love, they often become tongue-tied, unable to put whatever it is into words. Poems have been written about holding hands with the angels, about dancing with the clouds, about the utter freedom associated with being airborne. Most of this is sheer nonsense. You don't cavort with angels or eagles or what have you, and you don't dance with clouds. And about that freedom . . . true, you are released from the constraints of earth, of highways, speed limits, and traffic lights; but at the same time you are imprisoned in an often tiny cockpit, unable to move about, get up, or stretch, and are surrounded by never-ending noise.

Still, the view from this tiny cockpit, the myriad of impressions presented in a never-ending, always-changing panorama, is at least part of that great fascination. The earth below is a checkerboard of fertile fields, replaced by arid deserts, steep cliffs, and snow-capped mountains, the distant horizon, tiny puffballs of clouds below, or immense build-ups of ever-changing shapes with brilliant sun-caused highlights and deep black shadows, rivers, lakes, towns, cities, industries, railroads, and highways. And the ability to climb to great heights at will or to swoop down low, the mastery over a hostile environment, all this and more make up that elusive elation called flight.

PAUL GARRISON

Introduction to the Second Edition

TOO OFTEN MY CROSS-COUNTRY FLYING HAS CONSISTED OF A PREFLIGHT check, crank up the engine, takeoff to cruise altitude, lean out the engine, and wait to get there. *Cross-Country Flying* has reminded me there is more to it—whether it is getting around a TCA safely or coping with international travel. If you are a seasoned pilot, student, or regular passenger, hopefully this second edition will make cross-country flying more meaningful.

Please remember it has been published purely for the enlightenment of the reader. There is a continual effort to make flying safer and more efficient for pilots and passengers. Up-to-date information from flight instructors, the FARs, pilot's operating handbooks, and other sources may alter or affect the information published.

No individual, organization or company associated with this book assumes any liability arising out of reliance upon material contained herein.

Any navigation charts or other material resembling navigation charts in this book are supplied as reference material only; they are not for navigation purposes.

NORVAL KENNEDY

Introduction to the Third Edition

REVISING ANY BOOK IS LIKE GILDING A LILY. PAUL GARRISON'S ORIGINAL version of *Cross-Country Flying* and Norval Kennedy's first revision of it covered so much ground (pardon the pun) and did it so well that I felt my main task would be to update some regulations, embellish a few topics, rephrase a couple of sentences, and correct the occasional typo.

This turned out to be more work than I had originally expected, thanks mainly to general aviation's old friend, the FAA. During the course of updating and adding text, I had to rewrite parts of my own manuscript to contend with changes in the Mode-C requirement within 30-DME of TCAs, delays with the implementation of DUAT, and even a new FAR Part 91.

More interesting, but equally fast-paced, were new developments in equipment and avionics. Loran-C equipment required additional attention; it has become more commonplace in light aircraft and even portable. Hand-held transceivers and afford-able moving maps, which were unknown for private pilots when the earlier editions were written, are covered in this one.

As it turned out I also made extensive changes to the preflight, airspace, and TCA chapters, hopefully to the reader's benefit. Most of the other chapters received minor changes and additions; a new one on overwater flying was added. Three more cross-country "war story" flights, complete with analysis and lessons learned, found a place in the book, in the belief that, although it's good to learn from our own mis-takes, it's even better to learn from the mistakes of others. A number of photographs and tables were added; a few old ones recaptioned. Appendices were added about weather briefings, airports with Mode-C exemptions, and a suggested private aircraft survival kit. Finally, I took the liberty of changing the order of the chapters, with the goal of presenting all the information, both old and new, in a more logical format.

It sounds like a cliché, but it would be impossible to acknowledge all the people who helped me with this revision. I would like to particularly thank Bob Viscio for allowing me to pick his brain about general aviation, Dan Devine for his safety insights, Bill Comee and Mike DeSalvo for information about, respectively, flying in Alaska and the San Diego TCA, and Tom Stenhouse of Good Shepherd Industrial Services for help with photocopying. I also want to thank Airguide Publications, Jeppesen Sanderson, the Tacoma Mountain Rescue Unit, and the numerous avionics manufacturers (as noted in the photo captions) for allowing the use of their material. Last, but certainly not least, I want to thank my wife, Moira, for her continuous support, encouragement, and love.

To the best of my knowledge, this book contains the most complete and up-to-date information about cross-country flying of any book on the market today. One word of caution, however: book publishing lead times being what they are, some information in this book may already be outdated by the time it reaches your hands. Please don't use any of the maps for navigation, take the information concerning specific airports or TCAs as gospel truth, or bet your life on the FARs as quoted here. If revising this book has taught me anything, it's that aviation is in a constant state of flux.

Therefore, before you zoom off into the wild blue yonder based on what you learn in *Cross-Country Flying*, check that the aeronautical information you're using is current and correct.

If you're like me, you enjoy reading about flying almost as much as you enjoy flying itself. I sincerely hope this new edition of *Cross-Country Flying* will increase your enjoyment of both.

R. RANDALL PADFIELD

1
The Many Faces of Cross-Country Flight

TECHNICALLY, THE TERM *CROSS-COUNTRY FLIGHT* IS DESCRIBED BY THE FAA as *any flight other than a local flight, which requires some form of navigation, usually involving a landing at a point other than takeoff point.* In other words, every flight that starts here and ends somewhere else is a cross-country flight.

The airplane is basically a transportation machine, and as such, its primary purpose is to conduct cross-country flights, to move persons and/or freight from one place to another in a minimum of time at a reasonable cost and with an acceptable degree of safety. The vast majority of cross-country flights can be divided into two categories: recreational and business. The basic difference between the two is that recreational flights, those conducted strictly for the fun of it or to take families or friends on vacation or holiday trips, rarely involve firm schedules. They can be conducted at leisure because it usually matters little whether the destination is reached today or tomorrow. If weather is forecast to be troublesome, plans can be changed and rearranged with relative ease. There is little reason to press on when circumstances seem to dictate otherwise.

Business travel is another story. The businessman uses his airplane in order to maximize his effectiveness within a given time period. He has firm appointments to meet, sales to make, meetings to attend. His is a life in which meeting schedules may mean profit and missing them may mean irretrievable loss. He is a businessman first and a pilot second, and often he will utilize the time en route to think out complicated deals that must be consummated at the end of the trip. When weather or other circumstances interfere with his plans he is more likely to want to go on, to even take what appear at the time to be reasonable chances in order to get to where he feels he must be, on schedule. While this might seem to make the businessman-flier a less safe pilot, he usually flies a great deal more than the recreational flier and thus can be expected to be the more experienced and proficient of the two. Furthermore, his airplane is likely to be the better equipped machine, outfitted with the kinds of instruments that permit operation under adverse weather conditions (FIG. 1-1).

While the recreational pilot has little incentive, except maybe the pride of accomplishment, to spend the rather considerable amount of money associated with obtaining an instrument rating and subsequently maintaining instrument proficiency, the businessman-pilot will think of it as a necessity. He must be able to fly when the sky is full of clouds or rain or when the visibility is down to a mile or less. He must be able to control his aircraft by instruments alone, must be conversant with the rules governing IFR flight, must be comfortable in dealing with ATC, and must be capable of executing all manner of instrument approaches, often to unfamiliar airports.

Aside from the differences in the purpose of cross-country flights and the differences in pilot experience and proficiency, there is an infinite variety in the types of

Fig. 1-1. *Adverse weather conditions demand well-equipped airplanes for today's time-conscious businessman.*

Fig. 1-2. *Flights may be conducted in the perpetual industrial haze conditions in the Northeast . . .*

flying that might be involved. Flights may be over the flat terrain of the midwestern plains or in the perpetual industrial-haze conditions of the Northeast (FIG. 1-2). The route may force the pilot to decide whether to fly across one of the Great Lakes or to detour around its periphery. It may involve crossing the huge Okefenokee swamp in southern Georgia or the three-mile-high Rockies in Colorado (FIG. 1-3). There are the deserts of southern California, Arizona, Nevada, and New Mexico, the endless evergreen forests of Oregon and Washington, treacherous winds on the lee side of the Sierra Nevada and other mountain ranges. Summer thunderstorms and winter icing are extremely dangerous flight conditions. Variants of daylight, dawn, dusk, and night with or without the helpful light from a friendly moon all require individual piloting skills.

No two cross-country flights are ever alike. Like the human face, the features of each come in an endless variety, never to be repeated in the exact order or combination. No flight, no matter how short or long, should ever be undertaken without adequate preparation and the largest possible degree of foreknowledge of what might be encountered. Weather may mean a go or no-go decision. Winds will influence the altitude at which to cruise, the time en route, and frequently the selection of a refueling stop. Short winter days may force night flying on those who would prefer to do all their traveling during daylight hours. Excessive humidity can cause carburetor icing, and above-normal turbulence can turn even a short flight into an interminable nightmare.

Fig. 1-3. . . . . *or in the three-mile-high Rockies in Colorado.*

But it is exactly this plethora of possibilities—the knowledge that even though a certain route has been flown a hundred times, it will again be different during the hundred and first—that makes cross-country flying such a pleasurable challenge. So let's plot a course and take off into the famous wild blue yonder for one more flight that promises to be different from any other.

2
Preflight

WHILE A CERTAIN AMOUNT OF CONSCIENTIOUS PREFLIGHT PREPARATION is necessary for each and every flight, it takes on far greater importance when the flight involved is a cross-country over terrain and to a destination with which we are unfamiliar.

The longer the cross-country flight, the greater the chance that something not expected will occur. Good preflighting is the best way to prepare ourselves for the unexpected. Indeed, the *Airman's Information Manual* lists "inadequate preflight preparation and/or planning" as the most frequent cause of general aviation accidents that involve the pilot in command.

THE IMPORTANCE OF PREFLIGHTING

FAR 91.103 makes the FAA's standpoint on the importance of preflight action very clear. It states in part: "Each pilot in command shall, before beginning a flight, become familiar with all available information concerning that flight. This information must include—(a) For a flight under IFR or *a flight not in the vicinity of an airport*, weather reports and forecasts, fuel requirements, alternatives available if the planned flight cannot be completed, and any known traffic delays of which the pilot in command has been advised by ATC." (Italics added.) Paragraph (b) concerns information about runway lengths at airports of intended use.

Lest there be any doubt about the weight of the regulation on page 5, litigation lawyers have successfully used it in court to prove the negligence of pilots who failed to "become familiar with all available information concerning the flight." Granted, in reality this is an impossible task, but a pilot stands on much firmer legal ground if he at least makes the attempt to obtain "all available information" than if he does nothing at all.

The thoroughness with which preflight preparation is conducted depends to a considerable degree on the amount of experience of the pilot, the type of airplane to be flown, and whether passengers unfamiliar with light-aircraft travel will be carried.

An experienced pilot flying alone to a familiar destination over a familiar route in a high-performance aircraft with long-range tanks might be justified in taking off from an airport, where the weather is adequate, after just the usual preflight check of the aircraft and run-up of the engine, and leaving the chore of planning his route of flight, his fuel stops, and even weather checks until he is in the air and level at his cruising altitude. The high-performance capability of his airplane and the resulting high speed mean that adverse winds, in terms of percentages, have less influence on his range and ground speed than would be the case in a lower-performance slower aircraft. His long-range tanks provide him with a great variety of places where he can land in order to take on fuel, and his thousands of hours of experience permit him to be fairly casual about the whole thing because he knows that he is not likely to encounter any surprises that will tax his capabilities.

On the other hand, if this pilot really is serious about getting to a particular destination (as well as fulfilling the requirements of FAR 91.103 to the letter and not just in spirit), he certainly will not be as casual about the whole thing.

There's an old adage that you can hardly ever fly over 500 miles without a change in weather. Even if an experienced pilot is very familiar with the destination and the route, a quick check of the weather and NOTAMs before taking off is about the cheapest insurance he can "buy."

Waiting to check weather or talk to a Flight Service Station specialist until at cruising altitude is unprofessional for pilots at every experience level. At the very least, a pilot may save himself time and fuel by checking the weather before zooming off into the wild blue yonder. At best, he may escape taxing his capabilities to the limit because he encountered a few weather surprises or avoid inadvertently flying into an active restricted area because he didn't know it was "hot."

When carrying inexperienced passengers, this same pilot flying the same airplane does have additional preflight duties. First of all, two to three hours are about all such passengers can take without getting edgy and nervous. Furthermore, while nonpilot passengers rarely seem to be concerned about weather, which would cause second thoughts for a pilot, they generally tend to get spooked by even light turbulence. For these reasons the pilot should plan on a fuel stop that can be reached within a reasonable period of time, and he should obtain all available weather and wind information in order to be able to plan for an altitude at which the air can be expected to be reasonably smooth.

Again this same pilot flying, say, a Cessna 150 or a Piper Cub would have to pre-plan his route and fuel stops with great care because of the limited range of such aircraft plus the fact that adverse winds can easily reduce that range by an additional 25 percent or more. Flying long distances in such an airplane frequently involves a series of detours in order to make sure that there is always an airport available when it's time to replenish the fuel.

A less experienced pilot should always spend much time with his charts before embarking on any cross-country flight. He should mark his route and identify checkpoints in a way that will make them easy to find when looking at the chart during flight. In addition, he would do well to make a list of the radio frequencies he will need for navigation and communication so they are readily available when needed. And, further, adding the direction of flight to and from the nav aid associated with a given frequency would minimize the need to fumble with those awkward Sectionals in the cramped cockpit environment.

PREFLIGHTING STEPS

Let's say we want to plan a flight from Vero Beach, Florida, to Fulton County Airport at Atlanta, Georgia (FIG. 2-1). And let's further assume that the flight is to be made VFR in a Cessna Skyhawk.

Taking it one step at a time, the preflight activity should look something like this:

Step 1. Plan and plot the route.

Rather than look at a single Sectional, it's often convenient, if the route requires several Sectional charts, to take a look at a chart that covers a larger area, such as a World Aeronautical Chart (WAC) or a National Ocean Service Flight Case Planning Chart. Using one of these we decide our best route is from Vero Beach (VRB) to Ormond Beach (OMN) to Jacksonville (JAX) to Alma (AMG) to Macon (MCN) to Fulton County Airport-Brown Field (FTY)—a total distance of approximately 430 nautical miles (FIG. 2-2). The general direction of the flight is northwest, which means the proper VFR cruising altitudes (above 3,000 feet agl) will be 4,500, 6,500, 8,500, or 10,500 feet msl. For flight planning purposes, we decide to use 10,500 feet.

Knowing that a Skyhawk cruises at about 115 knots at 10,000 feet and 65 percent power, we figure the flight should take about three hours and 45 minutes, no wind. We estimate total fuel consumption will be about 25.5 gallons using a fuel flow of 6.6 gph, a figure we obtain from the flight manual. With 50 gallons usable fuel in the airplane, we can safely plan to make the flight without an en route stop.

Now we spread the current Sectional charts for Miami, Jacksonville, and Atlanta on a large flat surface. Using a nav plotter or ruler and a marking pen, we draw a line on the route to be flown, being careful to check for restricted and prohibited areas and other airspace that might have to be avoided.

The first leg from Vero Beach to Jacksonville is nearly a straight line, right up the coast. There are plenty of VORs and NDBs to help us keep track of our position as well as two highways, I-95 and Route 1, if the coastline and nav aids aren't enough.

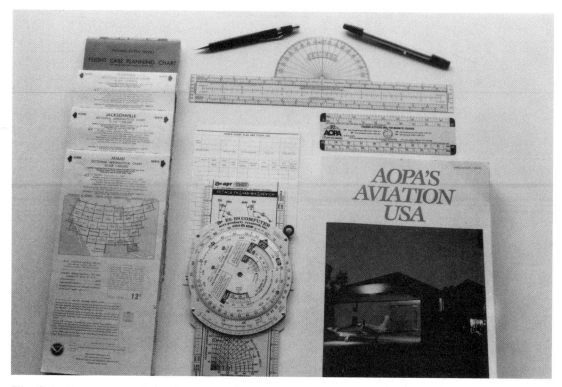

Fig. 2-1. *Cross-country flight planning tools needed for our flight from VRB to FTY. Do you know which chart we've forgotten?*

We note, too, that victor airways, V3, V3-533, and V51, are on the same track, so we'll stay alert for IFR traffic.

For ease of navigation, we decide to use Melbourne VOR (MLB), Ormond Beach VOR (OMD), and Craig VOR (CRG) for checkpoints. After takeoff from Vero Beach, we'll be sure to climb above the traffic patterns at Sabastian and Valkaria and the Airport Traffic Area (ATA) at Melbourne (FIG. 2-3). There's no requirement to talk to Melbourne Tower, but it wouldn't hurt to monitor their frequency (118.2) and tell them we're over-flying their ATA at whatever altitude we've reached by then.

Between MLB and OMN is a restricted area, R-2935 (FIG. 2-4). Checking the table at the bottom of the Jacksonville Sectional, we find out this is a Cape Canaveral restricted area that concerns altitudes from 11,000 feet msl to unlimited and is "intermittent activated by NOTAM normally 24 hours in advance." Since we plan to fly no higher than 10,500 feet, we don't have to worry about R-2935 on this flight.

As long as the weather is Visual Meteorological Conditions (VMC), we may fly over the Space Center Executive ATA (above 3,000 feet agl) and through the Control Zone without talking to anyone. But, like we did at Melbourne, we'll tune in tower frequency (118.9) and let Space Center Executive know who we are, where we are,

8

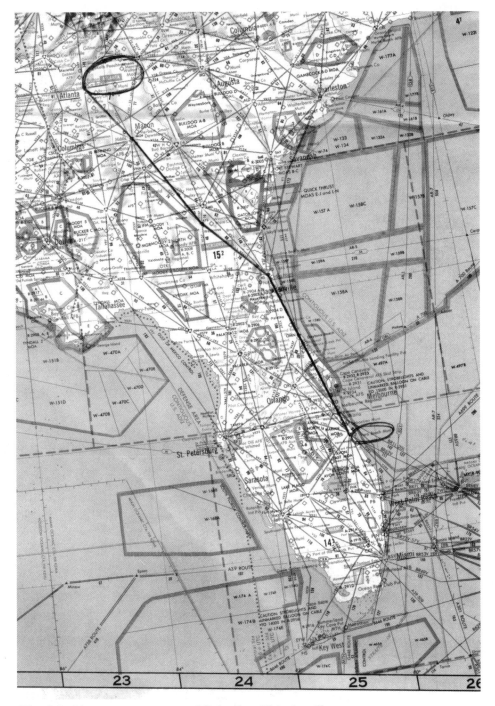

Fig. 2-2. *Plotting our route on a Flight Case Planning Chart.*

Fig. 2-3. *En route to Jacksonville we'll fly over the traffic patterns at Sabastian and Valkaria and the ATA at Melbourne.*

and where we're going. If the tower controller tells us to contact approach control on another frequency so they can identify us on radar and give us VFR traffic advisories, so much the better. It won't relieve us of the responsibility of "seeing and avoiding," but it won't hurt to have someone on the ground looking out for us, too.

About 28 nautical miles to OMN, we'll reach the Outer Area of the Daytona Beach ARSA (FIG. 2-4). Because we'll be flying well above the 4,000-foot upper limit of the ARSA, we won't be entering ARSA airspace and, therefore, contacting Daytona Beach Approach Control is not a VFR requirement. On the other hand, we know that ARSAs are established at airports that have a good deal of air traffic and that we can obtain traffic advisories within the Outer Area when two-way communications and radar contact are established with ATC. We decide to call up Daytona Beach (123.9) abeam Oak Hill and request traffic advisories.

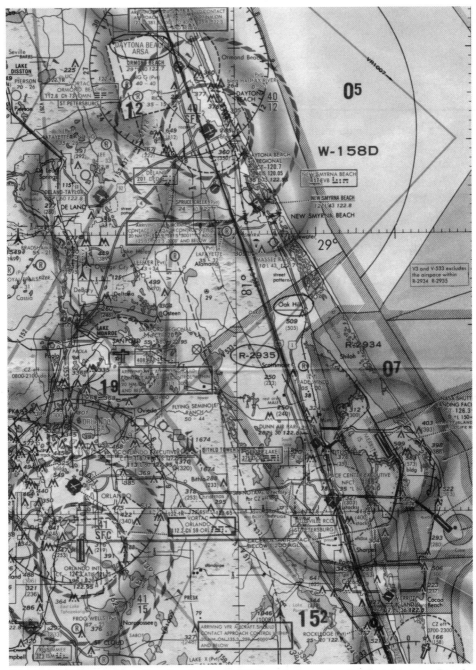

Fig. 2-4. *We'll fly below Restricted Area R-2935 and above the ARSA at Daytona Beach, but we'll contact Daytona Beach Approach Control abeam Vero Beach to get traffic advisories.*

From OMN to CRG there are no other airspace concerns to worry us, but shortly after CRG we'll come to the Jacksonville ARSA (FIG. 2-5). Like at Daytona Beach, we'll want to be well above the ARSA ceiling, but with 10 airports within about 10 miles of our route of flight through the Jacksonville area, we suspect we'll see a lot of other traffic. About 20 nautical miles from Jacksonville (10 DME from CRG), we'll contact Jacksonville Approach on 118.0 for traffic advisories.

At CRG we'll head inland and begin to pay closer attention to landmarks along the route. We'll still have a number of VORs and NDBs we can tune in and track, but it's always a good idea to maintain an awareness of our position with respect to topographical features, too.

The railroad and highway intersection at Folkston looks like an easily identifiable checkpoint and so does the town of Waycross (which also has an NDB at an airport) (FIG. 2-6). Alma has a VOR, and if we track about 320° from AMG, we'll cross the Ocmulgee River after 24 nautical miles.

Further on we'll pass near a sawmill by the town of Milan, which is also abeam the NDB at McRae, fly past Eastman (and its NDB), pick up Route 23, and soon come to the town of Cochran (FIG. 2-7). Here, we note, is the outermost ring of the Macon Terminal Radar Service Area (TRSA); 10,500 feet will keep us only 500 feet above the upper limit of this TRSA. It would be legal to maintain this altitude and not talk to Macon Approach Control, but it wouldn't be particularly safe because fast-movers could be climbing or descending through the ceiling.

Even if we were below 10,000 feet and inside TRSA airspace, we wouldn't be required to contact Macon Approach Control. (The *Airman's Information Manual* urges us to participate in the terminal radar programs for VFR aircraft, but pilot participation is not mandatory.) However, we know TRSAs, like ARSAs and TCAs, are established, not to harass pilots, but because there is much traffic around busy airports. The radar service is for our benefit, so we'll contact Macon Approach Control on frequency 119.9 (which we find on the frequency table on the Atlanta Sectional chart).

More likely than not, Macon Approach will give us vectors to Forsyth if we ask. If not, we can follow the highway and powerline out of Macon.

Approaching the Atlanta Terminal Control Area (TCA), we can choose one of two ways to fly to Fulton County-Brown Field (FTY). First, we could contact Atlanta Approach Control on 119.8 and request a clearance into the TCA and vectors to Fulton County field. Alternately, we could elect to stay below the floors of the TCA and navigate around the center portion of the TCA, which goes all the way to the ground.

To stay below the TCA, we'll have to descend below 10,000 feet msl before 35 nautical miles from the Atlanta VOR (ATL) and then below 8,000 feet msl before 29 nautical miles (FIG. 2-8). Griffin is a designated Visual Check Point, so it would be smart to use it, then fly west to Newnan, another Visual Check Point, being careful to descend below 5,000 feet msl before crossing the 218° radial from ATL. Between Griffin and Newnan we note a profusion of private and public uncontrolled airports,

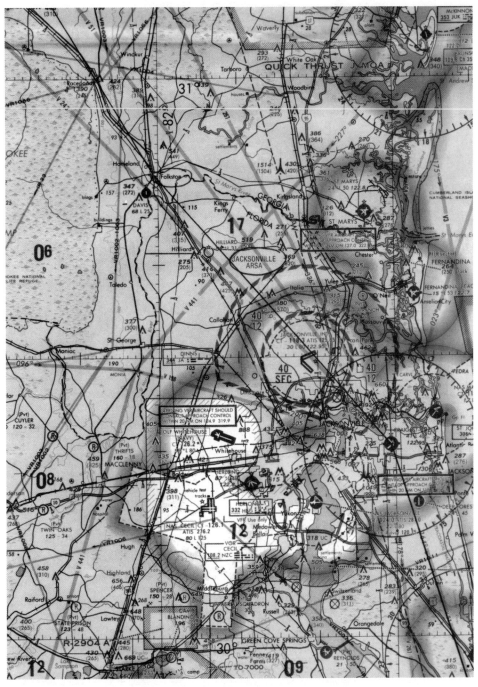

Fig. 2-5. *We'll fly over the Jacksonville ARSA, too, but with so many airports in the area it will be wise to contact Jacksonville Approach for advisories.*

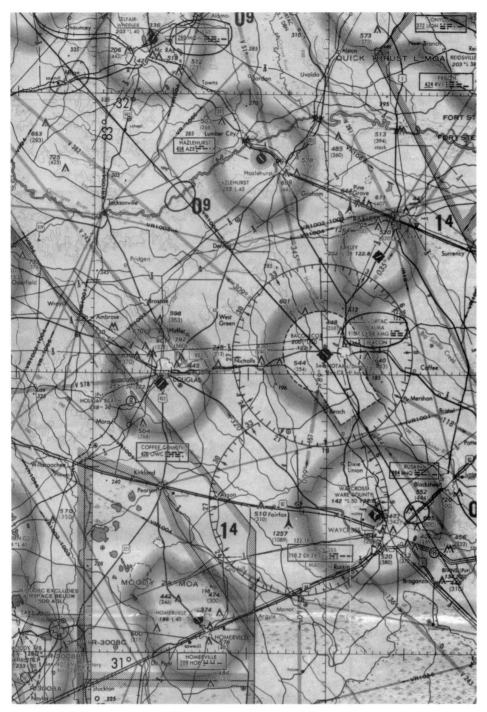

Fig. 2-6. *Waycross, Alma, and the Ocmulgee River look like good checkpoints.*

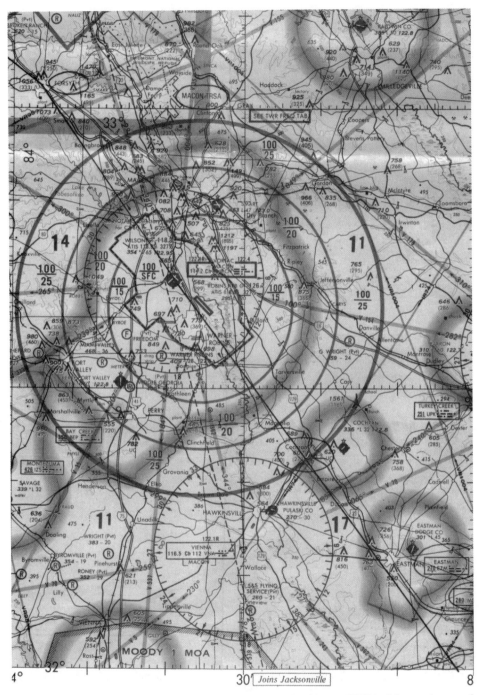

Fig. 2-7. *Soon after passing Eastman we'll reach the Macon TRSA. Macon Approach Control will provide us with radar service and vectors to Forsyth, if they're not too busy.*

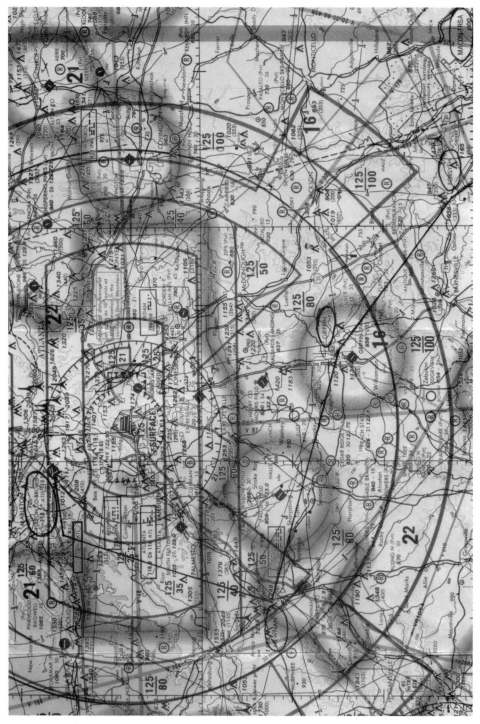

Fig. 2-8. *A route under the floors of the Atlanta TCA will require careful navigation and pre-planned descents.*

so we make a mental note to be extra alert for other traffic. From Newnan, we could fly direct to the FT locator outer marker (344) on a northeast heading, descending below 4,000 feet msl then 3,500 feet msl as required by the TCA sectors.

This route below the TCA floors may seem somewhat roundabout, but probably wouldn't be much longer than the vectors we'd get from Atlanta Approach Control. It could even be the shorter of the two routes, if Atlanta Approach has to vector us around a lot of IFR traffic going into Hartsfield-Atlanta International.

Of course, flying under the floors of a TCA will take us out of the radar service environment. Unless we're very low, the TCA controller will still be able to track us on his radar; if he isn't very busy, he may be willing to provide us with traffic advisories if we request them. But if he is busy, he probably won't want to talk to us and will tell us to remain outside the TCA and squawk VFR. Then we're on our own until we reach Fulton County-Brown Field.

Before reaching the airport, we'll be sure to listen to the ATIS on 119.0. This will tell us the weather and active runway. If we're being vectored to the airport by Atlanta Approach, we can expect to be released from the TCA in time to contact Fulton County Tower (118.5) before entering the Airport Traffic Area. If we're navigating to the airport on our own, we can use FT and the 245° radial/12 DME from Peachtree (PDK) VOR for additional guidance.

There's one last bit of information we need, which unfortunately we can't get from a chart: the Traffic Pattern Altitude (TPA) at the airport. We have to look this up in an airport directory, which is all right because we need the telephone number of an FBO at the airport anyway for Step 4. *AOPA's Aviation USA* tells us the TPA at Fulton County-Brown Field is 1,640 feet msl for light aircraft.

Step 2. Fill out a navigation or flight planning log.

We now take a piece of paper, or even more useful, a flight planning log, and write down the information as illustrated in FIGS. 2-9 and 2-10.

If the total of those mileages adds up to somewhat more than the original estimate of 430 nm, it is because of some minor detours necessary in order to make good the selected checkpoints. The purpose of making a note of all the distances between each of the checkpoints is to make it simple to figure out the actual ground speed for each leg; and with all this information written down, we minimize the need for fooling around with the charts during the actual flight.

It's also useful to write down the various frequencies we'll need during the flight. ATIS frequencies for airports we plan to overfly will make it easy to obtain the latest weather, including the local altimeter setting which is important so we can maintain the proper altitude.

There are numerous flight planning forms available, in addition to the ones illustrated, which present more or less the same information in different formats. Find one you like and buy it in bulk. Or devise your own and make copies of it. In a pinch, you can use a blank sheet of paper (lined is preferable when you're trying to read something quickly in the cockpit), but after using flight logs for awhile, you'll find printed flight logs much handier.

JEPPESEN NAVIGATION LOG

Aircraft Number:	N12345	Dep: VRB	Dest: FTY	Date:

Clearance:

VERO BEACH TWR 126.1 / ATIS 132.5 / FSS 122.5

MELBOURNE TWR 118.2 / ATIS 132.55

SPACE CENTER EXECUTIVE TWR 118.9

DAYTONA BEACH APPROACH 123.9 / ATIS 120.05

JACKSONVILLE APPROACH 118.0 / ATIS 125.85

Check Points (Fixes)	Ident / Freq.	Course (Route)	Altitude	Mag. Crs.	FUEL Leg / Rem.	Dist. Leg / Rem.	GS Est. / Act.	Time Off	
								ETE	ETA
								ATE	ATA
VERO BEACH	VRB 117.3					458			
MELBOURNE	MLB 110.0	V3		342	29 / 429	90	19		
ORMOND BEACH	OMN 112.6	V3- 533		341	76 / 353		51		
CRAIG	CRG 114.5	V51		342	66 / 287		44		
FOLKSTON		→D→		318	39 / 248		26		
CROSS RT 82 ABEAM WAYCROSS				329	30 / 218		20		
ALMA	AMG 115.1				20 / 198		13		
OCMULGEE RIVER				318	24 / 174		16		
ABEAM MC CRAE AT R.R.	MQW 280				17 / 157		12		

FUEL	Climb		Cruise		Apch.		Alt.		Res.	
	Cruise Burn/Hr		Block In		Block Out		Log Time			

AM436237D

Fig. 2-9. The second preflight step . . .

JEPPESEN NAVIGATION LOG

Aircraft Number: N12345	Dep: VRB	Dest: FTY	Date:

Clearance:

WAYCROSS CTAF 122.8

MACON APPROACH 119.6 / 118.95

ATLANTA APPROACH 119.8

FULTON COUNTY TWR 118.5/ATIS 119.0

" " FSS 122.6

Check Points (Fixes)	Ident / Freq.	Course (Route)	Altitude	Mag. Crs.	FUEL Leg / Rem.	Dist Leg / Rem.	GS Est. / Act.	Time Off	
								ETE	ETA
								ATE	ATA
ABEAM McCRAE	MQW 280					157			
ABEAM EASTMAN	EZM 270	▭→		323	12 / 145		90	8	
COCHRAN					15 / 130			10	
MACON	MCN 114.2				24 / 106			16	
FORSYTH				325	25 / 81			17	
GRIFFIN				308	21 / 60			14	
NEWNAN	CCO 210			286	28 / 32			19	
FULTON	FT 344			016	25 / 7			17	
FULTON COUNTY-BROWN	PDK 116.6	245R		081	7 / 0			5	

FUEL	Climb		Cruise		Apch.		Alt.		Res.	
	Cruise Burn/Hr		Block In		Block Out		Log Time			

AM436237D

Jeppesen Sanderson, Inc.

Fig. 2-10. . . . . *complete a navigation log.*

Fig. 2-11. *The third preflight step: Checking the weather by calling a Flight Service Station or one of the automated weather briefing services.*

Step 3. Check the weather (FIG. 2-11).

There are several ways to obtain weather information, but most experienced pilots usually do this in three steps.

The first step is to develop an awareness of the "big picture." A.M. Weather on public television stations, newspaper weather maps, and TV and radio weather reports are all good sources for preliminary flight planning. The evening before a flight is a good time to take a look at the weather and get oneself mentally prepared for the next day. This comes naturally to professional pilots because weather is such an intimate part of their jobs.

Sometimes, we might have to cancel or delay a flight based solely on this "big picture" information.

After we get the "big picture," we can obtain a more detailed analysis of the weather in a number of ways, many of them without even consulting a meteorologist or Flight Service Station weather briefer. We do this by calling an automated weather information service, such as 1-800-WX-BRIEF or the Interim Voice Response System (IVRS), by using the Direct User Access Terminal (DUAT) system with a personal computer, or by using one of the commercial computerized weather services, often available at FBOs. (For more information about how to use WX-BRIEF, IVRS, and DUAT see Appendix A.)

Whichever method we use to obtain a detailed weather briefing, our goal should be to find out the following information:

1. Adverse conditions—any significant meteorological and aeronautical information that might influence our proposed route of flight or even cancel the flight entirely.
2. Synopsis—a brief explanation of the general weather (fronts or pressure systems) that might affect the flight. (Not available from IVRS.)
3. Current conditions—a summary of the current weather at the departure point, destination, and points in between. Sequence Weather Reports (SAs) and current Pilot Reports (PIREPs) are the most common sources of current conditions.
4. En route forecast—a summary of forecast conditions along the route. By selecting airports along the proposed route that provide Terminal Forecasts (FTs), WX-BRIEF and IVRS users can obtain this information from automated briefings.
5. Destination forecast—the forecasted weather, including any significant changes, for the destination at the planned time of arrival, plus and minus one hour. Terminal Forecasts provide this information.
6. Winds aloft—forecast and observed winds and temperatures at desired altitudes along the route. Use the standard temperature lapse rate (2 °C per 1,000 feet) to help determine the freezing level, but be aware that temperature inversions are common in many parts of the country.
7. Notice to Airmen (NOTAMs)—relevant NOTAMs to the proposed route of flight. (Not available from IVRS.)

With the above information, we can usually make our "go-no-go" decision.

If the weather still seems "iffy," we take the third step and contact an FSS weather briefer in person or by telephone. Even the most sophisticated automated systems can't be compared to a human briefer. Often the briefer will be able to provide more timely and in-depth information than is available from the automated systems and will usually give a quite insightful analysis of the current weather situation, too.

Generally speaking, the longer our flight or the more changeable the weather, the more we'll need to talk to a briefer.

In the case of our example, the forecast calls for VFR conditions along our proposed route of flight, the only adverse feature being the forecast upper winds, which are reported to fluctuate between 15 and 30 knots and 290 to 340 degrees. Thus, assuming an average headwind component of some 25 knots, we find that our ground speed is likely to be reduced to 90 knots, increasing the ETE to just over five hours which, in turn, means that we'll be using about 35 gallons rather than the 25.5 originally estimated. Still, with 50 gallons available, this doesn't present a major problem.

The fact is that the headwind component would have to increase to an unlikely 40 knots before we would have to worry about reaching our destination with the available fuel.

Step 4. Call the destination airport.

Many pilots eliminate this step, or don't even think about it, but it can save a lot of trouble. NOTAMs are not always current or even available to the briefer we might have consulted, and there are often some hazards that never make it into "official" NOTAMs but could affect the flight. A quick conversation with the local FBO might yield something like, "Oh yeah, watch out for the crane workin' over at the Holiday Inn on downwind to one-four, 'specially if y'all come in from the west." One never knows.

A telephone call is also a good way to confirm the information about the field that you find in *The Airport Facility Directory*, Jeppesen, *Flight Guide, AOPA's Aviation USA,* or other publications. All try to stay as up-to-date as possible, but publication lead-times are long and even errata pages may be out-of-date.

We call to check that the field will be open when we arrive, that fuel will be available, that the runway lights will be working if we'll be landing after dark, and that the FBO will be open if we require any services. Uncontrolled airfields that are bustling with activity during the day often become dark and foreboding (and a long way from civilization) at night.

We make a quick call to one of the FBOs at Fulton County-Brown Field. There's nothing out of the ordinary happening, and their hours haven't changed since they were published in our airport directory.

It's a go.

Step 5. File a VFR flight plan (FIG. 2-12).

As explained in Appendix A, a VFR flight plan can be filed by calling the universal toll-free number for Flight Service Stations, 1-800-WX-BRIEF, and punching in "#*401" or "#*402" for Fast File. "401" is for filing both VFR and IFR flight plans when the expected departure time is within one hour and for closing flight plans; "402" is for filing flight plans when the expected departure time is greater than one hour from the time of filing.

Many pilots regard VFR flight plans as an unnecessary infringement on their freedom. This is utter nonsense. When we file a VFR flight plan, we still choose where we want to go, and if we change our mind, it's a simple matter to revise the flight plan in the air. Flight Service Stations are only too happy to help us with our flight plan and provide flight following; after all, that's their job.

Like checking the weather before departing, filing a flight plan is an inexpensive insurance policy. If we are ever forced down short of our destination, it will be extremely comforting to know that someone will soon be looking for us, especially if we don't manage to get out a "MAYDAY" call.

Step 6. Preflight the airplane.

While preflighting the airplane, we'll include a visual check of the fuel tanks to ensure they're topped off and that the fuel caps are secure. We'll also check the engine

Form Approved: OMB No. 2120-0026

U.S. DEPARTMENT OF TRANSPORTATION FEDERAL AVIATION ADMINISTRATION **FLIGHT PLAN**	(FAA USE ONLY) □ PILOT BRIEFING □ VNR □ STOPOVER			TIME STARTED	SPECIALIST INITIALS

1. TYPE	2. AIRCRAFT IDENTIFICATION	3. AIRCRAFT TYPE/ SPECIAL EQUIPMENT	4. TRUE AIRSPEED	5. DEPARTURE POINT	6. DEPARTURE TIME		7. CRUISING ALTITUDE
VFR IFR DVFR			KTS		PROPOSED (Z)	ACTUAL (Z)	

8. ROUTE OF FLIGHT

9. DESTINATION (Name of airport and city)	10. EST. TIME ENROUTE		11. REMARKS
	HOURS	MINUTES	

12. FUEL ON BOARD		13. ALTERNATE AIRPORT(S)	14. PILOT'S NAME, ADDRESS & TELEPHONE NUMBER & AIRCRAFT HOME BASE	15. NUMBER ABOARD
HOURS	MINUTES			
			17. DESTINATION CONTACT/TELEPHONE (OPTIONAL)	

16. COLOR OF AIRCRAFT	CIVIL AIRCRAFT PILOTS. FAR Part 91 requires you file an IFR flight plan to operate under instrument flight rules in controlled airspace. Failure to file could result in a civil penalty not to exceed $1,000 for each violation (Section 901 of the Federal Aviation Act of 1958, as amended). Filing of a VFR flight plan is recommended as a good operating practice. See also Part 99 for requirements concerning DVFR flight plans.

FAA Form 7233-1 (8-82)   CLOSE VFR FLIGHT PLAN WITH_____ FSS ON ARRIVAL

Fig. 2-12. VFR flight plan for our sample flight. Only blocks 2, 3, 9, and 10 will be transmitted to the destination FSS. For a complete explanation of flight plan items see AIM, para. 295.

oil quantity and add a quart or two as necessary. Remember that most aircraft engines burn oil at a greater rate than automotive engines, so we'll probably have to add oil after a long cross-country flight.

Step 7. Start the engine, check the radios, run-up, and take off.

Shortly after takeoff, we'll radio Vero Beach Flight Service Station on 122.5 and activate our VFR flight plan by giving them our departure time.

To close our flight plan, we'll notify Fulton County-Brown Field FSS either by radio on 122.6 or by telephone (1-800-WX-BRIEF, then #*401).

BE PREPARED

During the early portions of their flying careers, most pilots religiously perform all of these steps. Then, as the total of hours in the logbook builds up into the hundreds, and eventually the thousands, they tend to become somewhat more casual about their preflight preparations. Some experienced private pilots see nothing wrong with this because they feel that the more they fly, the less likely they are to be confronted by situations that cannot be handled easily based on past performance. On the other hand, professional pilots take a different point of view and tend to take things much less casually.

Most professional pilots would rather avoid situations that require them to use their skills to the limit, and they do this by stacking the cards in their favor as much as possible: double-checking the weather, adding extra fuel, using checklists.

As the old saying goes, "A superior pilot is one who uses his superior judgment to avoid having to use his superior skill."

Remember: The longer the cross-country flight, the greater the chance that something unexpected will occur. The better prepared we are before takeoff, the easier it is to complete each flight safely.

3
Flight Number One

Date: March 3, 1961.
Pilot: Male, age 35, photographer.
License: Private, SEL.
Pilot-In-Command Time: 48.5 hours.
Aircraft: Piper Tripacer.
Flight: From Santa Monica, California, to Seattle, Washington, and back.
Purpose of Flight: Visiting relatives and friends in Seattle and Portland.

This was going to be the pilot's first major cross-country flight. His only previous experience in cross-country flying amounted to one flight from Santa Monica to King City, California, and back, and another from Santa Monica to Apple Valley and back, both made as a student as part of his flight instruction, and one flight to San Diego and back after obtaining his license. All other flight time was either dual instruction or local solo. In those days flight instruction did not include any time under the hood, and this pilot was never called upon to fly an aircraft by reference to instruments alone.

The aircraft was equipped with a Narco Superhomer, a basic panel including a directional gyro driven by a venturi tube, but no artificial horizon.

During the days preceding the flight, the pilot had carefully studied the appropriate Sectional charts and, estimating his TAS at about 110 mph (it was only much later that he would start to think and figure in knots), he planned to head northwest from

Santa Monica to Santa Barbara and from there on past San Luis Obisbo and Paso Robles to Salinas, which was to be the first fueling stop. The distance to Salinas was 282 sm, calling for a little over two and a half hours of flight, or 2:34 to be exact. The next leg was to be from Salinas to Ukiah because he had decided to fly along the coast rather than to tackle the mountain ranges between Redding, California, and Eugene, Oregon, which looked rather forbidding on his charts. That distance was only 197 sm but the next logical stop would have been Eureka, 123 sm north of Ukiah, which would have left him with an uncomfortably skimpy fuel reserve.

He planned to spend the night in Ukiah and the next day to continue on via Eureka and Crescent City to North Bend, Oregon, a distance of 312 sm. He would refuel in North Bend and go on from there via Newport and Newberg to Portland, another 190 sm, where he would spend a day with friends and continue the following day up to Seattle, the final 117 sm. It all looked rather simple, and he was looking forward to it.

On the day of his planned departure he got up just before dawn and called Los Angeles Flight Service to check the weather and file a VFR flight plan. The weather in the Los Angeles Basin was the usual, low clouds and fog expected to burn off by midmorning. Farther north a frontal passage was expected by early afternoon, but ceilings and visibilities were forecast to remain comfortably above VFR minimums. He filed his flight plan to Salinas, giving his ETA as 2:45 and, though he knew that it was doubtful that Santa Monica Airport would be VFR for at least another hour or two, he left his home immediately after an early breakfast.

By the time he got to the airport he didn't have to look at the rotating airport beacon to know that it was still IFR. The fog lay heavy and damp over the entire airport, and from one end of the runway it was impossible to see the other. He parked his car, stowed his luggage in the airplane, untied it, and took his time in doing a very thorough preflight check. He then went to the coffee shop to have another cup of coffee and wait for the fog to lift.

By 9:45 the rotating beacon quit rotating, meaning that the visibility had improved to at least three miles, so he fired up the engine and taxied to the west end of Runway 21. (See note on page 35.)

"Santa Monica Tower, Tripacer Three-Two-Zero-Three Zulu ready for takeoff."

"Tripacer Zero-Three Zulu, cleared for takeoff."

He taxied onto the runway, fed in full power, and lifted off.

"Santa Monica Tower, Zero-Three Zulu requesting straight out departure."

"Straight out departure approved."

He continued his climb out toward the ocean and, once over the beach, changed course toward the north and Santa Barbara. He called Flight Service, asked that his flight plan be activated, and then concentrated on his navigation.

It must be remembered that there is little resemblance between the Superhomer in that Tripacer and today's average navcom. In order to receive either com or nav signals one had to crank a coffee-grinder-type handle to tune to the appropriate frequency, and the number of available transmission channels depended on the number of crystals installed in the unit. This one was equipped with 122.5, a frequency that in

Fig. 3-1. *Following the coastline on the way northwest to Santa Barbara.*

those days was guarded by virtually all control towers: 121.7 and 121.9 to be able to communicate with ground control; 122.1 for flight service stations; 122.8 for uni-coms; and, of course, 121.5, the emergency frequency. In addition, reception tended to be quite static laden and difficult, and reception distance was extremely limited by modern standards.

Making sure that he stayed over land in order to avoid accidentally straying into the restricted area at Point Mugu, he headed along the coast toward Santa Barbara (FIG. 3-1) and there changed course to a more northerly heading for San Luis Obisbo and Paso Robles. So far everything was working just fine, though each leg took a little longer than he had expected, indicating that there was probably a 10- to 15-knot headwind.

SUDDEN CLOUDS

Once past Paso Robles the first signs of deterioration began to appear. Heavy clouds were starting to show up everywhere ahead of him and to the right and left (FIG. 3-2), and for some reason he seemed unable to get a clear signal from Salinas. He was still in Visual Meteorological Conditions (VMC) and able to recognize the airport at King City below, which had been the destination of his first solo cross-country as a student. He followed the highway which, according to the chart, should lead him straight to his destination. But suddenly there were clouds below, obscuring the highway and most of the

27

Fig. 3-2. *Innocent-looking summer clouds may be the forerunners of a front.*

ground ahead. But the clouds were broken and seemed easy to circumvent, so he deviated from his course, climbed to stay above some of the lower scud, and flew on.

Exactly how he got himself into the fix in which he finally found himself, he doesn't remember. What he does remember is that eventually he found himself surrounded by clouds with no way out except to fly through some of them (FIG. 3-3). A quick look through a small hole below showed him that he was now over water rather than land, and he decided that he had better find a way to drop down to below the clouds in order to find an airport at which to land. At this point he had to admit to himself that he didn't have the faintest notion where he was, but he somehow convinced himself that if he could only get down below the clouds, he'd be able to locate the coastline and from there find one of the many airports in that area.

He had, of course, heard stories of how difficult it is to control an airplane without visual reference to the horizon, especially one not equipped with a gyro horizon. But he decided that if he kept the needle just one needle-width off center and his rate of descent at a steady 500 fpm down, he should be able to safely circle down. Though the palms of his hands were wet with perspiration, he was proud of the fact that he thought himself quite calm. He throttled back, pulled out the carburetor heat as a

Fig. 3-3. *A fast-moving cold front tends to envelop the airplane.*

precaution, and then banked to the left, keeping his eyes glued to the needle, the airspeed indicator, and the VSI. Considering the turbulence and his lack of experience it was doubtlessly a pretty sloppy spiral, but he did manage to ignore the gray mess racing by the windows and to keep the needle glued to a more or less standard-rate turn. Though it seemed like ages, it took, in fact, barely a minute until he could see the water below and the coastline not far away.

He turned toward the coastline, leveled off, and was about to follow it toward the north when out of the corner of his eye he saw a runway just a few miles inland. Hallelujah! He saw no tower, so he simply landed and for the first time in his flying career (though not the last), walked into the FBO and asked "Where am I?"

"Watsonville."

"Oh."

Having no idea where Watsonville was, he went to the wall chart and was somewhat startled to learn that he was a good 20-odd minutes north of Salinas. But at least he was safely on the ground.

STALLED FRONT

He asked to have the airplane refueled, ate a sandwich and drank a cup of coffee (both from automats), and called Flight Service to close his flight plan and ask about the weather toward San Francisco and beyond. The information he received was not what he'd been looking for. The front, instead of moving through, had stalled south of San Francisco with low visibilities and all mountaintops between Watsonville and San Francisco obscured by clouds. In other words, he was stuck.

Again, for the first time in his flying career (and again, not the last), he spent the afternoon in the flight lounge on a strange airport, listening to the adventures and non-adventures related by various other pilots who were in more or less the same boat as he. When it became obvious that there was no point in waiting for the weather to do anything constructive, he located a motel with a courtesy car and decided that he might as well hole up for the night.

The next day the weather reports were better, but not much. Watsonville was VFR, but the conditions in the direction of San Francisco were marginal at best. Still, sitting around at the airport was beginning to be oppressive, so he fired up his engine and took off, hoping that by flying east he would be able to pick up the highway and follow it north to San Francisco, beyond which the weather was reported to be improving rapidly.

He found the highway all right, but that's about as far as he got. The visibility toward the north was strictly zilch, and as far as he could tell the clouds were hanging right down on the ground. Well, the hell with that bit. He had had his fill of "dancing with the clouds" the day before, so he turned south, where things looked a lot better and, after less than an hour in the air, landed at Salinas.

As he watched the airplane being topped off it occurred to him that if he had driven he'd probably be farther ahead by now, but, oh, well . . . as they like to say: "Time to spare? Go by air."

Another night spent in a motel, this time in Salinas, he was hoping against hope that the optimistic forecast for the next day would hold up.

It did. He awoke to bright sunlight and blue skies, and as he climbed out toward the north he couldn't help wondering what had happened to all that ugly stuff from the day before. From here on the flight was smooth, beautiful, and uneventful. He refueled in Ukiah and North Bend and, after seven hours and six minutes of actual flight time, touched down at Portland International.

From the point of view of the navigation, the route from Portland to Seattle is simplicity itself. The direct route is 345 degrees out of Portland and passes over the foothills of the Cascades which, along that route, never rise over 4,333 feet. A simpler route, especially for our pilot with his dearth of navigation equipment, is along the highway that heads north from Portland to Olympia and from there along the Puget Sound via Tacoma to Seattle. This is the road he took when leaving Portland (FIG. 3-4). How he managed to get lost is a good question, but he did.

Along this route for some distance, the highway and a railroad run side by side. For some reason, he paid more attention to the railroad than he did to the highway and when, north of Longview, a spur branched off to the right (also paralleling a road, though a much narrower one), he followed the spur until it seemed to come to an abrupt end somewhere in the foothills. Realizing his mistake, he made a 180 and fol-

Fig. 3-4. *Following a highway can simplify the navigation chore for a pilot.*

lowed the spur back to the mainline and highway and then continued on toward Olympia and Seattle.

In Seattle his destination was the Boeing King County Airport, which he found without much difficulty. With its 10,000-foot runway clearly in sight, he called the tower.

"Boeing Tower, Tripacer Three-Two-Zero-Three Zulu just east of your airport at 6,500, landing Boeing."

He was given the current altimeter and wind at Boeing and told to continue the approach and to report on three-mile final for Runway One-Three Left.

Left? What left? All he seemed to be able to see was that beautifully long runway and so he aligned himself with it and when he thought that he was about three miles from touchdown he called the tower and told them so.

"Cleared to land One-Three Left." There seemed to be a certain amount of emphasis to the word *left*.

It is strange how the simplest, most common equations can become virtually unmanageable under conditions of minor stress. The fact is that the pilot kept searching on the *right* rather than the left of the long runway for the place on which the tower apparently wanted him to land. When he was once more admonished over the radio that he was aligned to the wrong runway, he simply veered to the right and landed on the two-mile-long taxiway that parallels the main runway.

"Zero-Three Zulu. After you've tied down, I wonder if you'd mind coming up to the tower."

The fellows in the tower were very nice. They asked if it was his first time into this airport and, when he said that it was, they gave him a chart of the airport and pointed out the 3,710-foot long second runway on which he should have landed. Feeling appropriately stupid, he thanked them and went on his way.

By now the total time in his logbook had grown from 49.5 to a respectable 63.7 and he was beginning to think of himself as a pilot with a certain amount of experience. Primarily, this experience had taught him to have somewhat more respect than he'd had just a few days earlier for weather, and the fact that navigating for real wasn't always as simple as it looked when studying the charts. With this in mind he decided that for the return trip he would fly around the south end of Puget Sound and west toward the Pacific, intercepting the coast at Hoquiam, and then follow the coast south. He figured that Newport, Oregon, would probably be as good a place as any to stay overnight before tackling the rest of the way back to Santa Monica the next day.

Now, as most everyone knows, Seattle is a great city if you like rain. Local citizens have been heard to boast that it has a wonderful summer, the only drawback being that it lasts only one day. Well, while that is an exaggeration, it does rain an awful lot, and when it doesn't rain, the sky is frequently covered with a solid overcast, though the visibility below that overcast, more often than not, is better than 15 miles.

And that was what it was like on his day of departure: Three thousand overcast, visibility 15. So he leveled off at 2,000 feet and, carefully avoiding the various Control Zones of Seattle-Tacoma International, McChord AFB, and Gray AAF and the adjoining restricted area, he snaked his way southwestward toward the Pacific. With the overcast extending as far as he could see, he continued southward at that altitude staying just off the coast.

PRESSING ON

The Oregon coastline is virtually straight and the flight would have been easy indeed if it hadn't been for a strong easterly wind that caused a fairly uncomfortable degree of turbulence on the lee side of the coastal mountains. He was still new enough to aviation to be bothered by turbulence, but there was no choice but to grit his teeth and press on.

Though there was sufficient fuel on board to fly the 280 miles to Newport, he landed at Astoria to have the airplane topped off and, above all, to give his shaken-up bones a rest. After lunch, with no change in the weather for either the better or worse, he took off and flew to Newport, where he decided he had had it for the day.

When he got up in the morning it was pouring rain. He called the weather station and was told that the rain extended only for some 20 or so miles southward, after which all stations reported CAVU conditions all the way to Los Angeles, with Los Angeles itself expecting three-mile visibilities in haze and smoke. Locally, despite the rain, the official report read 4,000-foot measured ceiling with visibility eight miles. The rain itself was expected to continue until the early afternoon and to be followed by a clearing trend.

But waiting until the afternoon would mean spending another night away from home, and that idea didn't appeal to him. So he arranged for the courtesy car to take him to the airport. There he conducted a rather cursory preflight, trying not to get drenched any more than necessary, and took off into the driving rain with water standing nearly an inch deep on the runway.

Luckily, airplanes don't really care whether or not it rains, and the Tripacer did just fine, leveling off at about 2,500 feet and heading south toward what its pilot hoped would soon be better weather. With the rain pounding the windshield, the forward visibility wasn't worth much, but using the coastline that was clearly to be seen out of his left window as a guide, he continued on his way without much difficulty. The wind, and with it the turbulence, had subsided and except for occasional drips of water running down his leg where the cockpit apparently leaked, he had a perfectly comfortable flight. And, true to the forecast, some 20 miles down the coast, the rain stopped, and soon he was flying under a bright blue sky.

He knew, of course, that the total distance from Newport to Santa Monica was slightly over 800 sm and that he'd therefore be arriving at his home airport after dark. But having made all of a half a dozen practice landings after sunset, though never in real darkness, he was confident that it would not pose any big problem. The flight back, with fuel stops in Ukiah and Salinas, was thoroughly enjoyable. Most of the time he cruised at 9,500 feet, and with no restrictions to visibility he could see the countryside for what seemed like hundreds of miles, making navigation easy despite the limited capability of his radio equipment.

By the time he took off from Salinas the sun was getting ready to drop into the Pacific Ocean. He turned on his navigation lights, confident that he'd have no trouble finding Santa Barbara and, subsequently, home. It worked out fine. The lights of Santa Barbara, slightly diffused by a thin layer of coastal fog, came into view on schedule and soon thereafter the glow ahead indicated that he was approaching the immense expanse of the Los Angeles megalopolis.

To the inexperienced, looking for a lighted airport in the sea of lights of a major city can be a confusing problem. It had never occurred to him that he might have difficulty finding Santa Monica Airport. He was beginning to realize that he was getting a bit tired and most likely his flying became somewhat erratic as he continued to search for the rotating beacon and the row of parallel lights that would indicate that he had spotted his final destination.

It took a considerable amount of time but eventually he did believe that he had spotted it (this was years before the VOR was installed at Santa Monica) and, relieved, he called the tower. No answer. He called again and again without getting any reply, and just as he was beginning to wonder what a pilot is supposed to do when he wants to land at a controlled airport when he is unable to contact the tower, another aircraft came on the line.

"Tripacer Three-Two-Zero-Three Zulu, this is Cessna Six Sierra Foxtrot. Santa Monica Tower closed 15 minutes ago. If you're planning to land, do so at your own discretion."

So that was it. He had never known that the tower wasn't operating around the clock. He thanked the Cessna, flew a careful pattern, and made what might be described as a good landing, considering that this was his first in real darkness.

Back in his car he realized that his hands and legs were shaking slightly; but, after all, he'd made it and there was nothing to be nervous about any longer.

ANALYSIS

In trying to analyze this flight, the thing that seems most obvious is the fact that for a pilot with his level of experience this was really much too ambitious an undertaking. With this in mind it must be admitted that he did remarkably well and made fewer serious errors than one might have expected.

His first, and by far the worst, mistake was on his first day when he decided to continue on despite the deteriorating weather conditions. With no instrument experience whatsoever and with an airplane that lacked the type of equipment that makes instrument flying relatively easy, especially with no artificial horizon, taking a chance on getting himself into Instrument Meteorological Conditions (IMC) could easily have resulted in a fatal accident. That it didn't was apparently a combination of luck, the fact that he forced himself not to panic, and most probably that the weather was, in fact, not as bad as it had appeared to him.

The next day, again faced by low clouds, he did make the right decision in turning back and landing at Salinas to wait things out.

Getting lost on the way from Portland to Seattle was probably the result of becoming fascinated with one particular ground feature, in this instance the railroad track, without relating it to other features clearly marked on the chart. Once having realized his mistake, he was right in turning back and retracing his steps to the point where he'd gone wrong, rather than trying a shortcut over unfamiliar terrain.

His failure to spot Runway 13L in Seattle is another case of a pilot having spotted what he believes he is looking for and somehow being either unwilling or unable to admit to himself that he could be wrong. This is a common phenomenon, and even experienced airline pilots have been known to land big jets at the wrong airport with the entire crew apparently convinced throughout the approach that they knew where they were.

On his way back he did fine, though it may be argued that taking off in heavy rain may not have been a brilliant decision. Even though the surface visibility was reported as eight miles, the in-flight visibility was much less because of the rain. Although officially VFR, the pilot was risking unintentional IMC again. In addition, flying off the coast with poor forward visibility wasn't too smart with respect to forced landing considerations.

What was perhaps even more foolish was his decision to continue home in one day. Actually, "foolish" would fit if such a decision were made by an experienced pilot. For a pilot still logging time in double digits, the decision was downright stupid. Logic should have told him that he would be tired and certainly not in top form by the time he got to his destination, and that he would be forced to make his first honest-to-goodness night landing under less-than-ideal conditions. Though everything did work out all right, it would probably have been a better idea to RON in Salinas and then to fly the rest of the way the next day.

Note: The extinguishing of the rotating beacon at Santa Monica airport may well have indicated that the visibility was greater than 3 miles, but pilots should realize this is not always the case. The *Airman's Information Manual* (AIM) makes this point clear:

In control zones, operation of the airport beacon during the hours of daylight **often** indicates that the ground visibility is less than 3 miles and/or the ceiling is less than 1,000 feet. . . . Pilots should not rely solely on the operation of the airport beacon to indicate if weather conditions are IFR or VFR. At some locations with operating control towers, ATC personnel turn the beacon on or off when controls are in the tower. At many airports the airport beacon is turned on by a photoelectric cell or time clocks and ATC personnel cannot control them.

Unless you are familiar with the procedure used at a particular airport, don't use the rotating beacon as an indicator of visibility.

4
Airports

THIS COUNTRY IS FULL OF ALL KINDS OF AIRPORTS. THERE ARE BIG ONES, little ones, hard- and easy-to-find ones. There are airports with elevations below sea level and others as high as 9,927 feet above sea level. There are public-use airports and private airports restricted to use by the owner. There are those with a profusion of mile-long paved runways (FIG. 4-1) and others consisting of poorly marked grass or a gravel strip (FIG. 4-2). Some are attended 24 hours, seven days a week; others, only during daylight hours; and some, not at all. There are one-way airports, controlled and uncontrolled airports, and huge ones surrounded by TCAs, TRSAs, or ARSAs. Some charge landing or takeoff fees, although most do not; tiedown, parking, or hangar fees may range all the way from zero to near-astronomical amounts.

Every cross-country flight involves at least two airports: the one being left behind and the one at the destination. Much of the time, we are likely to be familiar with both; and, in that case, neither departure nor arrival involves any particular problem. But when we are flying to an unfamiliar destination, it becomes a different story.

MORE THAN ONE AVAILABLE

The first question that must be answered is which airport to use if more than one is available. Let's take a few of the major cities and examine the choices.

Fig. 4-1. *All kinds of airports abound in the U.S.A., from mile-long paved runways to . . .*

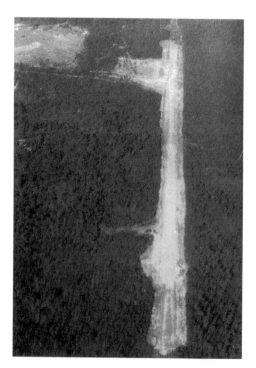

Fig. 4-2. *. . . gravel strips cut out of a forest.*

New York

Though New York is one of the most frequent destinations for cross-country flights, selecting the most convenient of its many airports can be a frustrating task. First, there are Kennedy International (JFK), La Guardia (LGA), and Newark (EWR), the three major airline terminals served by the New York TCA. At each, landing and tiedown fees are high, and general aviation traffic, other than corporate jets and turboprops, is discouraged. Of the three, Newark has traditionally been the least hostile to light aircraft, though none will actually refuse landing clearance to even an adequately equipped Cessna 150. (Mandatory equipment for operation to and from these airports includes a nav receiver, two-way communication radio, a transponder, and an encoding altimeter. The pilot must have a private license or better.) Common sense dictates that pilots flying aircraft that can't maintain at least 100 knots during the approach should avoid these airports unless there is an overwhelming need to land there. Slow aircraft tend to inhibit the acceptance rate at these busy terminals, and it is simply a case of having consideration for others to avoid using them unnecessarily. (For details of the appropriate technique to be used when necessary, see the chapter on TCAs.)

Next in line are the two airports used largely by general aviation and most of the corporate aircraft based in the New York area. They are Teterboro Airport, in New Jersey, and Westchester County Airport, northeast of White Plains. Both are equipped with instrument approaches including ILS and are, of course, attended 24 hours a day. Both charge fairly reasonable (for New York) landing fees and offer every conceivable service and maintenance capability. Neither has a VOR associated with the airport and, during the frequent conditions of reduced visibility due to haze, both can be hard to find by pilots unfamiliar with the area.

Each of the two underlies a portion of the New York TCA. VFR aircraft not wishing to fly through TCA airspace will have to approach Teterboro at an altitude below 1,800 feet and Westchester County at below 3,000 feet msl.

The most serious disadvantage of the two airports is that there is no transportation available to and from New York. The arriving pilot has virtually no choice but to rent a car, which becomes an expensive nuisance because cars are virtually unusable in Manhattan, where parking spaces are practically nonexistent and garages charge as much as $50 a day. With taxi fares to or from either airport being prohibitive, the most economical solution is to rent a car and then return it in Manhattan.

A similarly equipped airport, also with instrument approaches and ILS, is Republic Airport near Farmingdale on Long Island. Except for the fact that few corporate jets are based there and that, therefore, the traffic is usually somewhat less hectic, most everything that was said about Teterboro and Westchester can also be said for Republic, including the lack of available transportation to and from town. It, too, is located below the outer rim of the New York TCA, and VFR aircraft must stay below 4,000 feet msl.

The only other controlled airports in the area are Morristown and Essex County (formerly Caldwell), both with part-time control towers. Both have instrument approaches and charge landing fees. Again, getting into Manhattan from either is a major operation, best accomplished by rental car.

It should be pointed out that VFR aircraft, aside from staying out of controlled airspace (except when cleared by ATC and adequately equipped), must be exceptionally vigilant when operating within, say, 50 miles or so of the New York Metropolitan area. In addition, under certain weather conditions, visibility may be restricted because of industrial haze and pollution. Most VFR pilots familiar with the area prefer to stay quite low, within 1,500 to 2,000 feet of the surface, where one is unlikely to suddenly be confronted by a jet aircraft. On the other hand, as a result there is a great deal of VFR activity condensed within those low altitudes and constant attention is a must (FIG. 4-3). All studying of charts should be done in advance to minimize the time when the eyes must be used for something other than to look out for traffic.

Fig. 4-3. *Sightseeing around ''The Lady'' attracts a lot of traffic, both airplanes and helicopters, in the New York area.*

Los Angeles

Probably the second most frequent destination is Los Angeles. Though the problems awaiting the pilot here are entirely different from those described above, here, too, it helps to have a certain amount of advance knowledge of what one is getting into.

First of all, Los Angeles is a sprawling megalopolis with distances from one end to the other running as much as 50 miles. For this reason it would seem impractical to land at an airport on its west side if one's destination is to the east, or vice versa.

The primary airport is Los Angeles International (LAX), located at the Pacific coast southwest of downtown. Though surrounded by an elongated TCA, LAX had traditionally been one major jet terminal that has been most accommodating to general aviation aircraft. It has four over-two-mile-long runways plus a 3,000-foot STOL runway (all parallel) and charges no fees other than for overnight tiedown. It is surrounded by all manner of motels and hotels, and public transportation to various parts of the city is available at reasonable rates. Though all this may sound inviting, common sense, again, dictates that pilots flying aircraft incapable of maintaining adequate speed on approach and final should think twice before using the airport. Such aircraft disrupt the traffic flow and, with so many others to choose from, adding to LAX's problems seems unjustified. Therefore, LAX is not recommended for light aircraft.

Secondary airports within only a few miles of LAX are Santa Monica, Hawthorne, Compton, and Fullerton. Of these, Santa Monica (SMO) has a full-time control tower, and Hawthorne and Fullerton have part-time control towers. Compton is uncontrolled and has no IFR approach. Fullerton, Hawthorne, and Santa Monica all have instrument approaches. All are busy general aviation airports with appropriate services and reasonable charges for tiedown. Though public transportation is not far from any of them, it is relatively inadequate throughout Los Angeles. LA is an automobile city, and visitors should certainly consider renting cars in order to get around.

All four of these airports are located beneath the LA TCA, and VFR traffic must remain below 5,000 feet msl. In addition, Hawthorne is right next to the approach pattern for LAX, and aircraft operating to and from this airport should make certain to adhere to the pattern, which is to the south of the airport, away from the path of aircraft on approach to LAX.

The other major airline airport in the area is Long Beach. It is located southeast of LAX and east of Torrance and is outside the LA TCA. It is an extremely busy airport with about 80 percent or so of its traffic being general aviation. It has all manner of IFR approaches including an ILS. Every conceivable service and maintenance capacity is available, as are public transportation, taxis, rental cars, motels and hotels, restaurants, and so on (FIG. 4-4). Many general aviation aircraft dealers are located on this airport.

Farther south we have Torrance, and beyond that Orange County Airport, near Santa Ana and Newport Beach, primarily a general aviation airport although it does have some scheduled airline traffic. It has ILS, VOR/DME, and LOC approaches.

The three airports to the east are Fullerton (close to Disneyland), El Monte, more or less straight east of Los Angeles, and Brackett Field, adjoining the Pomona Fairgrounds. All three have part-time towers. El Monte and Brackett have VOR approaches, while Fullerton has an RNAV approach. All are general aviation airports with heavy student-training activities, reasonable tiedown charges, and most of the services needed by visiting pilots.

Fig. 4-4. *Long Beach Airport offers a wide variety of aircraft services.*

To the north there is Burbank, the Burbank-Glendale-Pasadena Airport, serving both general aviation and scheduled airlines. It has several IFR approaches, including ILS, and the tower is in operation 24 hours a day. Like most airports in the area, Burbank is especially busy during daylight hours when conditions are VFR. There are all manner of service and maintenance facilities, and tiedown fees are comparable to those at the other larger airports. Because of its proximity to three other airports in the area, all approaches and departures should be flown with considerable precision in order to avoid conflict with other traffic.

The other three airports in the area are Van Nuys, year after year the busiest general aviation airport in the world (FIG. 4-5), and Whiteman and San Fernando to the north. Van Nuys has a part-time tower and several IFR approaches including an ILS. It has two parallel runways with two different tower frequencies being used depending on the direction of the approach. Though arriving pilots might find that they are number six, seven, or eight in the pattern, the tower personnel at Van Nuys have always been outstanding in handling the huge volume of traffic, most of it compressed during the daylight hours.

Pilots arriving at VNY late at night may find it difficult to locate an FBO with anybody around. With many FBOs located on different parts of the airport, pilots

Fig. 4-5. *Heralded as the busiest general aviation airport in the world—Van Nuys.*

unfamiliar with VNY might do best to have ground control direct them to the one of their choice (FIG. 4-6).

Whiteman is a few miles northeast of Van Nuys. It has a part-time control tower and is quite active in the daytime, but after-dark arrivals might find it difficult to locate a warm body. There is no convenient public transportation available and, unless prior arrangements were made, one might have to phone for a taxi or rental car, which may take quite a bit of time.

As is well known by now, Los Angeles is afflicted with a disease called smog. It, and the frequent low fog that rolls in from the ocean during the early morning hours, can cause low-level visibility to be reduced to uncomfortable levels even though at altitudes of only a few thousand feet the sun is shining and the visibility unlimited. Pilots who are unfamiliar with the area would do well to stay above the smog level until they have found the airport of their choice and then try to keep it in sight while descending through the unsightly mess. It is usually quite easy to recognize airports and other landmarks from above, but it can become an exasperating experience to try and find what one is looking for when down in it (FIGS. 4-7 and 4-8).

Chicago

This is another city where deciding which airport to use can become complicated for pilots who are unfamiliar with the area. O'Hare, the primary airline terminal, is

Fig. 4-6. *FBOs, like this one at Van Nuys, often affiliate with manufacturers to attract those who fly a particular make airplane.*

Fig. 4-7. *It is usually easy to recognize landmarks when looking straight down through haze or smog . . .*

Fig. 4-8. . . . *but it can become exasperating trying to find an airport when flying low in smog.*

year after year the busiest in the world and, except under extremely pressing circumstances, it should not even be considered unless landing there is absolutely necessary. The same holds true for it that was advised previously about JFK.

Aside from O'Hare (ORD) there are four controlled airports and two uncontrolled ones. Of the four controlled airports the one most convenient to downtown Chicago is Meigs Field located on a small promontory on the coast of Lake Michigan. It offers no services other than fuel, tiedown, and a pilot lounge; and, due to the fact that tiedown spaces are extremely limited, the fees charged for using the airport are quite steep.

The advantage is that downtown is only a short taxi ride away. As a general rule it pays to fly into Meigs only if one has a business meeting or two downtown and plans to leave again the same day. For a longer stay the tiedown charges might be more than most pilots are willing to pay.

Landing at Meigs, at times, can be an interesting experience. If the wind blows from the west, as it often does, it tends to burble over the tall buildings along the lake shore, causing considerable low-level turbulence with sudden up and down drafts. It is always a good idea to use a certain amount of power during the final approach to be prepared to counteract the sudden gusts.

The next most convenient is Midway (MDW) on Chicago's south side. In the old days, Midway was the primary airline terminal for Chicago, and it is still being used by some airlines. It offers instrument approaches, including an ILS, and charges fees to all aircraft using the airport. All manner of service and maintenance facilities are available.

The most convenient transportation from the airport to downtown Chicago is probably by taxi. It's not a cheap ride but is likely to be less expensive than renting a car unless a rental car will be needed throughout one's stay in the city.

North of the city there is Pal-Waukee, a busy general aviation airport with a control tower which operates from 6 a.m. to 9 p.m. This is the most general-aviation-oriented airport in the area with all the services which might be needed. It has several instrument approaches, including an ILS. Transportation into the city is best accomplished by rental car via the freeway, which passes close by the airport.

Pal-Waukee is located relatively close to ORD under a cutout section of the TCA, and VFR aircraft must be on the lookout for O'Hare traffic and stay below 3,000 feet. Both Pal-Waukee and Midway have a profusion of runways, and it is advisable to study the runway layout before making the initial contact with the tower so that one has a reasonably clear idea of what to look for when the tower identifies the active runway.

The other controlled airport is the one farthest from the city. It is Du Page County Airport and is located some 45 nm west of downtown. It has IFR approaches, including an ILS, and the tower operates 24 hours. The airport, which is used by a number of commuter airlines, offers all manner of services and a choice of lodging facilities is nearby.

Schaumburg Air Park, an uncontrolled airport, is located about 15 miles west of downtown Chicago.

Dallas-Fort Worth

The Dallas-Fort Worth area is studded with over a dozen airports, the most convenient and frequently used of which are Love Field in Dallas and Meacham Airport in Fort Worth.

The major airline airport these days is, of course, the immense Dallas-Fort Worth International Airport, which is roughly the size of Manhattan and is designed strictly for jet traffic. While there is something that is laughingly described as a general aviation terminal, this airport does not encourage general aviation use and is only marginally equipped to handle general aviation aircraft. It is an interesting place to visit, but I wouldn't want to land there.

Love Field is practically right in downtown Dallas. While it is still used by one airline, it welcomes general aviation and offers all possible services, including some motels right on the airport (bring your earplugs!). The instrument approaches are an ILS or VOR/DME. With the close proximity to downtown, taxis are convenient transportation unless a rental car is needed during the stay.

Meacham Airport is to Fort Worth what Love is to Dallas. It is close to the city and offers all major and minor services, including an ILS and several other instrument approaches.

A look at the chart will show the location of all the other airports, any one of which may be selected if it happens to be conveniently close to the actual destination. Some are controlled and others are not, so the visitor can take his choice according to his preference.

San Francisco

San Francisco is a lovely city to visit, but when it comes to airports, the choice is somewhat limited. The most convenient, by far, is San Francisco International (SFO), the major airline terminal. Though not quite as attuned to general aviation as LAX, it does offer convenient facilities for general aviation. A variety of RON facilities are nearby, and there is convenient public transportation into the city.

The next most convenient is probably Oakland International (OAK), which is divided into two halves: one serves airlines and other jet traffic, and the other is used nearly exclusively by general aviation. It is an ideal airport for the visiting pilot and has all facilities including several instrument approaches and ILS. *Caution:* When approaching from either north or south, it is easy to confuse Oakland with the runway of similar length at Alameda Naval Air Station. Make sure you've got the right one.

The other airports in the area are Hayward, south of Oakland, and San Carlos and Palo Alto, south of SFO. All are controlled and all are busy, well-equipped general aviation airports. One other is Half Moon Bay on the Pacific Coast, south of the city. It is uncontrolled and frequently subject to fog.

Among the available airports, SFO and OAK will not accept requests for special VFR operations. The others will.

Boston

Boston is another one of those places where there is really no convenient airport except the primary airline terminal; in this case, Logan (BOS). It has general aviation facilities comparable to those at Newark, and the aircraft-equipment requirements are those applicable to all airports associated with a TCA. The city can be reached by taxi or public transportation.

The other three airports that might be considered are Norwood, Hanscom, and Beverly. Each is about 15 nm from the city, is controlled, and has instrument approaches. All are general aviation airports with fair amounts of student-training activity and all of the usual services. Transportation into the city is best accomplished by rental car.

It is beyond the scope of this book to examine the available airports at every major city. Suffice it to say that a careful study of up-to-date charts will show which airport is the most convenient at destinations where more than one is available. But, be sure that the charts are not outdated, otherwise you might start searching for an airport that has been recently closed, or be embarrassed by making an approach to an airport that was thought to be uncontrolled but that now has a tower.

UNCONTROLLED AIRPORTS

The choice between controlled and uncontrolled airports is one of personal preference. Some pilots prefer not to bother dealing with tower controllers, frequently because much of their flying has been done to and from uncontrolled fields and they feel a bit uncertain about their radio technique. Others like the order resulting from tower control and the fact that the tower is in a position to provide full information with reference to conditions at the airport.

An uncontrolled airport is one that does not have a control tower (indicated in magenta on aeronautical charts) or it is one with a control tower (indicated in blue on charts) when the tower is not in operation, i.e., "off the air." Such an airport may or may not also be in a Control Zone. Although a Control Zone has a direct bearing on the required weather minima (see chapter 16), it does not change how pilots should operate at uncontrolled fields.

The FAA tells us that most midair collisions occur within 5 miles of an airport during daylight VFR weather and below 3,000 feet agl. Nearly one-half of such collisions occur on final approach and usually involve a faster aircraft overtaking a slower one. Only 5 percent of all midair collisions occur head-on. It goes without saying that many midairs occur at uncontrolled airports and pilots should be extra vigilant when operating to and from these fields.

For safe arrivals at uncontrolled airports, make it a practice to apply the following steps.

1. Check an airport directory (such as the *Airport/Facility Directory* (A/FD), *Airguide Publications' Flight Guide*, and *AOPA's AIRPORTS USA*) before taking off for an uncontrolled airport—or any airport, for that matter. You want to find out a number of things, including the Common Traffic Advisory Frequency (CTAF). Does the field have an FSS or unicom, or should the multicom frequency be used? What are the hours of operation of the FSS or unicom? When you arrive at the airport, will you be talking to someone on the ground who can give you weather and traffic advisories or will you have to make all your calls "in the blind" to other pilots?

   What is the traffic pattern altitude? Unfortunately, this very important information is not provided on aeronautical charts. Since there is no standard traffic pattern altitude—it can vary from 600 feet to 1,500 feet agl for propeller-driven aircraft to as high as 2,500 feet agl for turbojet aircraft—it's a good idea to know what it is before arriving at the field.

Will the airport be open when you arrive? If you are arriving after sunset, does the airport have runway lights? Are the lights on all night, will you have to ask someone to turn them on, or can you turn them on yourself (pilot-controlled lighting)?

Also check the length of the runways to be sure you can safely land and take off from the airport.

2. When you are approaching the airport, select the CTAF while you are still 10 or 15 minutes away and no later than about 15 miles out. This will give you time to listen to the frequency and determine the level of activity and the runway in use. Turn on your landing light, both day and night. This makes it easier for other pilots to see you. Remember, you're in "see-and-avoid" territory.

3. Check the airport diagram and visualize the entry and traffic pattern you'll make. Broadcast your position and intentions when you're about 10 miles out. If there is someone on the ground monitoring the frequency (unicom or FSS), they should acknowledge you and give you advisories.

If you don't hear a reply, you're "in the blind." In this case, particularly if you are unfamiliar with the field, it's wise to remain at least 1,000 feet above the traffic pattern altitude (or at least 2,000 feet above field elevation) and fly over the airport. Check for other traffic, the traffic pattern, and the wind indicators. Then fly a safe distance away from the field before descending and returning.

4. Plan to descend so that you reach traffic pattern altitude at least 2 miles out. It's always safer to enter the pattern in level flight. Never descend into the pattern—that's how accidents happen. Reduce your airspeed to 1.5 V_{so} and trim for level flight.

5. Announce your type of entry on the CTAF; for example, "Bader traffic, 3-4 Mike entering on a 45 for runway 2-9." The standard entry is a 45-degree angle entry leg to midfield downwind, but direct downwind, upwind, or crosswind entries are also permissible. Never make a straight-in approach to an uncontrolled airport.

6. Check for traffic and turn downwind. Announce that you are on downwind and your intentions; for example, touch-and-go, low approach, or full stop. Depending on the traffic situation or local procedures, it may also be necessary to call base leg or final. However, sometimes such calls only serve to clog the CTAF. If there is other traffic in the pattern, your best bet is to do what everyone else is doing. If they are all calling base leg and final, they'll expect you to do it, too. If they're only calling downwind, that will be all you have to announce.

7. Taxi off the runway as soon as you safely can and, if there are other aircraft in the pattern behind you or waiting to take off, announce that you are clear of the runway.

When departing from uncontrolled airports, use the following steps.

1. Call taxiing out on the CTAF. If the field has an FSS, the radio operator will give you wind, altimeter setting, runway in use, and usually other traffic, too. Some unicom operators will provide you with the same information, too, without being asked. If not, you can request it. If there is no one monitoring a radio on the ground, you're in the blind again.
2. Check the traffic pattern while you taxi and be sure final approach is clear before taking the runway. If the wind is calm, final approach could be from either direction. Check both ways!
3. Turn on your landing light and announce your departure and direction of flight; for example, "Linden traffic, Cessna 1-6 Alpha is departing runway 2-7 southbound."
4. Depart the pattern by climbing straight out, or, upon reaching pattern altitude, by making a 45-degree left turn and then continuing your climb.
5. Monitor the CTAF, if it's not necessary to change to another frequency right away, until you're about 10 miles out. That way you'll be able to hear if other aircraft are approaching the field opposite to your direction of flight.

Remember, "seeing and avoiding" is paramount at uncontrolled fields, even when there is an FSS or unicom operator. Always be extremely vigilant when operating at one of these airports.

Under all circumstances, when an ATIS is associated with an airport, arriving pilots or those planning to depart should listen to the ATIS before contacting either tower or ground control and then when making the first contact, should acknowledge that they have that information. ("Cessna Six-Seven-Two-Three Uniform with Information Alpha, ten south at six thousand, over.")

ONE-WAY AIRPORTS

As long as we are on the subject of airports, we should mention one-way airports. One-way airports are those at which, for one reason or another, takeoffs and landings are made to and from the same direction: in other words, on opposite runways. There may be a variety of reasons for this. One may be the fact that the runway slopes downward at a rate that would make accelerating uphill or decelerating downhill difficult (such as at Prescott, Arizona). Another reason might have to do with noise, when there is a town or city close to one end of the runway (such as at Bader Field, New Jersey, an airport serving Atlantic City). (Figures 4-9, and 4-10.) A third reason may be steeply rising terrain in one direction (such as at Aspen, Colorado, and Los Alamos, New Mexico).

When such airports have a control tower or are served by a unicom, this should present no particular difficulty as the appropriate information will be transmitted to the arriving pilot. The difficulty arises when the information is not available. We are

Fig. 4-9. *Urban development near an airport . . .*

Fig. 4-10. *. . . often results in one-way runways.*

likely to arrive, watch someone take off in a certain direction, and logically decide, therefore, that we should land in the same direction. Information about one-way airports is hard to come by: the best suggestion is, if in doubt, contact the nearest FSS and ask them for information. They should be able to provide it.

In closing, one of the best aids in determining what is available at any given airport is the annually revised airport directory published by the Aircraft Owners and Pilots Association (AOPA). It is available free to members and lists all applicable information for over 13,000 landing facilities and includes approximately 3,000 runway diagrams.

5
Off-Airport Landings

THERE ARE TWO KINDS OF OFF-AIRPORT LANDINGS: THOSE THAT ARE THE result of an emergency and those that are planned. In the latter case there are, above all, legal questions to be considered. Different municipalities, states, or counties tend to look at off-airport landings with varying degrees of disfavor. In some cases pilots, after having made emergency off-airport landings, have had to pay stiff fines and, still worse, found that they had to have the airplanes dismantled and trucked away because they were not permitted to take off again. Therefore, if we plan to make an off-airport landing—say, at a lake in order to go fishing or some such—we should definitely make all necessary inquiries in advance to make sure that we don't find ourselves on the wrong end of some obscure local law.

Off-airport landings, as such—whether planned or the result of an emergency—require a combination of calm, common sense, and proficiency in handling the airplane. With reference to emergencies, few ever develop without warning; and, by being aware early that something is not quite the way it should be, a serious emergency can often be avoided. If the engine suddenly runs rough, sputters, or loses rpm for no apparent reason, it may be an indication that something is seriously going awry. But it may not be. Maybe all that is needed is carburetor heat. Try it. Pull it all the way out, and if, after a little while, the engine starts to run smoother, leave it out. There'll be some reduction in rpm but that's all. If that doesn't do it, try the mixture. Lean or enrich. It may do the trick. Also, flying briefly at full throttle, assuming we've been flying at partial power, may help to dislodge some junk that may have accumulated at the spark plugs. If none of this works and if the condition persists or continues to get worse, then we have to assume that it's something serious—in other words, an emergency.

Now check oil pressure and temperature and, if available, the cylinder head temperature. If all are reasonably normal and if we know of an airport fairly close by, we may be justified in attempting to nurse the engine along until we get there (which would be preferable to sitting in a sick airplane someplace out in the boondocks). If the oil pressure appears low but the temperature is normal and there is no change in rpm or the sound of the engine, then it is usually caused by a faulty gauge rather than an incipient engine failure. Still, a precautionary landing would be advisable, just to make sure (FIG. 5-1). If, on the other hand, the pressure drops and, at the same time, the temperature climbs to above normal, it most probably is an indication of an oil leak, which could result in a freeze up of the engine within minutes. When that happens, an immediate emergency landing, preferably with the engine shut down, is the only logical next step. Be aware, too, that with a complete loss of oil, and, therefore,

Fig. 5-1. *The track and field behind the plane's left wing might be a good place for a precautionary landing.*

oil pressure, an increase in oil temperature may not be indicated because there is no oil left to measure the temperature of.

Each year fuel exhaustion is much too often the cause of bent airplanes and injured or killed pilots and passengers. There is simply no excuse for running out of fuel. There are plenty of airports all over the place, and the slight inconvenience and loss of time associated with a precautionary fuel stop is certainly preferable to suddenly being caught up there with empty tanks. Worse yet, pilots insist on making emergency landings often with expensive or catastrophic results, simply because they *thought* they were out of fuel when the engine quit. Then, later on, it turns out that all they did was to run one tank dry while the other one was still full. So, if the engine sputters, switch tanks!

DESCENDING SAFELY

Regardless of the reason for wanting to make an off-airport landing, the first step calls for picking an appropriate landing site and gaining an awareness of the direction and velocity of the wind. For obvious reasons, the landing site should be picked as early as possible—before fuel exhaustion, a frozen engine, or some other calamity limits the available options.

If there is smoke nearby, it will give an indication of the wind direction and velocity, but it must be close to the selected landing site. A smoke plume some miles away may indicate an entirely different wind direction, especially in areas of hilly or mountainous terrain. If there is no smoke, check the degree of movement of trees or tall grasses to determine whether there is enough wind to worry about. Similarly, the surface of water, such as a lake or a pond or even a puddle, may serve the same purpose (rivers aren't much good). When trees show definite movement of branches and leaves or when the surface of a stationary body of water is ruffled by tiny waves, the indication is that the wind is of sufficient strength to warrant an attempt to land as straight into it as possible.

If there are cows around and all of them face in more or less the same direction, remember that cows (and horses) will always stand with their rear ends into the wind. But be sure to look for more than just one single animal. There's always a revolutionary around who stands the wrong way. Birds flying close to the ground can give an indication of the wind direction. If they seem to be crabbing or are flying too fast in one direction and too slow in the opposite one, it is a useful sign. Also, if there is time to maneuver, one can fly a straight line across the ground or head for a fixed landmark from different directions and watch the drift of the airplane. This, of course, must be done close to the ground in order to produce information about surface winds rather than those at higher altitudes.

Much to be preferred over all these rather unscientific means of checking the wind would be to have listened to the weather reports for the area and the wind-related figures. If the reported surface winds were more or less uniform for the area in which we were flying, it would be fairly safe to assume that the same would hold true for our selected landing site. This is more generally true in flat terrain than in the mountains but, with appropriate landing sites hard to find in mountainous terrain, landing into the wind may not be possible there anyway.

Now that we believe we know about the wind, the next step is to find a flat piece of real estate of adequate length. This is a lot more difficult than it seems. Depending on the shape of a field or the width of a road, one can easily misjudge the length of the areas available for landing. One good practice for pilots is to study runways of known dimensions from various altitudes to become familiar with what a given length looks like. In a tight emergency situation we tend to overestimate the length of a piece of ground that looks good, and it is depressing indeed to imagine making a perfectly good landing only to afterward roll into a fence.

If the airplane is still airworthy and there is enough fuel left, it is good practice to make a low pass over the selected landing site to look for holes, rocks, tree trunks, or any other obstacle that might be hard to see from higher up. Such a low pass will also help you to determine whether the ground rises appreciably in one direction or the other. A noticeable incline might indicate that it would be preferable to land uphill, no matter what the direction of the wind.

LANDING

Now it's time to land. We climb to about 800 feet agl, fly a standard pattern at the right speed, and make all turns and descents without rushing or shaving any portion. The aim is to try and touch down at the lowest possible speed which, in most aircraft, means full flaps and power. It must be remembered, though, that with some aircraft, such as the lower-powered Cessnas, a go-around with full flaps may be impossible unless the aircraft is very lightly loaded. In other words, when flying such an aircraft, full flaps should not be dropped until a successful landing is assured. Once the mainwheels have touched ground, keep the yoke way back to hold the nosewheel off the ground while, at the same time, retracting the flaps to increase the weight on the wheels and, in turn, the effectiveness of the brakes. Brake with care. A sudden, hard application of the brakes may cause the nosewheel to hit the ground and increase the danger of some damage due to terrain irregularities, holes, or small rocks.

Okay, so now we're on the ground. If this was a planned off-airport landing, fine. If, on the other hand, it was an emergency and we find ourselves miles from any sign of civilization, the next problem is to attract attention. Don't walk away from the airplane unless absolutely certain that a particular direction will lead to a village, farm, or traveled road. And if we do walk away, we must remember some recognizable landmarks so that we can find our way back to the plane. Since this was not a crash, the ELT will not be operating, so we should turn it on. This is assuming it is equipped with an on/off switch. If not, it can probably be activated by hitting it with a rock but, once it starts its whining, it will interfere with the other radios and render them practically useless. It might be preferable to hold off a while and try to establish contact with someone by radio. The best chance of success for this is to tune to one or another of the center frequencies for the area and listen. Transmitting in the blind is rarely effective and wears out the battery. The receiver, on the other hand, uses little electricity. Then as soon as we hear another aircraft talking to center, that is the time to transmit because we know that that aircraft is within reception distance. Once he replies, we can tell him our problem, ask him to tell the FAA, and then let them take it from there.

TAKING OFF

If this was a planned landing or if whatever was wrong was something minor that can be fixed on the spot, the next problem is getting out of there. Rough or soft ground or high grass, while useful in reducing the landing roll, increases the distance necessary for the aircraft to accelerate to liftoff speed. What we'll have to do is to walk the "runway" and look for ruts, rocks, sticks, or loose debris that might be picked up by the propeller. We clear that stuff away and, counting our steps at the same time, get an idea of the length of the "runway." Let's make sure that there are no trees or other obstacles in the takeoff direction. We will be lifting off at the very lowest possible flying speed and may have to stay for a certain distance in ground effect in order to gain sufficient speed to permit us to climb higher or make even shallow turns.

During the actual takeoff we start out with little or no flaps, stand on the brakes until the engine has developed full rpm, then let go and feed flaps in gradually. We hold the yoke all the way back in our lap to relieve as much pressure as possible from the nosewheel. As soon as the airplane seems to want to fly, we take it into the air but then hold it low (just a foot or two off the ground) until we've gathered sufficient speed to initiate a climbout.

In an emergency situation when flying an aircraft with a retractable gear there is always the additional question of whether to land gear up or gear down. In most cases we're likely to be tempted to land gear down as this seems, at least, to offer a chance of getting down without causing additional damage to the airframe and propeller. Still, if the available ground appears to be soft or freshly plowed, or the grass is exceptionally high or, of course, in the case of swamp or water, a gear-up landing is often the better choice. In such an event it helps if we are able to set up a controlled power-off glide. We then shut down the engine prior to touchdown with the prop in the horizontal position. (This can be achieved by hitting the starter button a couple of times. With three bladed props it is best to stop the engine with one blade pointing down, thus ruining only one of the three blades.) Seatbelt and shoulder harness should be tightly fastened to absorb the shock of the inevitable fast deceleration. In such a landing all control is lost once the aircraft hits the ground or water, and all we can do is sit there and wait for it to come to a stop.

In any emergency situation it is always a good idea to cut the master switch just before touchdown to minimize the chance of electrical sparks in case there is any fuel spillage.

The trouble with off-airport landings is that no amount of short-field practice on a smooth paved runway can adequately prepare us for the real thing. On the other hand, practicing actual off-airport landings is impractical in view of the attendant dangers. So all we can do when it happens is to stay calm and take our time. After all, a glide from 5,000 feet agl at 500 fpm takes 10 minutes and, at 80 mph, will cover 13 miles. So there is usually plenty of time to pick out a good spot and make all the necessary preparations.

6
Flight Number Two

Date: July 6, 1971.
Pilot: Male, age 42, salesman.
License: Private, SEL, MEL.
Pilot-In-Command Time: 2,852 hours.
Aircraft: Rockwell Commander 100.
Flight: Westchester County Airport, New York, to Baton Rouge, Louisiana.
Purpose of Flight: To set up a dealership.

The first part of the flight had been uneventful. The sky was clear, and above the layer of summer haze the visibility was unlimited. On board, in addition to the pilot, was one passenger—a friend who was hitching a ride as far as Chattanooga, Tennessee. The route would bypass Washington and then take them over most of the length of the Blue Ridge and Appalachian Mountains. Assuming no increase in the five-knot or so head winds, the fuel should be sufficient to take them all the way to Chattanooga.

By the time they had traveled about two-thirds of the way, clouds were beginning to build above the higher hills, and in the distance still-young anvil shapes were an indication of the thunderstorm activity that was to be expected during a hot and humid summer afternoon.

It wasn't long until they found themselves above a layer of scattered and occasionally broken clouds and, judging by the time it seemed to take to get from one nav aid to the next, the head wind had increased considerably. The pilot silently began to wonder whether he'd be able to make Chattanooga or whether it might not be a better idea to consider landing at some convenient airport along the way.

MIGHT AS WELL CONTINUE

He dug out his charts and looked for such an airport, without coming to a definite decision. Both his fuel gauges, though reading below half, were still comfortably in the black, so he figured he might as well continue on his course a while longer.

By now there were clouds above, as well as below, and the view ahead became less and less inviting. The clouds above were beginning to coalesce into a solid overcast, and those below became less and less scattered and more and more broken. And, to make things worse, straight ahead they appeared to be merging into a gray mess. The pilot briefly wished that he had spent more time working on his instrument ticket so that he could simply file IFR, but he hadn't and, on top of that, another quick look at his gauges indicated only too clearly that that wouldn't have been a good idea in any case.

Though he had flown this airplane—it was rented—before, he had never run either tank dry and could, therefore, not be completely certain of how much usable fuel could be counted on based on the needle indications. He tightened his seatbelt, expecting the inevitable turbulence below the clouds, throttled back, and, deviating from his course in order to make use of a good-sized clear area between the clouds, he dropped down to below and then turned back toward the row of hills that he would have to cross in order to get to one of several reasonably close airports. Though it was uncomfortably bumpy, the visibility down there was still quite good, and he expected no further difficulty, despite the fact that his OBI needle was acting up because the mountainous terrain ahead interfered with the reception. Then it went dead.

He pressed on for another 10 minutes or so only to then be faced suddenly with mountaintops obscured by clouds. Damn! There was no choice—he either had to detour or turn back, and do it right now. Well, maybe things around that hill would be better.

As should have been expected, one detour was followed by another and a third and fourth; it soon became perfectly clear that there was no way to get to those airports while staying VFR. He briefly considered simply climbing up into the clouds in order to pick up the VOR and to fly to it and then to let down to the associated airport but, aside from its being strictly illegal, another look at the fuel gauges killed that idea before he had time to consider all its ramifications.

What now? He was embarrassed to admit to himself (and, of course, said nothing to his passenger) that he had gotten himself into one of those classic situations that more often than not ends up as one more unpleasant statistic. Where the hell was he anyway, and where was an airport? He tried without success to relate some feature on the ground to something recognizable on his Sectional. He tuned the nav receiver to every frequency of any nearby VOR but was apparently too low to pick up a signal.

Should he expend some of the remaining fuel to climb as high as the clouds would permit in hopes of being able to establish some radio contact, or should he simply follow the road below in hopes that it would lead to a town and an airport? He switched his fuel selector from BOTH to LEFT, deciding to run one tank dry after which, he assumed, there would be sufficient fuel in the right tank to permit him to attempt a controlled landing on some road or field.

The road below was not a major highway but rather a country road, winding this way and that, accompanied by the usual telephone lines, making it an unlikely choice for an emergency landing, if that should become necessary.

A PLACE TO LAND

It did. The engine coughed, indicating there was fuel exhaustion on the left tank. He switched to RIGHT, the engine resumed its normal operation, and he began to search the surrounding terrain frantically for something straight and flat and devoid of power lines. Having made the decision to make the first off-airport landing in his 20-odd year flying career, he suddenly found that he was quite calm. There was no more uncertainty. And then he saw it: a dirt road, straight and apparently flat, with no trees or other obstacles on either side for a distance that seemed adequate for a short-field landing (FIG. 6-1).

He throttled back, dropped full flaps, flew a standard pattern and, ignoring the warning screams of the stall-warning, headed for the nonexistent numbers. The landing was hard but, with no flying speed left, he stayed firmly on the ground, stood on the brakes, and came to a stop opposite a driveway that led to a two-story home some 100 feet off the road.

A little girl, maybe 10 or 11 years old, appeared at the door and, when the pilot and his somewhat shaken passenger climbed out of the airplane, she asked if there was something she could do to help.

"Is there an airport nearby, do you know?"

"Oh yes, just a little ways down the road on the other side of the river."

"I wonder if I may use your phone."

"Yes, please come in."

He looked up the number of the FBO who, when he learned where they were, explained that the airport was barely five miles distant. He agreed to bring five gallons of fuel, as the pilot did not feel that he could safely attempt to take off and fly to the airport, being far from certain of how much usable fuel was left in that one right tank.

By the time the FBO arrived with his five-gallon drum, a number of local people had begun to gather to gawk at the airplane in those unlikely surroundings. A reporter-photographer from the local paper was using up a lot of film as the FBO poured the fuel into the tank while explaining exactly which direction to fly and what landmarks to look for in order to get to the airport. Then, with pilot and passenger back in the airplane, he helped to shoo the people a safe distance away from the road to permit them to taxi to the "approach end" of the road and then to take off.

Fig. 6-1. *Could the pilot safely land on a road or in a field below?*

It all worked perfectly. They took off, turned in the direction that had been indicated, found the river and the airport beyond, and landed without further incident. Then they topped off the tanks and thanked the FBO, who refused to be paid for his extracurricular aid, and flew on to Chattanooga the next morning in CAVU weather conditions.

ANALYSIS

Like most of us, the pilot had spent thousands of hours in the cockpits of light aircraft without ever seriously considering the necessity of landing anywhere other than on an airport. Oh, he might have looked at a road, an ocean beach, or a farmer's field, thinking that they would be acceptable in an emergency but, with the engine running smoothly, the thought was quickly put aside.

Of course, in decades past, when aircraft engines were quite unreliable and the number of airports limited to a very few, off-airport landings were nothing unusual. But then those airplanes were slow, landing even slower, and, with the conventional tailwheel gear, a few bumps or holes weren't as much of a problem as they tend to be for the modern tricycle-gear aircraft.

The kinds of aircraft we fly today are not too well suited to such unorthodox landings. They land at high speeds and need long, smooth surfaces on which to roll out without incurring damage. In addition, few of us ever bother to practice landing at the lowest possible speed. Full-stall landings are talked about a lot but rarely practiced except by students as part of their training.

In this specific instance the pilot, with close to 3,000 hours in his logbook, should never have gotten into the position in which he found himself. Knowing all along that the fuel on board (while sufficient to get him to his destination, assuming no head wind to speak of) did not include an ample reserve, he should have deviated from his course and landed as soon as he saw that the weather ahead was beginning to deteriorate.

As soon as he realized that he had to drop down to a lower altitude, he should have turned back and maintained radio contact with some nav aid, using it to get back to a safe airport. He didn't, and from then on the eventual need for an emergency landing was, in fact, a foregone conclusion.

Once having gotten himself into the fix of not knowing exactly where he was, where there was an airport, or how much fuel was left in his tanks, he did everything right. It was proper to use the fuel from one tank and run it dry first and then to use the remaining fuel in the other tank to make a controlled landing. If both tanks had run dry he most probably would not have been able to pick an appropriate spot and land without available power.

As it was, he used what time was left to locate a road on which to land. He then did the right thing by flying a complete standard pattern, which gave him the opportunity to set up the right landing configuration and an acceptable rate of descent while slowing the aircraft to its slowest controllable speed. He was also right in not attempting to take off again when he learned that the airport was only five miles distant even though the likelihood existed that he might have been able to make it. Then, again, he might not have. And, lastly, he made the right decision in staying overnight and continuing the next day, by which time the weather had cleared.

7
Dealing with Different Types of Airspace

ACROSS-COUNTRY FLIGHT WILL USUALLY TAKE A PILOT THROUGH MANY different types of airspace, all of which have different rules and requirements. It is the responsibility of the pilot to always know what kind of airspace he is flying in and to comply with the rules applicable to that airspace. As far as the FAA is concerned, ignorance is no excuse for violating a reg.

Without trying to reiterate all the applicable FARs, which are often quite difficult to understand, the following is an attempt to make meaningful sense of the U.S. airspace system (FIG. 7-1).

CONTROLLED AND UNCONTROLLED AIRSPACE

Take a look at any Sectional or World Aeronautical Chart. If your chart is from a part of the continental United States, most of what you see is controlled airspace.

Above 14,500 feet, everything is part of the Continental Control Area, except for the airspace less than 1,500 feet above the surface of the earth. From 18,000 feet to Flight Level 600 is the Positive Control Area, which means that all aircraft must be operated under Instrument Flight Rules. (Part of the Alaskan peninsula and some prohibited and restricted areas are excluded from the Continental Control Area, but this has little effect on the operation of most civilian aircraft.)

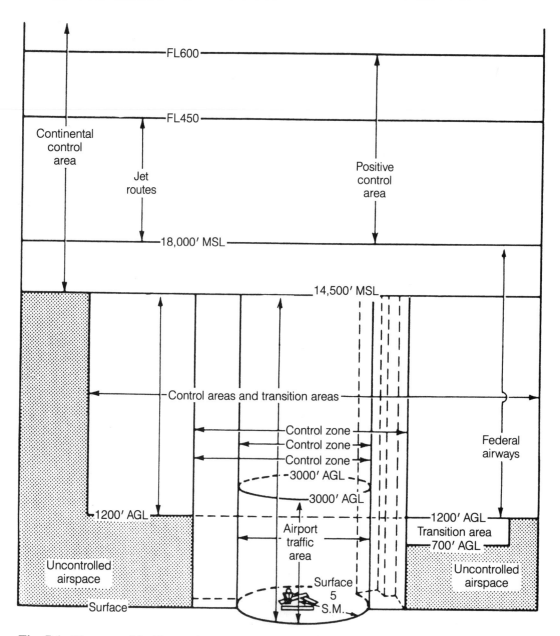

Fig. 7-1. *Elements of the National Airspace System.*

Below 14,500 feet, most of the airspace is designated as Control Areas, Control Zones, Transition Areas, Terminal Control Areas, and Airport Radar Service Areas. In fact, virtually *all* airspace in the United States east of the Rocky Mountains is controlled airspace above 1,200 feet agl. Those islands of uncontrolled airspace in the continental United States are few and far between.

There is, however, much airspace *below* 1,200 feet agl that is controlled, too.

Transition Areas (outlined in magenta on the charts) drop the floor of controlled airspace to 700 feet agl, and Control Zones (indicated by dashed blue lines around the airport) drop the floor of the controlled airspace all the way to the surface.

Transition Areas and Control Zones are both indicative of airfields with at least one instrument approach. ATC has the authority to issue clearances only in controlled airspace, which explains why airports that have instrument approaches need Transition Areas and Control Zones. If an airfield doesn't have an instrument approach, there is no reason for a Transition Area or a Control Zone at that airport.

Airfields with instrument approaches often (but not always) also have control towers. Some control towers have 24-hour operation; many do not. Airports with control towers are blue on Sectional charts and automatically have Airport Traffic Areas when the tower is open. Airports without control towers are magenta.

Of course, at busy metropolitan areas you also find Terminal Radar Service Areas, Airport Radar Service Areas, and Terminal Control Areas, which we'll cover later in this chapter.

CONTROL ZONES, AIRPORT TRAFFIC AREAS, AND "UNCONTROLLED" AIRPORTS

The different combinations of Control Zones, Airport Traffic Areas, and uncontrolled airports found throughout the United States are often a cause of confusion among many pilots, both inexperienced and experienced. This is not too surprising considering the way the FARs are written.

Control Zones are controlled airspace. Technically, Airport Traffic Areas are not controlled airspace, but rather "other airspace" (AIM, Section 5). However, three things make ATAs essentially controlled airspace.

First, to operate in an ATA you must have radio contact with the controlling ATC facility, usually (but not always) the control tower. Secondly, ATAs are often (but not always) found in conjunction with Control Zones. And finally, airports with operating control towers are referred to as "controlled airports," while those without control towers are referred to as "uncontrolled airports."

Let's look at the different combinations of airports and airspace and see what they mean in practice. For discussion purposes, each of the types of airports covered are considered to be isolated; in other words, far enough away from the airspace of other types of airports so as not to make them subject to different rules. In the real world, of course, uncontrolled airfields are often found within Air Traffic Areas or Control Zones and two or more ATAs and Control Zones sometimes coincide, overlap, or otherwise get in each other's way. Local agreements and procedures are worked out to take care of air traffic, and pilots are well advised to find out these procedures before blundering into the airspace.

Airports with neither Control Towers (Magenta Colored) nor Instrument Approaches

These quiet, uncontrolled airports are found all over the country and are havens for VFR pilots (FIG. 7-2). They have no control towers, no instrument traffic, and no Control Zones. The more active ones also tend to be the sites of many near misses and some midairs when the weather is either very good (and a lot of people are flying) or very bad (when the few who are flying think no one else is).

Fig. 7-2. *Uncontrolled airports with no instrument approaches are often havens for VFR pilots.*

Above them, controlled airspace doesn't start until 1,200 feet agl. (The controlled airspace could be VOR Airways, Additional Control Areas, Transition Areas, or Control Area Extensions. For the sake of simplicity, I will refer to all controlled airspace between 1,200 feet agl and 14,500 feet msl as "Control Area," with the exception of Control Zones.)

Legally, during daylight hours you may fly as low as 500 feet agl over an uncontrolled airport in an uncongested area or 1,000 feet over an uncontrolled airport in a congested area (FAR 91.119) if you have a flight visibility of 1 statute mile and remain clear of clouds (TABLE 7-1). You don't even need com radios or have to turn them on if you have them. You may also land and take off at such an airport under the same conditions without talking to anyone. At night, you may legally do the same thing if

Table 7-1. Basic VFR Weather Minima (FAR 91.155).

Minimum VFR Visibility and Distance From Clouds

Altitude		Outside Controlled Airspace		Controlled Airspace	
		Flight Visibility	*Distance from Clouds*	***Flight Visibility*	***Distance from Clouds*
1,200' or less above the surface, regardless of msl altitude	DAY	*1 statute mile	Clear of clouds	3 statute miles	500' below 1,000' above 2,000' horizontal
	NIGHT	3 statute miles	500' below 1,000' above 2,000' horizontal		
More than 1,200' above the surface but less than 10,000' msl	DAY	1 statute mile	500' below 1,000' above 2,000' horizontal	3 statute miles	500' below 1,000' above 2,000' horizontal
	NIGHT	3 statute miles	2,000' horizontal		2,000' horizontal
More than 1,200' above the surface and at or above 10,000' msl		5 statute miles	1,000' below 1,000' above 1 statute mile horizontal	5 statute miles	1,000' below 1,000' above 1 statute mile horizontal

* Helicopters may be operated outside controlled airspace below 1,200 feet agl when the visibility is less than 1 mile during day hours or 3 miles during night hours provided they are operated clear of clouds and at a speed that allows the pilot adequate opportunity to see any air traffic or obstruction in time to avoid a collision.

Airplanes may be operated outside controlled airspace below 1,200 feet agl in an airport traffic pattern when the visibility is less than 3 miles, but not less than 1 mile during night hours, provided they are operated clear of clouds and within one-half mile of the runway.

** In addition, when operating within a control zone beneath a ceiling, the ceiling must not be less than 1,000 feet. If the pilot intends to land or takeoff or enter a traffic pattern within a control zone, the ground visibility must be at least 3 miles at that airport; if ground visibility is not reported at the airport, 3 miles flight visibility is required.

you have 3 statute miles visibility and standard VFR cloud clearance (i.e., 500 feet below, 1,000 feet above, and 2,000 feet horizontally). This is not a safe way to operate, but it would be legal. The safe thing to do would be to use the Uncontrolled Airport Procedures described in chapter 4.

Remember that as soon as you climb above 1,200 feet agl you will be entering controlled airspace (the Control Area) and will need 3 statute miles visibility and VFR cloud clearance (500 feet below, 1,000 feet above, and 2,000 feet horizontally—up to 10,000 feet msl) in order to be legally VFR.

It should be noted that an airport without a control tower that has a Flight Service Station on the field has an Airport Advisory Area (AAA). AAAs have a radius of 10 statute miles and no particular altitude limit. Flight Service Stations will provide advisories much like a unicom within this area—but there is no legal requirement for a pilot to talk to the FSS. AAAs are not marked on charts.

Airports without Control Towers (Magenta Colored), but with One or More Instrument Approaches

You can generally expect to find more traffic at these uncontrolled airfields than the ones in the first category because the FAA has deemed them busy enough to qualify for at least one instrument approach. Notice the circular or key-shaped magenta area around these airports. This means that controlled airspace (a Transition Area) starts at 700 feet over the airfield.

Legally, you may still fly over such an airport at 500 feet agl if it is in an uncongested area (but not at or above 700 feet agl), with a flight visibility of 1 statute mile and clear of clouds, with your radios turned off—but, really, you would be asking for trouble.

With such a low visibility, it wouldn't be unlikely that another pilot, wiser than you, had filed IFR to the airport and was approaching the field in the clouds and under the control of ATC. Of course, ATC has no authority in the uncontrolled airspace below 700 feet agl, and even with radar the controller may not know you are there. The best the controller could do is advise the IFR pilot to "Change to advisory frequency," and that pilot should broadcast his intentions and position and monitor reports from other pilots on the CTAF frequency. If your radios are off, you won't know he's coming in and he won't know you're there if you don't tell him—but you will be legal!

If the airport is in a congested area, you must maintain at least 1,000 feet agl above it, which now puts you in controlled airspace. VFR minima in controlled airspace are 3 miles visibility, and 500 feet below, 1,000 feet above, and 2,000 feet horizontally from clouds. Practically speaking, you therefore need a 1,500-foot ceiling and 3 miles visibility to overfly such an airport VFR.

Airports without Control Towers (Magenta Colored), but with One or More Instrument Approaches and a Control Zone

These uncontrolled airfields are relatively rare, but some can be found. The reason they are rare is that the basic requirements for a Control Zone (communication capability with aircraft to the surface of the primary airport and federally certified weather observers that take hourly and special weather observations) usually dictate the presence of a control tower. However, if the airport has a weather observer at the field and remote rapid relay communications capability to the ATC facility having jurisdiction over the area, a Control Zone can be approved for the field (FIG. 7-3).

Controlled airspace starts at such an airport at the surface, as in all Control Zones. Surrounding the airport with a radius of five statute miles, plus any extensions for instrument approach and departure paths, is a cylinder of controlled airspace you may not legally fly into when the weather is below VFR minimums (1,000-foot ceiling, 3 miles

Fig. 7-3. *Since the control tower at Bader Field in Atlantic City has been shut down, the airport no longer has an ATA, but it still has an instrument approach and is inside the Atlantic City Control Zone.*

visibility) unless you have a clearance from the controlling ATC facility. You can tool around all you want at 500 feet with 1 statute mile visibility below the 700-foot floor of the Transition Area and the 1,200-foot floor of the Control Area—but stay out of the Control Zone.

To land at or take off from an airport in the Control Zone or to transit through the Control Zone when the weather is less than 1,000-foot ceiling and 3 miles visibility, you need what is called a Special VFR clearance. AIM paragraph 264 should be read and understood if you intend to ask for a Special VFR clearance because special rules apply. Basically, you'll need a minimum of one mile visibility and be able to remain clear of clouds. The section about Special VFR doesn't specifically say it, but since FAR 91.119 requires a basic safe altitude of 500 feet agl over uncongested areas, you may find yourself bending the regulations, if not breaking them, if you fly at a lower altitude. Special VFR operations are also prohibited at night unless the pilot is instrument rated and flying an aircraft equipped for IFR flight.

What happens to a Control Zone when the weather is greater than that required for VFR flight, in other words, when the ceiling is at or above 1,000 feet and the visibility at or above 3 statute miles?

This is the old $64,000 question. It is often stated and sometimes written that Control Zones do not exist when the weather is VFR. This is an oversimplification of the truth.

The truth is Control Zones are still there, during their respective operating hours, even if the conditions are VMC. However, when the weather is VMC, the controlled airspace in Control Zones is no different than, say, the controlled airspace in the Control Area above 1,200 feet agl up to 14,500 feet msl. You can fly in the Control Area VFR without a clearance and without radio communications as long as you maintain VFR minima and don't infringe on other controlled airspace, such as ARSAs or TCAs. You can likewise fly through a Control Zone, land and take off at the airport (if it doesn't have a control tower) in the Control Zone, and not talk to anyone on the radio. It's perfectly legal, if not perfectly safe.

All IFR traffic will, of course, still be conversing with the ATC facility that has control over the zone, but there is no requirement for VFR traffic to even turn on their radios—as long as the ceiling is 1,000 feet or better and the visibility is at or above 3 statute miles.

A more prudent procedure is to monitor the ATC facility in charge as you approach the field and then follow the procedures for operating at uncontrolled airports outlined in chapter 4.

Another catch with the statement "Control Zones don't exist when the weather is VFR" is that the primary airport in most Control Zones usually has a tower. When an airfield has an operating tower, it automatically has an Airport Traffic Area regardless of the weather, and flying in ATAs requires two-way radio communication.

So be careful about busting into a Control Zone when you are VFR—unless you are at or above 3,000 feet agl (the ceiling of an ATA)—because chances are you will be entering an ATA, as well, and you need contact with the tower to do that.

Airports with Control Towers (Blue Colored), but No Instrument Approaches

These are also few and far between because it costs money to keep controllers in a tower, and the utility of an airport is greatly increased when it has an instrument approach. The opposite, an airport with an instrument approach and no control tower, is more common because it's much less expensive to run. But for the sake of explanation, let's talk about it.

As stated above, an airport with an operating control tower is a controlled airport and therefore also has an Airport Traffic Area. *Operating* is a key word because when the tower controllers go home the ATA disappears.

An ATA, by definition, extends to a radius of 5 statute miles from the center of the field (the same as a Control Zone) and up to an altitude of (but not including) 3,000 feet. ATAs are not indicated on charts except by the fact that all blue-colored airports have them.

As stated in *AIM*, "When operating at an airport where traffic control is being exercised by a control tower, pilots are required to maintain two-way radio contact with the tower while operating within the airport traffic area unless the tower authorizes otherwise. Initial call-up should be made about 15 miles from the airport."

Generally speaking, clearance to take off, land, and transit an ATA must be obtained from the control tower.

What about weather minimums?

Strictly speaking, an airport with a control tower but without a Control Zone is in uncontrolled airspace. Therefore, VFR minima in uncontrolled airspace apply; i.e., 1 statute mile visibility and clear of clouds during day hours and 3 statute miles and 500 feet below/1,000 feet above/2,000 feet horizontal distance from clouds at night.

The new (1990) FAR Part 91 added a new wrinkle to these VFR weather minima. Specifically, 91.155(b) states, ". . . the following operations may be conducted outside controlled airspace below 1,200 feet above the surface: (1) Helicopter . . . (2) Airplane. When the visibility is less than 3 miles but 1 mile or greater during night hours, an airplane may be operated clear of clouds if operated in an airport traffic pattern within one-half mile of the runway" (TABLE 7-1).

What this means is that you may shoot touch-and-gos, remaining within one-half mile of the runway, at any airport that is not inside a Control Zone or other controlled airspace (such as a TCA) regardless of whether or not it has an operating control tower (remember an ATA is not technically "controlled airspace") as long as you remain clear of clouds and, during night hours, have at least 1 statute mile visibility. Presumably doing the above during the day requires no specific minimum visibility, although to stay within one-half mile of a runway it would help if you could see it. You must also be careful with the phrase "outside controlled airspace below 1,200 feet above the surface" because an airport with an instrument approach will have a Transition Area, which will bring the floor of controlled airspace down to 700 feet agl.

This new rule isn't particularly beneficial to the cross-country pilot and, in fact, may cause him some distress, particularly at airports without control towers. It's not difficult to imagine a pilot descending through the clouds on an instrument approach to an uncontrolled airport only to find two or three student pilots in the traffic pattern, all trying to remain within one-half mile of the runway in low visibility and below 700 feet. If nothing else, such a situation would certainly raise everyone's blood pressure.

Airports with a Control Tower (Blue Colored) and One or More Instrument Approaches, but No Control Zone

Such airports are theoretically possible and there are, in fact, a few military airports fitting this description (for example, Olf Whitehouse Field in the Jacksonville Navy Airport Traffic Area in Florida). However, if any such civilian airports exist, I haven't been able to find them. If you ever happen to run into one, just remember that ATAs are considered outside controlled airspace with respect to VFR weather minima, but that you must maintain two-way radio contact with the tower inside the ATA.

Because of the instrument approach, controlled airspace at such fields would start at 700 feet agl.

Airports with a Control Tower, One or More Instrument Approaches, and a Control Zone

This is by far the most common combination found at busy airfields (FIG. 7-4). In fact, because both ATAs and Control Zones have the same horizontal radius (5 statute miles) and Control Zones are marked with dashed blue lines on charts while ATAs are not marked at all, it's easy to start to think of the two as being one and the same. As we have seen, they aren't.

However, for all practical purposes, at airports that have both ATAs and Control Zones, they may as well be the same. At such airports, the ATA is now officially controlled airspace because it is co-located with the Control Zone. And at these airports you must always contact someone (the control tower or approach control) before entering the Control Zone, even when the weather is VFR.

If conditions are VFR (ceiling 1,000 feet and visibility 3 statute miles), you need clearance from the control tower to take off, land, or transit the ATA (ATA rules).

If the conditions are less than VFR (the ceiling is less than 1,000 feet and the visibility is below 3, but not less than 1 statute mile), you still need a clearance from the control tower to take off, land, or transit the ATA, but you also need to obtain a Special VFR clearance to fly within the Control Zone (Control Zone rules). The tower can usually obtain this clearance from the ATC controller for you, although sometimes you may have to talk to approach or departure control to get it. You must

Fig. 7-4. *Busy airports usually have a control tower, a control zone, and one or more instrument approaches.*

remain clear of clouds in the Control Zone and at a safe altitude, i.e., not less than 500 feet over uncongested areas and 1,000 feet over congested areas.

If the visibility is less than 1 statute mile or the ceiling is below 500 feet, you'd better be IFR if you are flying inside a Control Zone cum ATA.

(Note that fixed-wing Special VFR flight is not allowed in Control Zones that are indicated on charts by blue T T T T T T T.)

Once you are outside the Control Zone (and, therefore, the ATA as well), you enter uncontrolled airspace if you remain below the floors of the Transition Area (700 feet) and the Control Area (1,200 feet). Above those altitudes, you are in controlled airspace, and VFR minima in controlled airspace apply.

When flying VFR and maintaining VFR minima, you may legally fly over an ATA at or above 3,000 feet agl, and consequently through the Control Zone associated with the ATA, without obtaining any clearance. In this case, it would be safer to contact the appropriate ATC facility (in most cases approach control) for advisories because IFR traffic may be transiting the same airspace. As the *Airman Information Manual* points out, "A high percentage of near midair collisions occur below 8,000 feet agl and within 30 miles of an airport," so it's always a good idea to broadcast your position.

TERMINAL RADAR SERVICE AREAS, AIRPORT RADAR SERVICE AREAS, AND TERMINAL CONTROL AREAS

More often than not when you operate near an airport with a control tower and Control Zone, you'll also find yourself in a Terminal Radar Service Area, an Airport Radar Service Area, or a Terminal Control Area, and you'll be required to talk to someone.

Terminal Radar Service Areas (TRSAs)

All commissioned radar facilities, in addition to controlling IFR traffic, provide basic radar services (traffic advisories and limited vectoring) to VFR aircraft. At many airports with relatively heavy traffic, the FAA has established Terminal Radar Service Areas. TRSAs are indicated on Sectional and other charts by solid magenta lines around airports.

Originally when the STAGE services were developed, these two radar services were identified as STAGE I. Over the years, as STAGE II and III services came into being, this definition became unnecessary. As a result, STAGE I has been eliminated from use and in handbooks.

The difference between STAGE II and STAGE III service is that while both provide traffic advisories, limited vectoring, and sequencing of both IFR and VFR traffic, only STAGE III TRSAs provides separation for IFR and participating VFR aircraft. This is of little practical consequence to the VFR pilot—all he need remember is that he can obtain traffic advisories, vectoring, and sequencing in all TRSAs, if he wants it.

When a pilot is approaching a TRSA or getting ready to depart from an airport in a TRSA, he is requested to contact approach or departure control, after which he will be in radar contact with ATC and be vectored to the final approach or out of the TRSA in a manner that assures safe operation from other participating aircraft. The important phrase here is *participating*.

The radar service is not mandatory. A pilot may refuse it by simply informing ATC with the phrase "Negative Stage Three" and then continuing his approach or departure completely oblivious to everyone else. Some pilots habitually refuse the radar service, feeling that in many cases it results in a waste of time and fuel. As a consequence, all pilots, participating and nonparticipating, must still maintain visual surveillance in order to be sure that ATC does not inadvertently vector them into a conflict with a nonparticipating aircraft.

Airport Radar Service Areas (ARSAs)

By the middle 1980s TRSAs were beginning to disappear—only to reappear as Airport Radar Service Areas (ARSAs) that require radio contact with all aircraft in the prescribed airspace.

In August 1982, a National Airspace Review task group recommended discontinuance of the TRSAs and implementation of Model "B" Airspace. Test airports for one year were Robert Mueller Airport in Austin, Texas, and Port Columbus Airport in Columbus, Ohio. At the close of a one-year study of "B" airspace the FAA confirmed the concept and renamed it "Airport Radar Service Area."

ARSAs are indicated on charts by dashed, magenta lines around the primary airport. They are a kind of a middle ground between TRSAs and TCAs. Their dimensions compare interestingly to Airport Traffic Areas.

While an ATA has a radius of 5 statute miles and an upper limit of 3,000 feet, the "Inner Circle" of an ARSA has a radius of 5 nautical miles and a vertical limit of 4,000 feet agl. In addition, an ARSA has an "Outer Circle" with a radius of 10 nautical miles, which starts at 1,200 feet agl (the floor of most Control Areas) and extends to 4,000 feet agl (FIG. 7-5).

Finally, an ARSA has an "Outer Area" with a radius of 20 nautical miles, which "extends from the lower limits of radar/radio coverage up to the ceiling of the approach control's delegated airspace, excluding the ARSA and other airspace as appropriate" (AIM, para. 100). In this "Outer Area," nothing special is required of the pilot and, like TRSAs, basic radar service is available, but not mandatory. Unlike TRSAs, the "Outer Areas" of ARSAs are not indicated on charts.

Each person operating an aircraft within the "Inner" and "Outer" Circles of an ARSA (which, to repeat, are both indicated on charts by dashed magenta lines) must maintain two-way radio communications with ATC and comply with all ATC clearances and instructions. Obviously, you need an operable two-way radio to do this.

Airport Radar Service Area (ARSA)

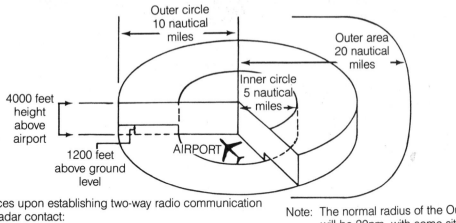

Services upon establishing two-way radio communication
and radar contact:
Sequencing arrivals
IFR/IFR standard arrivals
IFR/VFR traffic advisories and conflict resolution
VFR/VFR traffic advisories

Note: The normal radius of the Outer Area,
will be 20nm, with some site specific
variations.

IFR: Instrument Flight Rules
VFR: Visual Flight Rules

Fig. 7-5. *Basic ARSA dimensions.*

The requirement to establish radio communications with ATC before entering an
ARSA has come under close scrutiny and interpretation by the FAA. Use the following rules to stay out of trouble.

1. If, on your initial radio call to ATC, the controller responds with "(your aircraft call sign) standby," or "(your aircraft call sign), go ahead," or something
   similar, radio communications have been established, and you may legally
   enter the ARSA. The controller does not have to say "radar contact" or give
   you a clearance in order for radio communications to be established between
   you and him—he just has to say your call sign.
2. If, on your initial radio call to ATC, the controller responds with, "Aircraft
   calling Metropolis Approach Control, standby," or any other reply *without*
   your specific aircraft call sign, radio communications have not been established and you must remain outside the ARSA.
3. If, on your initial radio call to ATC, the controller responds with, "(your aircraft call sign) remain outside the ARSA and standby," you have established
   radio communications, but workload or traffic conditions prevent immediate
   provision of ARSA service. Follow the controller's instructions, and don't
   enter the ARSA until he says you may.

The controller will call you back as soon as he can. In most cases, he won't establish radio communication with you (by responding with your call sign) until he has positively identified you on his radar screen. He must do this because ARSA rules require him to maintain separation for all aircraft in the ARSA, and he obviously can't do this unless he knows where you are. The controller's not being nasty—it's simply that his workload or traffic conditions in the ARSA make it difficult or impossible to add you to the mix just yet.

Beginning December 30, 1990, a transponder with Mode-C capability also became required for operations within and above an ARSA.

Terminal Control Areas (TCAs)

TCAs are the big daddies of controlled airspace. Their establishment around the airports in large metropolitan areas is primarily to provide for the safe and efficient flow of commercial air traffic. General aviation traffic, including private, corporate, and charter flights, are allowed into TCAs, if not always particularly welcome. Student pilots are not allowed in many TCAs at all, and those that do permit student pilot operations have special requirements.

Flying even in the vicinity of a TCA has special requirements and hazards. If you are within 30 nautical miles of the center of the TCA, you are required to have a transponder with Mode-C (altitude reporting) capability, no matter what your altitude. Fortunately, this 30-nm line is marked on charts with a solid, blue line. (See Appendix C for exceptions to this rule.)

Another rule is a speed limit of 200 knots in the airspace underlying a TCA. The reason for this is air traffic that, in order to avoid the TCA proper, tends to concentrate in the airspace underlying the TCA (FIG. 7-6).

To enter a TCA, you must have a clearance from ATC. You also must have a private pilot certificate, although certain exemptions for student pilots in some TCAs are permitted. You must have two-way communication available for the appropriate frequencies required, and the aircraft must be equipped with a VOR receiver and a transponder with Mode-C. DME, although useful to have, is not required.

It's a good policy to take along extra fuel whenever you expect to encounter a TCA en route because chances are you'll find yourself on a detour even if you do get a clearance into the TCA as soon as you request it. The reason is simple: When you're in the TCA, the controller must keep you separated from other traffic, VFR and IFR alike. If your straight-line track takes you through a busy instrument approach corridor, which is quite possible, the controller must vector you around it.

TCAs are depicted on Sectional and other charts with solid, blue lines. The VFR Terminal Area Charts (TACs) give a much more detailed depiction of the areas and are, therefore, a must when flying in a TCA. Helicopter Route Charts, which are available for the Chicago, Washington, Los Angeles, New York City, and Boston

Fig. 7-6. *Bridges often confront VFR pilots when flying under the floors of TCAs.*

areas, give even more detail than the TACs and are recommended if you plan to fly often within these TCAs. They also give you a better idea of where you'll encounter low-flying helicopters and a more precise location of the landmarks used for position reporting.

Presently only available for the Los Angeles terminal area is a new type of chart called the Jeppesen Sanderson VFR NavService. These charts detail arrival and departure routes for 18 airports in the Los Angeles area, and an overflight chart. They use VORs and visual checkpoints to depict recommended routes and altitudes through and around the TCA, the ARSAs, and the ATAs. Jeppesen is reportedly working on VFR NavService charts for other terminal areas, as well.

With respect to weather, TCAs are obviously controlled airspace, so VFR minima in controlled airspace apply. It's important to remember that adhering to an assigned heading or altitude is no excuse for violating VFR minima. The ATC controller gives you instructions based on other traffic, not weather. He cannot see where the clouds are, and it is the pilot's responsibility to avoid them. When weather is a problem, it is helpful to the controller if the pilot suggests a heading or altitude that will work better for him.

It goes without saying that lower ceilings and visibilities make it all the more difficult for TCA controllers to vector VFR aircraft through their sectors—the available airspace just becomes that much smaller. It's not surprising, then, that VFR aircraft are often denied entry into TCAs when the weather is marginal.

Don't ever get angry with a controller when this happens. He or she is doing a difficult job made more difficult by the weather. Be prepared to hold outside the TCA until a traffic "window" opens for you, or fly around or under the whole area. If you get angry and insist on a clearance, you may find yourself vectored all over the sky or you may never get one at all. Controllers are only human. Be civil to them, and they'll be as helpful to you as they can.

Many VFR pilots consider TCAs a real hassle, but, on the other hand, TCAs are the closest thing a VFR pilot can come to the radar-protected environment of IFR flying. With all aircraft inside a TCA under the control of ATC, the likelihood of a midair collision in heavy traffic areas is reduced. "See and avoid" is still a good policy, of course, because a controller may miss a conflict, or some oddball might come busting through the area without a clearance or transponder, but TCAs are generally safer than TRSAs, in which participation is recommended but not mandatory.

AIRSPACE ABOVE 10,000 FEET MSL

All aircraft operating above 10,000 feet msl, except when within 2,500 of the terrain in mountainous areas, must be equipped with a functioning transponder and encoding altimeter. When thus equipped, pilots—for the time being, at least—may operate above 10,000 feet but below 18,000 feet msl VFR without obtaining a clearance or maintaining contact with ATC, assuming that they remain in VFR conditions.

SPECIAL-USE AIRSPACE

The country is dotted with areas that are shown and identified on the charts as *Prohibited, Restricted, Warning,* or *Alert Areas.* Most of these are related to a variety of military activities, and warnings or instructions given on the charts should be heeded. Inadvertent or unauthorized penetration of the airspace within the altitude limitations shown may put the aircraft in serious jeopardy.

Prohibited Areas are definite no-nos. Such areas are established for security or other reasons associated with national welfare. Flight of aircraft in these areas is absolutely prohibited.

Flight in Restricted Areas is not quite as prohibitive as in Prohibited Areas, but penetration of active Restricted Areas without authorization may be extremely hazardous. Restricted Areas denote the existence of unusual, often invisible, hazards to aircraft, such as artillery firing, aerial gunnery, or guided missiles.

If a Restricted Area is not active, ATC will allow aircraft operating IFR to fly through the area without a specific clearance. If the area is active, ATC will issue a clearance to ensure that the aircraft avoids the restricted area.

Aircraft operating VFR, on the other hand, are on their own. Pilots are advised to contact the nearest ATC agency to find out if an area is active or inactive. If it is inactive, you may safely fly through it. If it is active, avoid it. You cannot operate an aircraft in an active Restricted Area unless you have obtained permission from the using or controlling agency.

Warning Areas are essentially Restricted Areas established outside the coastal 3-mile limit. Because they are in international airspace, they cannot legally be designated Restricted Areas. The hazards associated with Warning Areas, however, can be just as dangerous as those associated with Restricted Areas. All aircraft should obviously avoid these areas when they are active.

Military Operations Areas (MOAs), though not quite as restrictive as Restricted and Warning Areas, can also be quite hazardous. IFR flights may be cleared through an MOA if ATC can provide IFR separation between participating and nonparticipating aircraft. If ATC cannot do this, the flight will be vectored around the area.

Pilots flying VFR may legally fly into an MOA when it is active, but they must be extra alert for military aircraft, which could be doing virtually anything military aircraft do: high and low altitude dogfighting, bombing runs, aerial refueling, nap-of-the-earth, all-weather insertions, etc. Military pilots flying military aircraft in MOAs are exempted from the FARs, which prohibit acrobatic flight within Federal airways and Control Zones. A prudent policy is to avoid MOAs when they are active, and if you must fly through one, contact the controlling agency for traffic advisories.

Alert Areas are not quite as dangerous as MOAs because all activity within an Alert Area should be conducted in accordance with the FARs. Their existence, however, does designate the presence of a high volume of pilot training or other unusual types of activities. Alert Areas often, but not always, are under the radar coverage of a military radar facility. For example, Alert Area A-220 in New Jersey is controlled by McGuire Approach Control. Flying VFR, you may legally enter an Alert Area without contacting anyone, but it is always more prudent to contact the controlling agency and request radar advisories. The service is there, so why not use it? Besides, Alert Areas are often found in conjunction with restricted areas or MOAs, and the military controller can vector you around these when necessary.

For safety's sake, always make it a policy to check your route for any Prohibited, Restricted, Warning, or Alert Areas and to contact ATC before penetrating any special use airspace.

FUTURE AIRSPACE

Early in 1990, the FAA published a notice of proposed rulemaking proposing that U.S. airspace be redesignated in accordance with ICAO standardization. In addition to the name changes proposed below, the ceiling of Airport Traffic Areas would be raised from 3,000 feet agl to 4,000 feet agl.

Present name	ICAO designation
Positive Control Airspace (above 18,000 ft msl)	A
Terminal Control Area	B

Present name	ICAO designation
Airport Radar Service Area	C
Airport Traffic Area	D
All Other Controlled Airspace	E
Uncontrolled Airspace	G

Whatever they end up being called, the number of TCAs and ARSAs is expected to increase. In 1990 there were 24 TCAs and 125 ARSAs. By 1992 the FAA expects totals to rise to 34 and 130, respectively.

8
Flight Number Three

Date: April 28, 1973.
Pilot: Male, age 26.
License: Commercial, SEL, MEL, instrument.
Pilot-In-Command Time: 535 hours.
Aircraft: Grumman American Yankee.
Flight: From Farmingdale, New York, to Nassau, the Bahamas.
Purpose of Flight: Vacation.

The weather in the Northeast was grey, overcast, and wet, and the pilot and his girlfriend thought it was a perfect time for a sunny vacation in the south. They filed an IFR flight plan from Farmingdale to Salisbury, Maryland, and flew two hours of the 2:45-hour flight IMC. After topping off the tanks and adding a quart of oil, they walked over to the Flight Service Station to get a preflight briefing.

At that time there were Flight Service Stations at many airports. The briefer told them it was VFR to Wilmington, North Carolina, their next en route stop, and they shouldn't have any problems with weather all the way south. They gathered all the information they thought they would need and made a VFR departure from Salisbury.

As they flew into the Carolinas, they observed a large number of military aircraft, both at high and low altitudes. There were all sorts of helicopters and fixed-wing aircraft, even paratroopers. Although so much activity seemed unusual, the pilot didn't think it was of any particular concern to him.

"EXOTIC DANCER"

For whatever reason, perhaps higher winds than forecast (the pilot can't remember exactly), he decided to divert to Ellis Airport, a small airport in North Carolina, to take on more fuel before continuing to Wilmington. After landing and taxiing to the ramp, they were met by a group of aviators clad in olive-drab flight suits. These Army helicopter pilots informed the pilot and his girlfriend that Ellis Airport, along with a good number of other airports in the area, was closed for a major military exercise (called "Exotic Dancer") and would remain so for a week. Since the airport was closed to civilian traffic, they couldn't allow the pilot and his girlfriend to take off.

The pilot didn't care to spend his vacation in a hole-in-the-wall airport surrounded by Army aviators, so after a fairly lengthy discussion he convinced them he was adamant about not staying at Ellis. The Army pilots eventually consented and coordinated with their command to obtain a clearance for the pilot to fly to Newburn Airport, about 30 miles northeast of Ellis.

Unfortunately, there was the problem of fuel. The Grumman American Yankee carried 24 gallons of fuel, 22 of it usable, but the pilot wasn't sure how much he had because the fuel sight gauges in the Yankee were highly unreliable. The gauges were inside the cabin walls in the wing roots and had a tendency to show a high fuel indication with just a few gallons and vice versa. For this reason, the pilot usually relied on elapsed flight time as his main way of judging how much fuel he had. Obviously, this wasn't too reliable either because different altitudes and power settings give varying rates of fuel consumption, so he liked to give himself a large margin for error. His personal rule of thumb was three hours and 30 minutes. After that he liked to have the Yankee at the fuel pumps.

The sight gauges didn't show much fuel. Up to that point they had been airborne just over two hours. Although the pilot knew he had enough fuel to make it to Newburn, he wasn't sure if he'd be landing with legal VFR reserves. Because Ellis was closed, the pilot couldn't buy fuel there.

In any case, the Army assigned the pilot a VHF frequency to communicate with the airborne command post, a helicopter, which would coordinate their route from Ellis to Newburn. The point was to give the pilot vectors away from dangerous goings-on. But the pilot's fuel situation was such that he didn't want to do as much S-turning as the command post wanted. He flew a more or less direct track to Newburn and kept his eyes open for hazards like paratroopers, artillery, and low-flying aircraft.

The flight was even more difficult for his girlfriend because the pilot was wearing a headset and as a consequence she couldn't hear his conversation with the Army command post. He had also decided to allow one tank to run completely dry and should have told her, but he got too busy talking on the radio to the command post and forgot.

When the engine did quit 1,000 feet over the trees, she was so surprised she banged her head on the canopy. The pilot switched tanks quickly and got the engine restarted right away, but his girlfriend was still shaken up. Finally, they landed uneventfully at Newburn Airport.

They were met by one of the local FSS specialists, who was then acting as an investigator. He was very polite about the incident and informed the pilot what he already knew, that they had flown into a major military exercise.

What the pilot didn't know was that Exotic Dancer occurs every spring. If he had checked the NOTAMs and the JEPP revisions, he would have found that they put out quite a bit of information about it. It normally covers the Carolinas and a hundred or so miles out to sea with the Naval Task Force.

The FSS specialist told the pilot that he might later receive a phone call from the FAA. The pilot accepted responsibility for the mistake but did mention that he had had a face-to-face briefing at the Flight Service Station in Salisbury, Maryland, and they had a full record of his briefing. The pilot felt the briefer should have known the exercise was going on and should have told everyone going south about it; therefore, the mistake was at least partly the briefer's, too.

As it turned out, the FAA never called, and the pilot chalked the incident up to experience.

ANALYSIS

One would think that a face-to-face briefing with a Flight Service specialist would certainly include information about an extensive military operation in one's route of flight. As this experience proves, however, this is not always the case.

Although the briefing didn't provide the pilot with all the information he needed to know, at least it allowed him to "spread the blame" for the incident. This shouldn't be your motivation for obtaining a briefing, but on the other hand, in these "sue-'em-for-all-their-worth" times, a briefing may be all that's between you and a court case. Of course, if you're shot down by a ground-to-air missile because the briefer forgot to tell you a restricted area was active, it's going to be a moot point anyway. Maybe your survivors can try to sue the government for neglect.

Seriously, this flight reinforces an important point this book is trying to stress, namely, preflight planning. Flying an airplane on a cross-country flight certainly requires a lot more planning than driving a car over the same route. Unfortunately, many private pilots seem to forget this.

It's also unfortunate that it's no longer possible for most pilots to receive face-to-face briefings from a Flight Service specialist. This flight notwithstanding, there's nothing like such briefings for thoroughness and sheer educational value. One always seems to learn a little more about weather, ATC procedures, or the National Airspace System after talking to a briefer. If you ever do find yourself at an airport that still has an active Flight Service Station (and there are many of them still around), take the time to get a preflight briefing from one of the specialists. You'll be surprised at what you've been missing.

Today's methods for obtaining preflight information are a lot more passive and require more work from the pilot. The information is there, but you have to know what you need, request it verbally or by punching keys, sometimes sift it out of a mass of other information, and evaluate it. We don't have the luxury of an experienced briefer second-guessing what we forget to ask him and volunteering information we don't even know we need.

Lessons to learn from this flight?

1. Check NOTAMs thoroughly for your destination, route, and alternate.
2. Double-check your chart for special-use airspace, i.e., Prohibited, Restricted, Military Operating, and Alert Areas.
3. Call ahead to your destination and intermediate stops to find out any last-minute information.

In two words: PLAN AHEAD!

EPILOGUE

The pilot's girlfriend obviously was not all that shaken up because she eventually became his wife, even though they didn't make it to the Bahamas that time. The pilot decided then and there the Yankee was not a long-range, cross-country aircraft. It was fun to fly, zipping around New York, but its 24-gallon fuel tanks were too limiting. They flew to Myrtle Beach, overnighted, and returned the next day to Farmingdale, keeping well clear of the exercise area.

On the basis of that trip, the pilot sold his Yankee and bought a Piper Arrow. He has kept it in mint condition ever since.

9
TCAs Made Easy

IF YOU READ ONE OF THE EARLIER EDITIONS OF *CROSS-COUNTRY FLYING*, you'll notice the title of this chapter was "Those Pesky TCAs." That title, although catchy, implied a less than friendly attitude toward TCAs.

True, operating near and inside a TCA might be considered an inconvenience to some, especially those pilots who pine for the thrilling days of yesteryear, when the Great Waldo Pepper plied the skies of the U.S. of A., but the fact is the sheer volume of air traffic these days—we're talking about nearly a million aircraft movements per year at some airports—makes the establishment of TCAs a virtual necessity. Whether you agree with this assessment or not is immaterial. TCAs are here to stay, and more are coming: We may as well learn how to live with them.

HOW TO SURVIVE TCAs

The way to live with TCAs is to use the system the way it's designed to be used. For the VFR pilot, there are four ways to get into, out of, or through a TCA, and all four require prior planning. (For the IFR pilot, TCAs are a minor concern because ATC will simply handle the flight through the airspace in a routine manner, assuming the aircraft is suitably equipped.)

Prior planning means you know what you want before you get to the TCA boundary and you know how to tell the controller you want it. If you've flown frequently into TCAs, you may have noticed that many commercial pilots seem to get preferential treatment from the controllers. In fact, they do; but not because controllers are particularly prejudiced against noncommercial aircraft.

Commercial pilots usually operate on the same routes day in and day out. As a result, they know where they want to go and how to ask for it properly. Just as important, the controllers know from experience that these pilots know more or less what's expected of them. (In addition, operators often establish Letters of Agreement with ATC facilities that specify exact routes and altitudes for their flights.) Thus, commercial pilots become, as far as the controllers are concerned, "known entities," which means the controllers can safely spend a little less time monitoring their blips on the radar screens.

On the other hand, an aircraft arriving out of nowhere with an unfamiliar call sign or tail number is an "unknown entity" to the controller. He or she has no other way of knowing the competence of the pilot at the controls other than by the way he or she speaks on the radio. If the pilot isn't sure what he wants or demonstrates a lack of knowledge of the area, the controller will have to spend a proportionately greater-than-normal amount of time watching that radar return to be sure the pilot does what he's told to do.

(Of course, private aircraft can also become "known entities" to controllers. After a short while at a particular facility, controllers begin to recognize call signs and tail numbers that frequent their airspace. If you demonstrate your competence often enough, the ATC specialists will reward your professionalism with respect and be more willing to accommodate your requests. The opposite is also true.)

It's the controller's responsibility to keep all aircraft in his sector clear of all other aircraft, and sometimes there isn't too much room for error. If the controller happens to be exceptionally busy, he may decide to avoid the extra workload (and headache) by keeping a pilot who doesn't seem to know what he's doing outside the TCA airspace until the traffic situation improves.

It makes sense, therefore, to make a good impression on the TCA controller the first time you call him up. By using a current Terminal Area Chart (TAC) or Helicopter Route Chart, you can find the correct frequency and a known VFR checkpoint. Use these and the correct terminology, and chances are you'll get what you request if it is at all possible.

Perhaps the most efficient way to transit a TCA is to use an established VFR route. The route could be under the TCA floors (the New York TCA's Hudson River Route), in a "tunnel" of VFR airspace through the TCA (the San Diego VFR Corridor), or in the TCA airspace proper (the Biltmore Route in the Phoenix TCA).

If you stay under the floor altitudes or fly in a corridor, you don't need a clearance, but you won't receive traffic advisories either. Check the chart for "self announce" or "pilot-to-pilot monitor" frequencies for the TCA. Be sure to broadcast your position, altitude, direction of flight, and destination at regular intervals and to keep your eyes wide open. If the route is popular (and it probably is since it was established in the first place), expect to encounter other traffic.

If the route is inside the TCA, find the appropriate TCA frequency on the chart, ask the controller for the route you want, and follow his instructions. It's as simple as that.

The second way to transit a TCA is to construct your own route between designated or well-known landmarks and request this route from the controller. Don't be surprised if you don't get it or if the controller revises it for you. In most cases, however, you will get something that at least approximates the route you asked for. By giving the controller a specific request, you'll also give him the impression that you know what you're doing and he'll probably do his best to get you to your destination using the most direct route possible while keeping you clear of other traffic.

The third way is to plan to fly under and around the controlled airspace inside the TCA. Because TCAs are shaped like upside-down wedding cakes, the further one is from the center of the TCA (which is controlled all the way to the surface), the higher the altitude one may fly and still avoid the floor of the overlying TCA segment. Of course, the closer one is to the center of the TCA, the lower the floor of controlled TCA airspace. Obviously, the closer-in segments often present greater traffic congestion because aircraft are squeezed into a smaller space.

Be aware, too, that ATC may legally vector aircraft inside the TCA on a floor or ceiling altitude of the TCA. Therefore, consider all the airspace inside these "wedding cakes" as "hot" and fly accordingly: Stay at least a mile or two from the vertical boundaries and 300−400 feet, preferably 500 feet, below the floors.

Of course, you should increase your "see and avoid" vigilance anytime you're in or near a TCA, but be particularly vigilant when your main reason for selecting a particular route is to avoid TCA airspace. Chances are, a lot of other pilots have noticed the same route, too, know they can legally fly it without talking to ATC, and may not be watching out for other traffic as well as you are. Unfortunately, there are still some pilots who subscribe to the "Big Sky" theory of collision avoidance, even near TCAs.

The fourth way to avoid a TCA is to fly over the top of it. Although legal, this option may also be dangerous if you fly only 100 feet or so above the TCA ceiling.

Turbine engines are more efficient at higher altitudes, and pilots flying turbine-equipped airplanes want to get to a high cruising altitude as soon as possible. One of the reasons for establishing TCAs is to provide for the safe transition of these aircraft between the airport environment and the higher altitudes. Skimming just over the ceiling of the TCA is asking for trouble and will also cause controllers considerable work as they stop climbs and descents of other traffic in order to protect you. (Just because you're not talking to ATC doesn't mean they can't see you on radar.) Additionally, controllers can and often will assign IFR traffic to the ceiling altitude of a TCA. Therefore, overfly a TCA by at least 1,000 feet, more if you're able.

Depending on the height of the TCA and the type of aircraft you're flying, it may take some time to climb to a safe altitude, or it may not be possible at all, which is why you'll need to do some prior planning. If the top of the TCA is 12,500 feet and the service ceiling of your aircraft is only 11,000 feet, for example, avoiding the TCA by overflying it is not one of your options. You'll have to choose another way.

A FEW MORE TRICKS

For the uninitiated, one of the most frightening aspects of operating in TCAs is the radio chatter. During busy hours, it is virtually nonstop. Pilots accustomed to the more casual pace of non-TCA environments usually find it hard to get a word in edgewise. It takes some practice to find them, but there really are pauses between transmissions. They're just shorter than in less hectic areas.

The trick is to pay close attention to what is being said and to know exactly what you want to say before keying the microphone. Tune in to the frequency five or ten minutes before you need to call up the TCA controller. Listen to the exchanges of information to get a feel for the pattern. Without too much difficulty, you'll be able to detect when the controller's conversation with one pilot is over and how long the other pilots wait before jumping in.

The first few times you try you'll probably hear someone else transmit just as you're about to key the microphone. This is quite normal because most of us are reluctant to cut another pilot off in the middle of his conversation with ATC and it is often hard to know when the conversation is over. Listening to the frequency some minutes before you need your clearance is the only way to get a feel for the pace of the transmissions and the information being passed to each aircraft.

Don't despair if you don't catch on at first. It will come with practice and after a while even gets to be fun.

Another trick of the trade used by many commercial operators is the "sterile cockpit" principle. Simply put, air crews cut out the intracockpit BS when inside or near a TCA and pay full attention to the chatter on the radio. En route they may discuss everything under the sun, but in TCAs the talk is (or should be) all task oriented. It may take some effort for a private pilot to convince his companion to stop gabbing about the sights or complaining about the lack of amenities, but it's worth the effort. A missed radio call is not only irritating and time-wasting to the controller and other pilots, it may also make the difference between a near-miss and a midair in a busy TCA.

One last—magic—word about entering TCAs: The word is *clear*, and derivations thereof. If you don't hear the word *clear* from the controller, as in, "N23456, *cleared* into the Metropolis TCA, maintain 3,000 feet directly to the Daily Planet," don't enter TCA airspace. The term "radar contact" is not a clearance, nor should a transponder squawk, heading instruction, or altitude assignment be construed as an authorization to enter the TCA unless it is accompanied by the word *clear*.

Be aware that controllers are human and sometimes forget to use the correct terminology. If you're unsure whether or not you've received a clearance, be polite and ask the controller to confirm that you are cleared in.

One more tip: Turn on your landing light in TCAs, day and night! It's the best, and cheapest, way to increase your own visibility to other aircraft—and to birds, too, for that matter. In the 1970s the Air Force experienced a significant decrease in bird strikes after all aircraft were required to fly with landing lights on all the time. Think of it this way: TCAs are near big cities, big cities have garbage dumps, garbage dumps attract birds, and no one complains about aircraft overflying the local trash heap. Therefore, there's a good chance a low altitude VFR TCA route will be in the vicinity of at least one garbage dump and a large breakfast flock.

SOME RULES

In order to operate within a Terminal Control Area, the aircraft must be equipped with an operable two-way radio capable of communications with ATC on the appropriate frequencies, at least one VOR or TACAN nav receiver, and a transponder with automatic altitude reporting equipment (Mode-C).

The speed limit inside a TCA and below 10,000 feet is 250 knots. Above 10,000 feet, even inside TCA airspace, there is no speed limit. Within the lateral limits of a TCA, but below TCA airspace (in other words, under the outer portions of the upside-down wedding cake), the speed limit is 200 knots.

With respect to pilot qualifications within TCAs, the rules haven't changed, but the names have. Originally, the FAA started out with Group I, II, and III TCAs. Group IIIs never materialized, and because there was little practical difference between Group I and Group II TCAs, the FAA decided to do away with the Group designations and, effective January 12, 1989, to refer to all TCAs as simply . . . TCAs. However, the slightly stricter pilot requirements that differentiated Group I TCAs from Group II TCAs were kept at all the primary airports that were formerly in Group I TCAs.

To take off or land at a primary airport in what used to be a Group I TCA, the pilot in command must hold at least a private pilot certificate (FAR 91.131). To transit a former Group I TCA, take off or land at a nonprimary airport in a former Group I TCA, or operate in all other TCAs, the pilot in command must have at least a private pilot certificate *or* be a student pilot who has received special TCA training as specified in FAR 61.95.

So although all TCAs are now called the same thing, they are not all equal. There are still two kinds (or groups, if you prefer to use that word), just as there were before: Those that require the PIC to have a private certificate to land or take off at the TCA's primary airport and those that require the PIC to have only a student certificate with an endorsement. If you think it made more sense designating the first kind of TCA as "Group I" and the other kind as "Group II" to emphasize this difference, I couldn't agree with you more.

Whatever the FAA calls a TCA, it remains the pilot's responsibility to stay clear of clouds (if operating VFR inside TCA airspace) and to immediately inform ATC if a given vector will take you into below-VFR-minimum weather conditions.

In the following pages we'll examine each of the existing TCAs in the Continental United States (the Honolulu TCA is not included) with respect to the best ways to bypass them or land at airports other than the primary ones for which the TCA was established (TABLE 9-1). The charts accompanying the text were provided by Airguide Publications and should not be used for navigation.

Table 9-1. TCAs Included in This Chapter.

TCA	Primary Airport(s)	Certificate required*
Atlanta	Hatsfield-Atlanta	Private
Boston	Logan	Private
Charlotte	Charlotte/Douglas	Student
Chicago	Chicago O'Hare	Private
Cleveland	Cleveland-Hopkins	Student
Dallas-Fort Worth	Dallas-Fort Worth	Private
Denver	Stapleton	Student
Detroit	Detroit Metro Wayne	Student
Houston	Houston	Student
Kansas City	Kansas City	Student
Las Vegas, Nevada	McCarran	Student
Los Angeles	Los Angeles	Private
Memphis	Memphis	Student
Miami	Miami	Private
Minneapolis	Minneapolis-St. Paul	Student
New Orleans	New Orleans	Student
New York	Kennedy, La Guardia, Newark	Private
Philadelphia	Philadelphia	Student
Phoenix	Phoenix Sky Harbor	Student
Pittsburgh	Greater Pittsburgh	Student
Salt Lake City	Salt Lake City International	Student
St. Louis	Lambert-St. Louis	Student
San Diego	San Diego-Lindbergh	Student
San Francisco	San Francisco	Private
Seattle	Seattle-Tacoma	Student
Washington, D.C.	Washington National	Private

* Student pilot certificate requires a "TCA" endorsement from a Certified Flight Instructor.

ATLANTA

Airports:

Hartsfield-Atlanta International (ATL/primary)
Cobb County McCollum Field (RYY/uncontrolled)
Covington (9A1/uncontrolled)

Dekalb-Peachtree (PDK/controlled)
Falcon Field (2A9/uncontrolled)
Fulton County-Charlie Brown Field (FTY/controlled)
Gwinnett County-Briscoe Field (LZU/controlled)
Henry County-Morris Field (4A7/uncontrolled)
Newman-Coweta County (CC0/uncontrolled)
South Expressway (9A7/uncontrolled)

VORs:

ATL - Atlanta (116.9)
PDK - Peachtree (116.6)

Top of TCA:

12,500 feet

Atlanta is one of three TCAs with a top of 12,500 feet. For that reason, and because over-flying a TCA with much jet traffic entering and exiting that airspace through the top is a fairly chancy undertaking, we have concentrated entirely on low-level operations (FIG. 9-1).

In order to bypass Atlanta east-west or west-east all we need to do is stay below 6,000 feet and at least nine nm north or south of Hartsfield-Atlanta International, the primary airport. Using the bypass to the north is somewhat easier, as there we can use the PDK VOR as a nav aid to keep us out of trouble. There are neither nav aids nor meaningful landmarks to the south. Therefore, if that route is chosen, it would be a good idea to fly somewhat farther south than we have indicated on the chart.

When flying north-south or south-north it is advisable to miss the primary airport by somewhat over 20 miles and to stay as low as practical even though the floor of the overhanging TCA is 6,000 feet.

For those who want to land in Atlanta without entering the TCA, Charlie Brown and DeKalb-Peachtree are the two most popular general aviation airports, though we have also listed several uncontrolled fields for those who prefer not to get involved with tower controllers. Check in advance, or by unicom, to make sure that rental cars or other convenient forms of transportation are available to your final destination.

BOSTON

Airports:

Logan International Airport (BOS/primary)
Beverly (BVY/controlled)
Hanscom Field (BED/controlled)
Norwood Memorial (OWD/controlled)

VORs:

BOS - Boston (112.7)
LWM - Lawrence (112.5)

Top of TCA:

7,000 feet

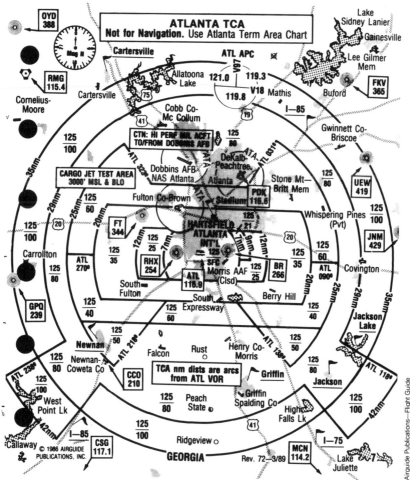

Fig. 9-1. *Atlanta TCA. Top is 12,500 feet.*

Boston presents few problems for the VFR pilot other than the fact that the three general aviation airports are all a considerable distance from the city. To bypass the TCA when traveling north-south or south-north, the only sensible procedure is to stay to the west of it, using either one or several of the VORs for navigational guidance (FIG. 9-2).

The three general aviation airports are all located beneath the outer rim of the TCA, where the base of the positive control airspace is at 3,000 feet. As a result, a fair amount of VFR traffic is likely to be compressed at that low altitude on days when the flying weather is good. In other words, vigilance is called for.

Anyone planning to overfly the TCA at an altitude above 7,000 feet should monitor the approach and departure control frequencies for Logan International to keep

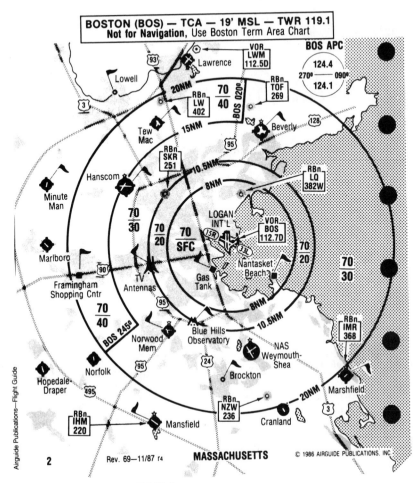

Fig. 9-2. *Boston TCA. Top is 7,000 feet.*

track of the direction of flight used by the arriving and departing jet aircraft, most of which will enter or leave the TCA through the top. On a clear day this should not present too much of a problem, but it would be less than advisable to attempt such overflights on top of an overcast where the jets might suddenly pop up just about anywhere.

CHARLOTTE

Airports:

    Charlotte/Douglas International (CLT/primary)
    Gastonia Municipal (0A6/uncontrolled)
    Lincoln County (5N4/uncontrolled)
    Monroe (EQY/uncontrolled)

Rock Hill Muni/Bryant Field (29J/uncontrolled)
Wilgrove (A86/uncontrolled)
VORs:
    CLT - Charlotte (115.0)
    FML - Fort Mill (112.4)
    RUQ - Rowan County (111.0)
Top of TCA:
    10,000 feet

    Upgraded from an ARSA in 1990, Charlotte is one of the newer TCAs. Bypassing it to the north is relatively simple if we use RUQ VOR for east/west vectors and Lake Norman as a visual checkpoint. Do not stray too far south over Lake Norman because

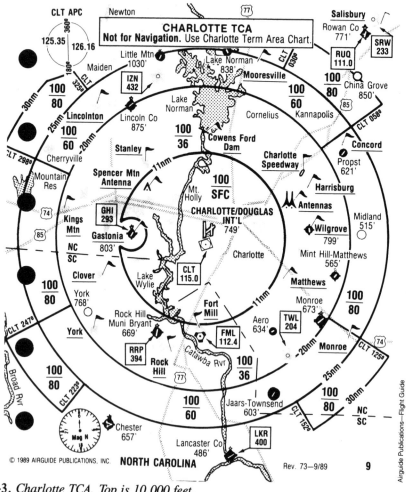

Fig. 9-3. *Charlotte TCA. Top is 10,000 feet.*

the floor of the TCA drops from 6,000 feet down to 3,600 feet msl. Flying north or south, RUQ VOR can also be used to bypass Charlotte TCA to the east (FIG. 9-3).

To the south LKR NDB will keep us out of the TCA, but to the west there aren't any nav aids we can use. Navigation will have to be by map reading or Loran-C, if we are so lucky.

Gastonia, Monroe, and Wilgrove are the most convenient uncontrolled airports to Charlotte. Notice the TCA "cutout" around Gastonia. If we stay below 3,600 feet we can fly in and out of Gastonia without contacting Charlotte Approach Control, but we must be careful not to enter the TCA airspace to the north, east, and south of the field.

CHICAGO

Airports:
>   Chicago O'Hare International (ORD/primary)
>   DuPage County (DPA/controlled)
>   Midway (MDW/controlled)
>   Meigs Field (CGX/controlled)
>   Pal-Waukee (PWK/controlled)
>   Schaumburg Air Park (06C/uncontrolled)
>   Waukegan Regional (UGN/uncontrolled)

VORs:
>   CGT - Chicago Heights (114.2)
>   DPA - DuPage (108.4)
>   JOT - Joliet (112.3)
>   OBK - Northbrook (113.0)
>   ORD - Chicago O'Hare (113.9)

Top of TCA:
>   7,000 feet

Chicago is pretty much a mess, and unless it is simply impractical, VFR pilots might do best to simply give it a wide berth. O'Hare is always the busiest airport in the world, and airline jets arrive and depart in all directions, frequently at a rate of several each minute. In addition, there is the Glenview Naval Air Station north-north-east of O'Hare, which spits out military jets that usually fly inland along the coast of Lake Michigan to and from the north (FIG. 9-4).

Below the outer rims of the TCA a great deal of VFR traffic, including student-training activity, is concentrated on the north side in the Pal-Waukee area, on the west in the DuPage area, and to the east over the water just on the edge of the lake. VFR pilots coming from the southeast and wishing to continue north-westerly without landing in the Chicago area would do best to use the Chicago Heights and DuPage VORs for navigational guidance around the southern and western rims of the TCA and the Chicago Midway ARSA. If their destination is to the north, they might prefer the route along the lake. Either way, there is likely to be a considerable amount of traffic below 3,000 feet, so the eyes should be kept on a constant swivel.

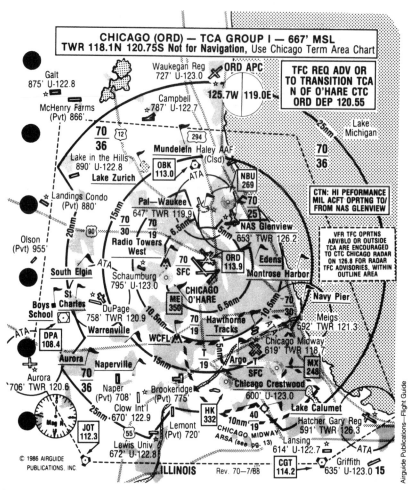

Fig. 9-4. *Chicago TCA. Top is 7,000 feet.*

Those who want to land in the area have a choice of the various airports we have listed on the chart, each of which can be reached from the indicated flyways without the necessity of dealing with the TCA controllers by staying below 3,000 feet (except in the case of Schaumburg, where the last mile or so has to be flown below 1,900 feet).

One of the worst features of flying around Chicago is the fact that it and the surrounding cities produce heavy industrial pollution, often resulting in marginal visibility. The worst offenders are the steel mills in and around Gary, Indiana, just to the southeast of Chicago. Their smoke can turn even a perfect VFR day into a reddish-brown mixture of smoke and haze which, for all practical purposes, is IFR. In addition, on gray overcast days (and there are many of those) flying along the lake can be an unpleasant experience because the sky and water are more or less the same color and tend to become indistinguishable from one another.

CLEVELAND

Airports:

    Cleveland-Hopkins International (CLE/primary)
    Burke Lakefront (BKL/controlled)
    Columbia (4G8/uncontrolled)
    Cuyahoga County (CGF/controlled)
    Elyria (1G1/uncontrolled)
    Freedom Liberty Airpark (7D6/uncontrolled)
    Lost Nation (LNN/controlled)
    Lorain County Regional (22G/uncontrolled)

VORs:

    ACO - Akron (114.4) (Not shown.)
    DJB - Dryer (113.6)
    CXR - Chardon (112.7) (Not shown.)
    LNN - Lost Nation (110.2)
    MFD - Mansfield (108.8) (Not shown.)

Top of TCA:

    8,000 feet

Cleveland is another city sitting right next to a lake, in this case Lake Erie, but it presents a lot less trouble than does Chicago (FIG. 9-5). On east-west or west-east flights the VFR pilot has a choice of flying around the inner rings of the TCA on either the south or north side. Using the north side will take him a fair distance out over the water unless he wants to stay below 1,900 feet. The best thing to do is to fly outbound on the 280- or 285-degree radial from the Chardon VOR (when westbound) until intercepting the 040-degree radial from the Cleveland VOR, at which point it is safe to turn to a more southerly heading in order to again intercept the coastline. When flying in an easterly direction, this route is a little more complicated. The best procedure would probably be to fly along the coastline until intercepting the 040-degree radial from Dryer VOR, then follow it until reaching the 280-degree (or so) radial *from* (or the 100-degree bearing *to*) the Chardon VOR, and then follow it back to dry land. On a nice, clear day there is nothing much wrong with that; but, when things are a bit murky, the southern detour must be considered preferable.

For those who want to land in Cleveland, the Burke Lakefront Airport is the most convenient to downtown, and Cuyahoga County would seem to be second best. All others are quite considerable distances away.

DALLAS –FORT WORTH

Airports:

    Dallas-Fort Worth International (DFW/primary/private required)
    Addison (ADS/controlled)

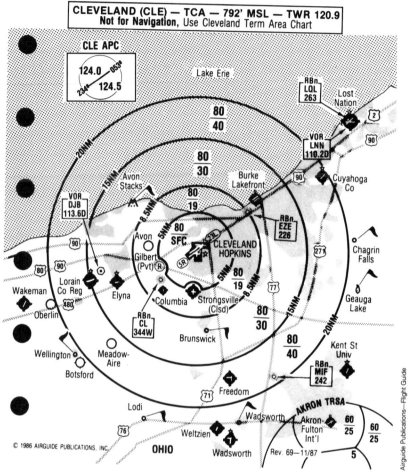

Fig. 9-5. *Cleveland TCA. Top is 8,000 feet.*

Love Field (DAL/controlled)

Meacham Airport (FTW/controlled)

Redbird (RBD/controlled)

(The uncontrolled airports around the periphery of the Dallas-Fort Worth area are too numerous to list. Consult Sectional and TAC charts.)

VORs:

DFW - Dallas-Fort Worth (117.0)

LUE - Love (114.3)

Top of TCA:

8,000 feet

This is a big one (FIG. 9-6), but it doesn't present any great problems for north-south or south-north flights except that when bypassing the area to the east, a heavy

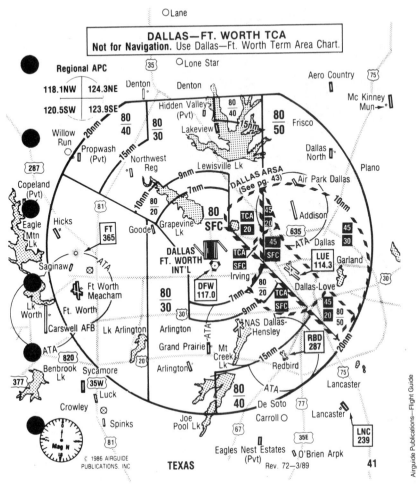

Fig. 9-6. *Dallas-Ft. Worth TCA. Top is 8,000 feet.*

amount of both VFR and IFR traffic, going to and from Love, Addison, and even Redbird may be encountered.

To accommodate this traffic, as well as help pilots through the Dallas ARSA, a north-south VFR corridor was created (FIG. 9-7). Also keep in mind that the top of airport traffic areas is 3,000 feet agl, which puts it at 3,643 at Addison, 3,660 at Redbird, and 3,487 at Love when converting to feet msl. With the base of the ARSA outer circle at 3,000 feet msl over Addison, the base of the TCA at 4,000 and 3,000 feet msl over Redbird, and the ARSA inner circle extending from the surface to 4,500 feet msl over Love Field, trying to find an altitude and route through the area that doesn't require radio contact with approach control or a control tower is more trouble than it's worth. The only way to do it is to stay well east of the TCA, ARSA, and ATAs, but this will require careful navigation, too, and may not be as fuel efficient.

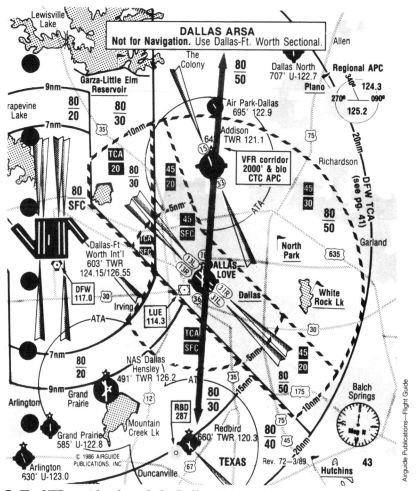

Fig. 9-7. *The VFR corridor through the Dallas ARSA and below the eastern portion of the Dallas-Ft. Worth TCA. Contact with Dallas Approach Control is required.*

When wishing to pass the TCA east-west or west-east, flying around the southern periphery is probably the better choice; but be sure to stay out of the way of the Airport Traffic Areas of Dallas Naval Air Station and Carswell Air Force Base. In the event that our east-west (or west-east) route is somewhat to the north of the Dallas-Fort Worth metropolitan area, then bypassing the inner portions of the TCA to the north should be preferred.

There are no VORs available to guide us on either of those two routes. On the southern route the most convenient landmark is a four-lane divided highway that passes in a more or less straight line just south of the Redbird Airport.

North of the TCA there is no such convenient highway. The best landmark is probably the huge Garza-Little Elm Reservoir/Lake Lewisville (not to be confused with Lake Grapevine to the southwest of it, which underlies the inner portion of the TCA). By flying right over the middle of the widest portion of the Garza-Little Elm Reservoir at an altitude below 3,000 feet msl we will be able to stay out of trouble.

DENVER

Airports:

Stapleton International (DEN/primary)
Boulder Municipal (1V5/uncontrolled)
Centennial (APA/controlled)
Front Range (FTG/uncontrolled)
Jeffco (BJC/controlled)

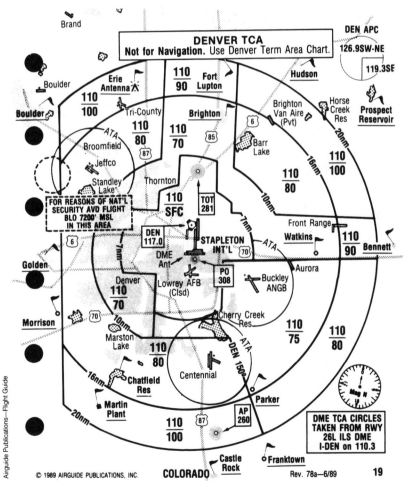

Fig. 9-8. *Denver TCA. Top is 11,000 feet.*

VORs:

DEN - Denver (117.0)

Top of TCA:

11,000 feet

This is the mile-high city; hence, the 11,000-foot TCA top (FIG. 9-8). Since it is located a considerable distance from any other major city except Colorado Springs to the south, most pilots flying into the Denver area will most likely want to stop for food and fuel. Those who do want to simply bypass it will find it fairly easy. On flights from the south northward to, say, Wyoming, or coming from up north and flying south along the eastern slopes of the Rockies, the best suggestion is to use Boulder as a landmark and stay west of the cutoff portion of the TCA until crossing the four-lane, divided highway at Golden. Then head southeastward away from the higher mountain, staying below 8,000 feet msl until leaving the TCA south of Centennial Airport.

Flying east-west from, say, Akron, Colorado, via the Kreminling VOR to Grand Junction and Las Vegas, it is simple to pass under the very outer ring of the TCA below 9,000 feet msl and once past Boulder to climb to roughly 14,000 to clear the mountains.

Those who want to land in Denver will find that none of the available airports are close enough to downtown to be considered convenient. The fact is that the closest and most convenient airport is Stapleton, and all manner of general aviation pilots are treated extremely well there, but it does require appropriate instrumentation in the aircraft and the necessity to deal with the TCA controllers. Pilots who cannot or do not wish to fly into the TCA itself have no choice but to pick one of the outlying general aviation airports.

DETROIT

Airports:

Detroit Metro Wayne County (DTW/primary)
Ann Arbor Municipal (ARB/controlled)
Custer (D92/uncontrolled)
Detroit City (DET/controlled)
Grosse Ile Municipal (2G5/uncontrolled)
Mettetal-Canton (1D2/uncontrolled)
Troy-Oakland (7D2/uncontrolled)
Willow Run (YIP/controlled)

VORs:

CRL - Carleton (115.7)
SVM - Salem (114.3)
YIP   - Willow Run (110.0)

Top of TCA:

8,000 feet

Though Detroit has a nice and convenient downtown airport (Detroit City), it is a miserable place to fly to or through. Bordering, as it does, on Canada (at Detroit, Canada is *south* of the U.S.) and with both major airline airports to its west, all VFR traffic is either forced to fly a huge westerly detour or to squeeze through a narrow corridor over the Detroit River, which is also the Canadian border. When taking the westerly detour, the Salem VOR is useful for navigational guidance in both the north-south and east-westerly directions. In the vicinity of Salem we can expect to run into heavy student-training activity if the weather is reasonably good (FIG. 9-9).

The trouble with that Detroit River flyway is twofold. One, it is quite narrow, pilots should be careful to stay on the right side of the river in order to minimize the danger of running into another airplane head-on. With the base of the overlying TCA being around 2,500 feet and elevations on Grosse Ile going up to 600 feet, there isn't

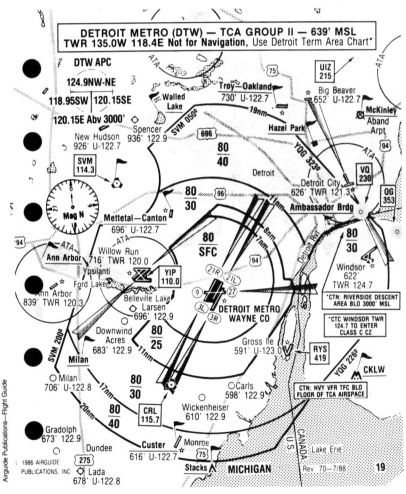

Fig. 9-9. *Detroit TCA. Top is 8,000 feet.*

much room for vertical separation. The second problem is great amounts of ever-present smoke that often reduces visibility to an unacceptable minimum. Still, for pilots coming from the south (and most around here do), using the river flyway on the way to the Detroit City Airport or destinations beyond cuts some 30-plus nm off the distance. Whether those 30 nm are worth taking a chance for is something each pilot must decide for himself.

HOUSTON

Airports:

    Houston Intercontinental (IAH/primary)
    Andrau Airpark (AAP/uncontrolled)
    David Wayne Hooks Memorial (DWH/controlled)
    West Houston-Lakeside (IWS/uncontrolled)
    William P. Hobby (HOU/controlled)

VORs:

    HUB - Hobby (117.6)
    IAH - Humble (116.6)

Top of TCA:

    7,000 feet

Houston, though one of the fastest growing cities in the country, is one of the easiest to deal with for the VFR pilot (FIG. 9-10). With the TCA cut off at the bottom, east-west flyers can simply bypass it using the Hobby VOR for navigational guidance and flying above 4,000 feet msl to stay above the Houston-Hobby ARSA. Those who come from the north, like Dallas, for instance, will find it easy to stay to the west of the inner rings of the TCA and then to home in on Hobby either to land there or to continue on south toward Galveston and the Gulf of Mexico. Hobby, by the way, is a fine airport attuned to efficiently deal with general aviation traffic. It is more convenient to downtown than any of the other airports, all of which are a considerable distance from the city.

KANSAS CITY

Airports:

    Kansas City International (MCI/primary)
    Kansas City Downtown (MKC/controlled)
    Lawrence Municipal (LWC/uncontrolled)

VORs:

    MKC - Kansas City (112.6)
    RIS - Riverside (111.4)

Top of TCA:

    8,000 feet

Flying into Kansas City used to be a fascinating experience in the days when all airline traffic was using the Downtown (then Municipal) Airport. The final approach, nearly always from the south, took you virtually within spitting distance of the upper

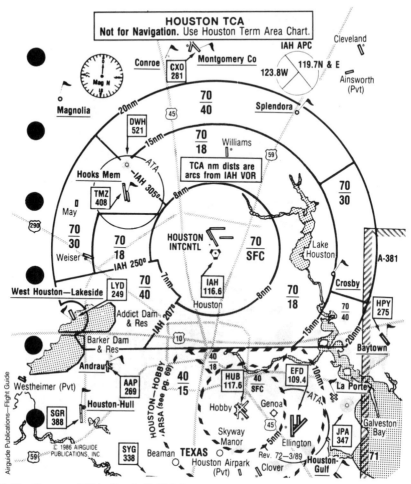

Fig. 9-10. *Houston TCA. Top is 7,000 feet.*

floors of some of Kansas City's higher skyscrapers, and there was plenty of activity to keep those two runways busy. Now that Kansas City International has been built some 20 miles north of downtown, most of the airline traffic uses it and general aviation has inherited the downtown airport (FIG. 9-11).

For those who want to bypass Kansas City in a north-south direction, the best advice is to simply stay clear of the TCA. East-west, at the southern portion of the TCA, things get a little more complicated. Unless a landing is planned for Downtown, the better part of valor would be to stay well south of the whole area.

LAS VEGAS

Airports:

McCarran International (LAS/primary)

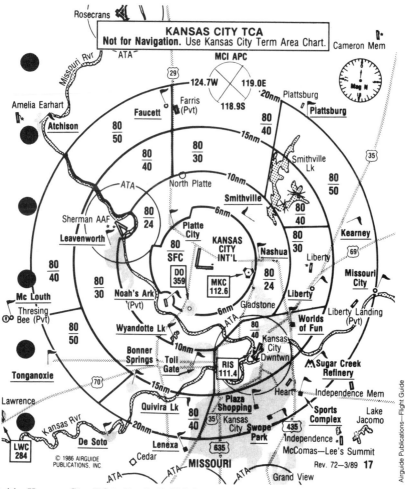

Fig. 9-11. *Kansas City TCA. Top is 8,000 feet.*

Boulder City Municipal (BLD/uncontrolled)
Las Vegas-Henderson Sky Harbor (L15/uncontrolled)
North Las Vegas (VGT/controlled)
VORs:
LAS - Las Vegas (116.9)
BLD - Boulder City (116.7)
Top of TCA:
9,000 feet
For most pilots Las Vegas is not a place to bypass but, rather, a location to or from which to fly. Even those who don't go there to gamble and lose their shirts usually land at Las Vegas simply because the distances in all directions to any major cities are such that it is usually time to top off the airplane and defuel the pilot (FIG. 9-12).

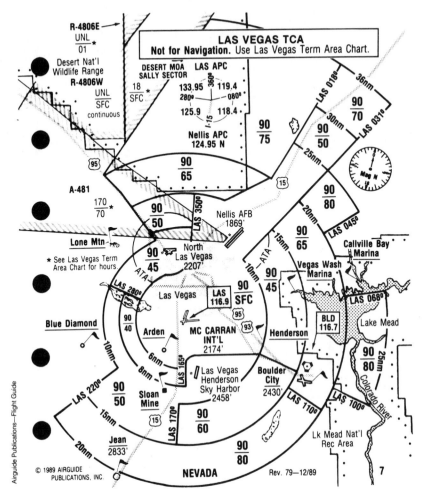

Fig. 9-12. *Las Vegas TCA. Top is 9,000 feet.*

If the shape of the Las Vegas TCA seems more convoluted than most, it is caused by the 10,000-foot Spring Mountain range directly to the west, the equally high Sheep Mountain range to the north, and the extremely active Nellis Air Force Base just northwest of the city. The TCA is designed both to serve McCarran and Nellis and to keep us general-aviation types separated from all that high-performance jet activity.

In the days before the establishment of the TCA, McCarran was the ideal airport for visitors to Las Vegas, and it still is for those who don't mind dealing with the TCA controllers. For those who prefer to avoid that, there is North Las Vegas, which requires a bit of navigating in order to get there without accidentally flying into the inner portion of the TCA. Then there is Henderson to the south, some 10 miles from downtown, and Boulder City near Hoover Dam, some 20 miles away.

Those who do want to bypass the city and its much-touted attractions altogether on their way from, say, Salt Lake City or Grand Junction to Los Angeles (or vice versa), are best served by using the Boulder City VOR as a navigational guide and either staying east of it and out of the TCA altogether or overflying it at below 6,500 feet. (The highest peak in the area is 3,789 feet.) With the weather in the area usually (though not always) amply VFR, navigating by such landmarks as Lake Mead is relatively easy.

Flights over the mountains northwest of Las Vegas—though this may look like the shortest route to Reno or San Francisco—should be avoided. This is where the Nellis Air Force Base boys do their thing, not to mention the fact that it is unfriendly country in which to find oneself in the event of an emergency.

LOS ANGELES

Airports:
> Los Angeles International (LAX/primary)
> Burbank-Glendale-Pasedena (BUR/controlled)
> Compton (CPM/uncontrolled)
> El Monte (EMT/controlled)
> Fullerton Municipal (FUL/controlled)
> Hawthorne Municipal (HHR/controlled)
> Long Beach (LGB/controlled)
> Santa Monica Municipal (SMO/controlled)
> Torrance Municipal (TOA/controlled)
> Van Nuys (VNY/controlled)
> Whiteman (WHP/controlled)

VORs:
> LAX - Los Angeles (113.6)
> POM - Pomona (110.4)
> SLI - Seal Beach (115.7)
> SMO - Santa Monica (110.8)
> VNY - Van Nuys (113.1)

Top of TCA:
> 12,500 feet

There are probably more active general aviation airplanes per square yard in the Los Angeles Basin than anywhere else in the world. Among the collection of airports are four or five that are each year among the busiest anywhere. For this reason, the designers of the Los Angeles TCA had to structure it in a manner that would create a minimum of interference with VFR traffic (FIG. 9-13).

The TCA around LAX is extremely complicated, and its design should be carefully studied before any flight is made even near the airspace. The midair collision over Cerritos, California, in May 1986 serves as example enough for strict adherence to rules of TCA flight, and for constant practice of the see-and-avoid technique.

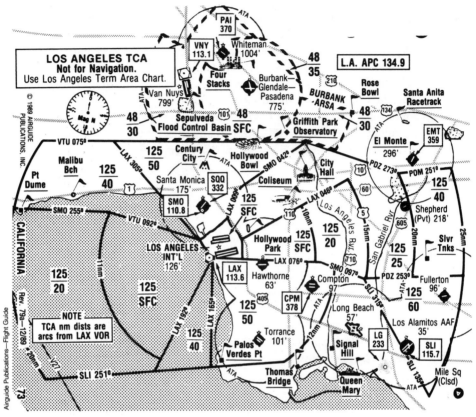

Fig. 9-13. *Los Angeles TCA. Top is 12,500 feet.*

Aircraft arriving from the east, in order to either land at one of the general aviation airports or to continue on toward Santa Barbara, will find that they have no trouble staying out of TCA airspace by navigating by the many available VORs. The east-west flyway north of the city is defined by the Brackett, Van Nuys, and Fillmore VORs. Arriving from the south or southeast, the Seal Beach VOR effectively helps us in locating any one of the five airports in that area—four of which sit under outer portions of the TCA, with altitude limits at 5,000 and 6,000 feet.

The only airport that requires a bit of circuitous navigation is Santa Monica. To reach it from the north, we have to contend with the TCA, the Burbank ARSA, and the Van Nuys ATA. Considering the complexity of the airspace and the amount of traffic, it probably makes most sense to contact Los Angeles Approach and request vectors to Santa Monica when arriving from the north.

To get to Santa Monica from the south we can use the Los Angeles Special Flight Rules Area (SFRA), which takes us right over Los Angeles International Airport. Flying through this "tunnel" of VFR airspace does not require a clearance, but other requirements must be met. These can be found in more detail on the Terminal Area Chart, the Airguide Flight Guide, and the Jeppesen Sanderson VFR NavService chart. After arriving over Santa Monica Airport from the SFRA, we can expect to descend to the west over Pacific Palisades before entering the airport traffic pattern.

The LA TCA also has two TCA VFR routes, the Shoreline Route and the Hollywood Park Route, both of which require a TCA clearance. Again, details of these routes can be found in the above-mentioned publications.

It goes without saying that there tends to be a lot of traffic compressed into these narrow bits of airspace. Constant vigilance is required at all times. And remember to turn on that landing light to make it easier for other people to see you!

MEMPHIS

Airports:
Memphis International (MEM/primary)
Arlington Municipal (LHC/uncontrolled)
Charles W. Baker (2M8/uncontrolled)
General Dewitt Spain (M01/uncontrolled)
Isle-A-Port (TN43/uncontrolled)
Olive Branch (OLV/uncontrolled)
Twinkletown (2M6/uncontrolled)
West Memphis Municipal (AWM/controlled)
Wolf River (54M/uncontrolled)

VORs:
MEM - Memphis (117.5)
GQE - Gilmore (113.0)
HLI   - Holly Springs (112.4)

Top of TCA:
10,000 feet

Memphis, "Home of the Grand Ole' Opry," is another former ARSA that just became a TCA in 1990. It can be easily bypassed from any direction by using the GQE or HLI VORs and remaining below 5,000 feet msl (FIG. 9-14).

The most prominent land feature we can use to transit through the TCA is the Mississippi River, which runs southwest to northeast on the western side of the TCA. To follow it northward and remain outside of TCA airspace, we must descend below 5,000 feet, then 3,000 feet, then 1,800 feet. We'll have to watch out for ultralight activity and the occasional blimp near Isle-A-Port, particularly during the weekends. Alternatively, we could avoid the last descent by flying due north just south of West Memphis Municipal, getting clearance through their ATA, and picking up the river again just north of General Dewitt Spain.

With eight smaller airports within 20 miles of Memphis International, the general aviation pilot has plenty of landing sites from which to choose when going to Memphis and should have no difficulty avoiding the primary airport.

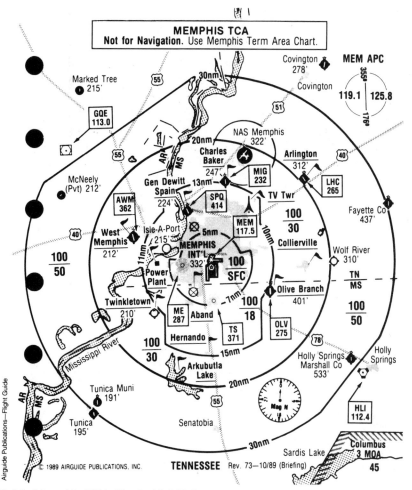

Fig. 9-14. *Memphis TCA. Top is 10,000 feet.*

MIAMI

Airports:

Miami International (MIA/primary)
Fort Lauderdale Executive (FXE/controlled)
Fort Lauderdale-Hollywood International (FLL/controlled)
North Perry (HWO/controlled)
Opa Locka West (X46/uncontrolled)
Opa Locka (OPF/controlled)
Tamiami (TMB/controlled)

VORs:

BSY - Biscayne Bay (117.1)

FLL - Fort Lauderdale (111.4)

MIA - Miami (115.9)

Top of TCA:

7,000 feet

Miami, sitting between the Atlantic Ocean on one side and the Everglades on the other, must be looked at primarily from the point of view of how to bypass it in a north-south direction (FIG. 9-15). Navigation by pilotage is simple, using the ocean front as a guide when passing east of the city or staying between the populated areas and the edge of the swamp when passing to the west. The trick, even when still north of the TCA, is to stay low. Fort Lauderdale-Hollywood International and West Palm Beach (some distance to the north) are both airline airports with ARSAs, and VFR traffic is better off to be safely below the various approach and departure paths. But in each case the ARSA

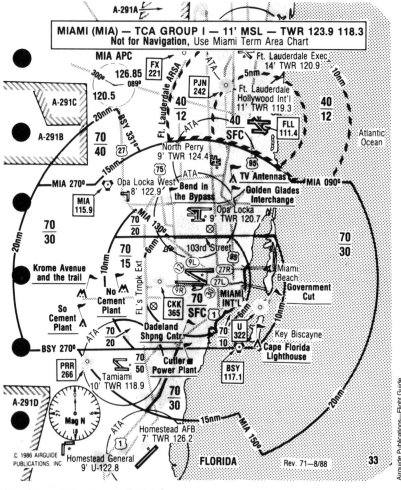

Fig. 9-15. *Miami TCA. Top is 7,000 feet.*

reaches several miles out into the ocean, which means that approach control must be contacted for clearance to fly through. Since most of the local pilots habitually fly at altitudes between 1,000 and 1,500 feet, the controllers are used to being contacted by VFR pilots and can be counted on to be quite helpful. "No-radio" airplanes or pilots who prefer to do their flying in silent splendor virtually have no choice but to either stay at least five miles to either side of those controlled airports and below 1,200 feet or to climb to above 7,000 feet and fly right over the top of the whole array. Since the prevailing winds are such that most arrivals and departures by jet aircraft are made in east-west directions, flying north-south over the top is relatively safe. Still, monitoring the tower frequencies of the airline airports (and possibly the approach- and departure-control frequencies) will help to avoid unpleasant surprises.

MINNEAPOLIS

Airports:
>   Minneapolis-St. Paul International (MSP/primary)
>   Anoka County-Blaine (ANE/controlled)
>   Airlake (Y12/uncontrolled)
>   Crystal (MIC/controlled)
>   Flying Cloud (FCM/controlled)
>   Lake Elmo (21D/uncontrolled)
>   St. Paul Downtown Holman Field (STP/uncontrolled)
>   South St. Paul Municipal-Richard E. Fleming Field (D97/uncontrolled)

VORs:
>   FCM - Flying Cloud (111.8)
>   FGT - Farmington (115.7)
>   GEP - Gopher (117.3)
>   MSP - Minneapolis (115.4)

Top of TCA:
>   8,000 feet

This is one TCA that is quite easy to avoid regardless of the direction of flight. When flying east-west, the Farmington VOR will keep us in the clear as long as we are flying below 4,000 feet. On the north-south heading the best choice is to bypass the TCA on the west using the Gopher and Flying Cloud VORs for guidance; although, if we decide to actually overfly the Flying Cloud VOR, we have to drop down to below 3,000 feet, which would take us right through the Airport Traffic Area and require communication with the tower. If we want to avoid that, we'll have to fly outbound on the 200-degree radial from the GEP VOR until we intersect the 290-degree radial *from* (or the 110-degree bearing *to*) the Farmington VOR, staying below 4,000 feet while under the outer overhang of the TCA (FIG. 9-16).

For those who wish to land at Minneapolis, the St. Paul Downtown Airport is the most convenient to downtown Minneapolis and St. Paul. It is best approached from an easterly direction, which will reduce to a minimum the time spent under the inner ring

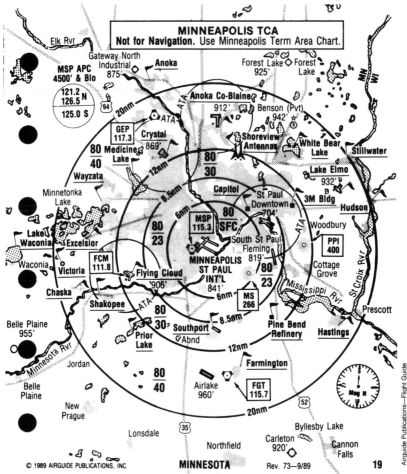

Fig. 9-16. *Minneapolis TCA. Top is 8,000 feet.*

of the TCA and below 2,300 feet. Located in a bulge of the Mississippi River, it can easily be found by pilotage. In addition to the river there are two four-lane divided highways, one from the east and the other from the southeast, which join just northeast of that airport.

NEW ORLEANS

Airports:

New Orleans International (MSY/primary)

Lakefront (NEW/controlled)

Westwego (2R3/uncontrolled)

VORs:

MSY - New Orleans (113.2)

HRV - Harvey (112.4)

Top of TCA:

7,000 feet

In view of its location, New Orleans is nearly always a destination and rarely a place we simply want to fly by (FIG. 9-17). For those wanting to go to New Orleans, the only logical airport is Lakefront, which is built on the shore of Lake Pontchartrain, with one runway going right out into the lake. Arrivals from the north should use the 25-mile-long, ruler-straight causeway across the lake as a guide, staying to the right of that causeway and dropping down to below 2,000 feet. Once the airport comes into view it is time to turn off to the east and head straight for it. Arrivals from the east are best advised to fly over the Triple Bridges, again keeping to the right, and then follow the edge of the lake right to the airport. On this route aircraft can stay at any altitude below 4,000 feet until ready for the approach.

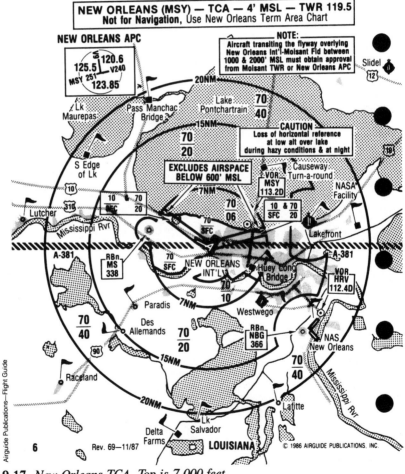

Fig. 9-17. *New Orleans TCA. Top is 7,000 feet.*

Arrivals from the west have a slightly more complicated problem. Even though there is a narrow VFR tunnel through the center of the TCA, it does require contact with, and clearance from, New Orleans Approach Control and, being only one mile wide with VFR traffic compressed between 1,000 and 2,000 feet, it is a less than comfortable choice. The better part of valor would seem to be to fly out over the lake at approximately the point where Interstate 10 crosses a railroad and then bends south-ward along the edge of the lake toward New Orleans. From there we take up a heading of 065 degrees until we intersect the 330-degree radial from New Orleans, at which point we turn right to approximately 115 degrees, which takes us straight to the air-port. All of this has to be done at an altitude below 2,000 feet.

The New Orleans TCA chart contains this warning: *Caution: Be prepared for loss of horizontal reference at low altitude over lake during hazy conditions and at night.* This can be a serious problem, and pilots who don't feel comfortable with the thought of having to control the aircraft at such a low altitude by reference to instruments alone might be better advised to stay away from the lake under such haze conditions.

To bypass New Orleans on the south side when coming from the west or to get to Lakefront without passing over the lake, we can use the Harvey VOR for reference while flying under either one of the two outer rings of the TCA and then either con-tinue east or break off for an approach to the airport from the south.

NEW YORK

Airports:
John F. Kennedy International (JFK/primary/private required)
La Guardia (LGA/primary/private required)
Newark International (EWR/primary/private required)
Essex County (CDW/controlled)
Lincoln Park (N07/uncontrolled)
Linden (LDJ/uncontrolled)
Morristown Municipal (MMU/controlled)
Republic (FRG/controlled)
Teterboro (TEB/controlled)
Westchester County (HPN/controlled)

VORs:
COL - Colt's Neck (115.4)
CRI - Canarsie (112.3)
DPK - Deep Park (117.7)
JFK - Kennedy (115.9)
LGA - La Guardia (113.1)
SAX - Sparta (115.7)
TEB - Teterboro (108.4)

Top of TCA:
7,000 feet

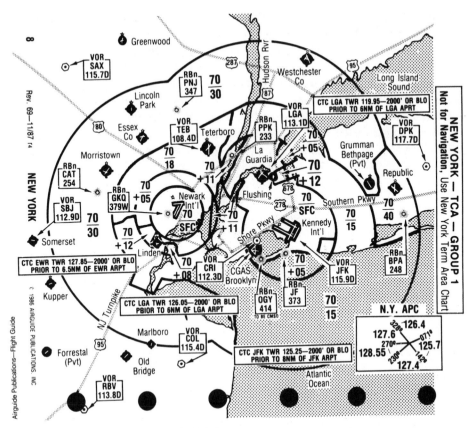

Fig. 9-18. *New York TCA. Top is 7,000 feet.*

The New York TCA is really a "lulu" (FIG. 9-18). The simplest approach to the New York area is from the west. Regardless of whether we want to land or continue on toward New England, it is fairly simple to stay out of the inner portions of the TCA and to fly at an altitude below 3,000 feet below the outer overhang. On the other hand, if we want to go to Long Island it gets more complicated. We can follow that same route and then, from some point southeast of the Westchester County Airport, turn right and fly over the Long Island Sound. If we would prefer to avoid that detour, we can drop down to below 1,800 feet and head toward Teterboro. Here we have to contact Teterboro Tower for clearance to fly through the Airport Traffic Area. Once past Teterboro, as we approach the Hudson River, we have to descend further to below 1,500 feet and stay at that altitude until we have passed over a narrower portion of the Long Island Sound. Once again over land we can then climb to below 3,000 feet until we have reached the Deer Park VOR, which is just outside the TCA.

Coming from the north or south and simply wishing to continue on we have two choices. One, involving a rather extensive detour, takes us over Essex County and

Morristown airports below 3,000 feet (again necessitating getting tower clearances to fly through the airport traffic areas) and around the inner rings of the TCA. The other, and shorter, route is a rather interesting experience, which might best be reserved for pilots with a fair degree of proficiency. This route takes us up or down the Hudson River at an altitude below 1,100 feet over the George Washington Bridge, past the sky-scrapers of Manhattan (some of which rise considerably higher than our flight alti-tude), past the Statue of Liberty, over the Verrazano Bridge, and on. At several points the Hudson is somewhat less than a mile wide, and this is again an instance where it is vitally important to stay on the right side of the river in order to avoid head-on con-flicts. There is nearly always a great deal of helicopter traffic along the Hudson, and one should use the "self announce" frequency (123.05) to broadcast type aircraft, position, altitude, direction of flight (south or north), and destination. The altitude, too, is critical. The superstructure of the George Washington Bridge rises to 612 feet, meaning that between it and the base of the TCA airspace there are only 488 feet of available VFR airspace. In addition, La Guardia arrivals cross that bridge at about 1,300 feet, meaning that cheating upward can be rather chancy.

One word of warning: In the entire area that encompasses New York, Philadel-phia, and the area down to Washington, we are likely to encounter high-performance airline and corporate jets at relatively low altitudes. Therefore, even when flying out-side of the various TCAs, it is advisable to stay below 3,000 feet. Also always take great care in navigating with maximum precision, as landmarks tend to be confusing.

PHILADELPHIA

Airports:
>   Philadelphia International (PHL/primary)
>   Greater Wilmington New Castle (ILG/controlled)
>   Northeast Philadelphia (PNE/controlled)
>   Wings (N67/uncontrolled)

VORs:
>   ARD - Yardley (108.2)
>   MXE - Modena (113.2)
>   OOD - Woodstown (112.8)
>   PNE - North Philadelphia (112.0)
>   PTW - Pottstown (116.5)
>   VCN - Cedar Lake (115.2)

Top of TCA:
>   7,000 feet

With this profusion of VORs, it is a cinch to bypass Philadelphia, giving it as wide a berth as we like (FIG. 9-19). The decision of whether to fly under the outer rims of the TCA or to bypass it altogether will depend to some degree on the available visibil-ity at low altitudes. But remember that even when staying amply clear of the TCA, it is not advisable to fly much above 3,000 feet in this area. The airport most convenient to

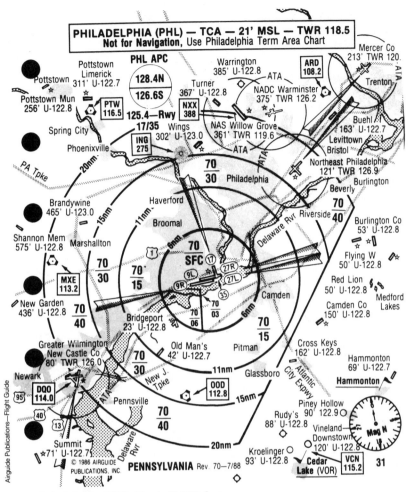

Fig. 9-19. *Philadelphia TCA. Top is 7,000 feet.*

downtown Philadelphia is Northeast Philadelphia which, with a VOR on the field, is easy to find and easy to get to from all directions except west—in which case the inner portion of the TCA must be detoured.

PHOENIX

Airports:

Phoenix Sky Harbor International (PHX/primary)
Chandler Municipal (P10/uncontrolled)
Phoenix-Deer Valley Municipal (DVT/controlled)
Falcon (FFZ/controlled)
Glendale Municipal (GEU/controlled)

Goodyear-Phoenix Municipal (GYR/controlled)
Scottsdale Municipal (SDL/controlled)
Stellar Airpark (P19/uncontrolled)

VORs:

SRP - Salt River (115.6)
CHD - Chandler (113.3)

Top of TCA:

10,000 feet

Phoenix, another new TCA, has a number of unusual features (FIG. 9-20). Most striking, perhaps, is the shape of the innermost TCA airspace areas: They're rectangular instead of circular. There are good reasons for this.

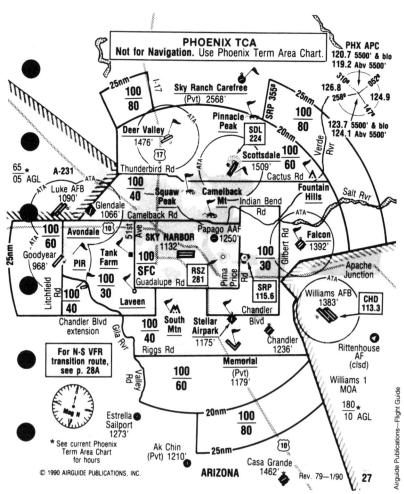

Fig. 9-20. *Phoenix TCA. Top is 10,000 feet.*

First, unlike most other primary TCA airports, Sky Harbor International does not have a VOR located on the field. This obviously makes it more difficult to determine one's position with respect to the airport. The wisely chosen alternative was to use land features to define the boundaries of a few of the sectors. As a result, the boundaries of the innermost sector are Camelback Road (north), Prima Price Road (east), Guadalupe Road (south), and 51st Avenue (west). Similarly, other sectors use roads for boundaries, too, and give new meaning to the old saw about IFR (I Follow Roads) pilots.

The Phoenix TCA also has a VFR transition route that runs north-south called the "Biltmore Route," (FIG. 9-21). The route takes you right over the top of Phoenix Sky Harbor International and therefore inside TCA airspace, so a clearance is required. You will receive an assigned altitude, probably between 3,500 and 5,500 feet, and be provided radar service.

Biltmore VFR Transition Route
(3500'—5500')

Clearance Required. Remain outside TCA until receiving clearance.

If above 5500' ctc:

PHX APC
North of TCA 119.2
South of TCA 124.1

At 5500' & below ctc:

PHX APC
N of TCA, southbnd 120.7
S of TCA, northbnd 123.7

NOTE: TCA extends from 6000' to 10,000' in the sectors north and south of depicted route-arrows. *Remain below floor of TCA until you are cleared into the TCA* and/or cleared to follow the Biltmore route.

1. Contact PHX Approach on appropriate frequency. *See above.*

2. Advise APC of your

   • position
   • altitude
   • desired route
   • direction of flight (e.g. "Biltmore route northbound")

3. Maintain assigned altitude (3500'-5500')

   Note: Clearance to fly a VFR transition route **is not** clearance to fly into IFR weather conditions. You must remain VFR. Advise the controller if your route & altitude will take you into clouds. Suggest a heading or altitude that will keep you VFR. (*You* can see the clouds; he can't.)

28   ARIZONA   Rev. 79—1/90   © 1990 AIRGUIDE PUBLICATIONS, INC.

Airguide Publications—Flight Guide

Fig. 9-21. *Biltmore VFR Transition Route procedures. Clearance is required from Phoenix Approach to fly the route.*

To the northwest of the TCA is Alert Area A-231 associated with Luke AFB, and to the southeast is the Williams 1 Military Operations Area associated with Williams AFB. Expect to encounter numerous low-time student pilots in fast-movers operating from both of these bases. In other words, don't stray into the areas, and maintain good "see-and-avoid" procedures when you're in the vicinity.

PITTSBURGH

Airports:

> Greater Pittsburgh International (PIT/primary)
> Allegheny County Airport (AGC/controlled)
> Beaver County Airport (BVI/controlled)
> Wheeling-Ohio County (HLG/controlled)
> Zelienople Municipal (8G7/uncontrolled)

VORs:

> AGC - Allegheny (110.0)
> EWC - Elwood City (115.8)
> HLG - Wheeling (112.2)
> MMJ - Mountour (112.0)

Top of TCA:

> 8,000 feet

Pittsburgh is easy to miss but hard to get to (FIG. 9-22). Bypassing it either beyond the outer perimeter of the TCA or by flying under the outer rim at below 4,000 feet is easily accomplished with the help of all those VORs. In the event that one wants to fly over the top of it, approach- and departure-control frequencies should be guarded to keep track of approaching and departing jets, which normally operate in an east-west direction.

To land at an airport other than the primary one the best choice is probably Allegheny County, which is closest to the city. Located under the southeast portion of the outer rim of the TCA, it can be approached at any altitude below 4,000 feet. (The airport itself is at 1,252 feet.)

ST. LOUIS

Airports:

> Lambert-St. Louis International (STL/primary)
> Arrowhead (02K/uncontrolled)
> Creve Coeur (1H0/uncontrolled)
> St. Louis Downtown-Parks (CPS/controlled)
> St. Louis Regional (ALN/controlled)
> Spirit of St. Louis (SUS/controlled)
> St. Charles (3SQ/uncontrolled)
> St. Charles County Smartt Field (3SZ/controlled)
> Weiss (3WE/uncontrolled)

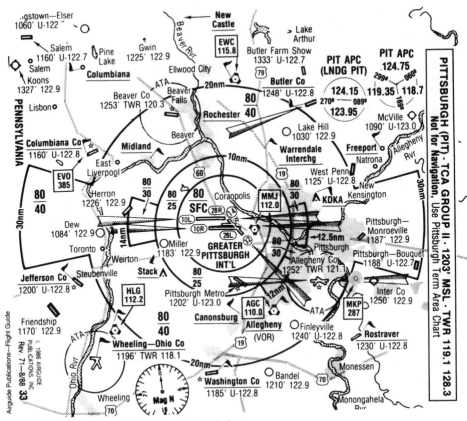

Fig. 9-22. *Pittsburgh TCA. Top is 8,000 feet.*

VORs:

STL

TOY - Troy (116.0)

Top of TCA:

8,000 feet

Bypassing St. Louis in an east-west direction is best accomplished by flying south of the city under the outer or second rim of the TCA below either 4,500 or 3,000 feet. Radials from the Troy and Foristell (not shown) VOR's offer ample guidance in navigation (FIG. 9-23).

Flying around the north, one can use the Mississippi as a landmark. With no appropriate nav aids in that area, one may end up flying a greater detour than is necessary.

On a north-south heading it is again possible to use the rivers as landmarks. On the west side we can stay clear of the inner ring of the TCA by following that bulge in the river and then overflying the Spirit of St. Louis Airport (getting tower clearance) before getting back on course. On the east side we can accomplish the same thing by staying just east of the river all along the way.

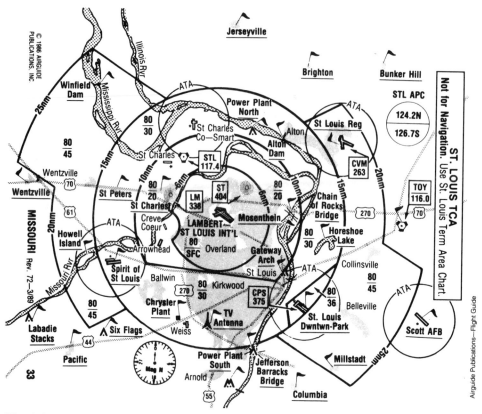

Fig. 9-23. *St. Louis TCA. Top is 8,000 feet.*

Finding a convenient airport for downtown St. Louis is a bit of a problem. The most convenient one is, in fact, the primary airport, but using it will involve dealing with the TCA controllers. Next closest is probably St. Louis Downtown-Parks, near East St. Louis, which requires a drive over one of the bridges over the Mississippi in order to get to St. Louis proper. An excellent airport is Spirit of St. Louis, but that's about 17 miles from downtown.

SALT LAKE CITY

Airports:

Salt Lake City International (SLC/primary)
Bolinder Tooele Valley (UT29/uncontrolled)
Morgan County (42U/uncontrolled)
Ogden Municipal (OGD/controlled)
Salt Lake Skypark (BTF/uncontrolled)

Salt Lake City Municipal No. 2 (U42/uncontrolled)

Tooele Municipal (U26/uncontrolled)

VORs:

SLC - Salt Lake City (116.8)

OGD - Ogden (115.7)

Top of TCA:

10,000 feet

Salt Lake City, another of the newer TCAs, is one of the easiest to negotiate (FIG. 9-24). The area is, of course, dominated by the Great Salt Lake and the Wasatch mountain range to the east, but there are numerous other easily identifiable landmarks throughout the area, making VFR navigation relatively simple.

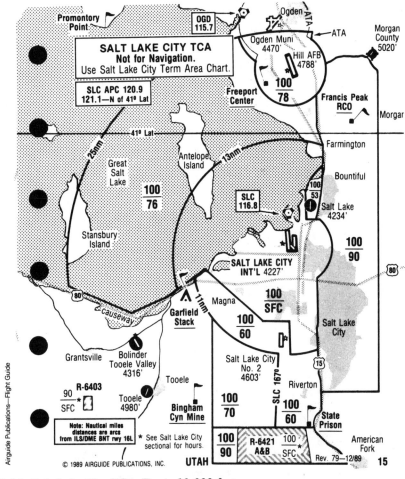

Fig. 9-24. *Salt Lake City TCA. Top is 10,000 feet.*

Given its isolated location, most light aircraft approaching the Salt Lake area would probably be landing (for fuel, if nothing else) instead of just transiting. However, if we wanted to bypass the area east-west, it is perhaps best done north of the TCA via the Ogden VOR. Avoiding the area to the south is trickier but not difficult if the state prison and Bingham Cyn Mine are used as checkpoints. Restricted Area R-6421, if active, should be avoided.

Transiting the area in a north-south direction can be done over the Great Salt Lake, using DME information from the ILS (IBNT/111.5) to runway 16L at SLC and Stansbury and Antelope Islands for landmarks. One can also fly on the eastern side of the TCA, but the mountains rise up rapidly to peaks in excess of 10,000 feet on that side of the Great Salt Lake. The Wasatch Range is great for skiing, but, flying over it requires the same caution and skill necessary with mountain flying anywhere.

Although none of the airports are really close to downtown Salt Lake City, the interstate highways criss-crossing the area allow one to drive anywhere in the basin without much hassle. Salt Lake Skypark in Bountiful and Salt Lake City No. 2 are both uncontrolled and welcome general aviation aircraft wishing to avoid the international airport.

SAN DIEGO

Airports:

    San Diego International-Lindbergh (SAN/primary)
    Brown Field Municipal (SDM/controlled)
    Gillespie Field (SEE/controlled)
    Montgomery Field (MYF/controlled)

VORs:

    MZB - Mission Bay (117.8)
    PGY - Poggi (109.8)

Top of TCA:

    12,500 feet

The popularity of flying in Southern California—especially VFR activity due to generally good weather conditions—has made some areas, like San Diego, extremely congested (FIG. 9-25).

In this case the FAA has a designated area for use by VFR aircraft operating near Lindbergh—the VFR Corridor. Flight Guide's San Diego corridor information (FIG. 9-26) puts the operating procedures in an easy-to-understand format.

If you want to avoid the big airport, San Diego can be reached through either Montgomery or Gillespie airports, located north of Lindbergh and south of Miramar NAS. Fortunately, they lie under the TCA; just be sure to remain below 4,800 feet. And considering the wide variety of traffic—civil and military—using the airspace, it would be worthwhile to enlist the eyes of any passengers along with your own to scan for traffic.

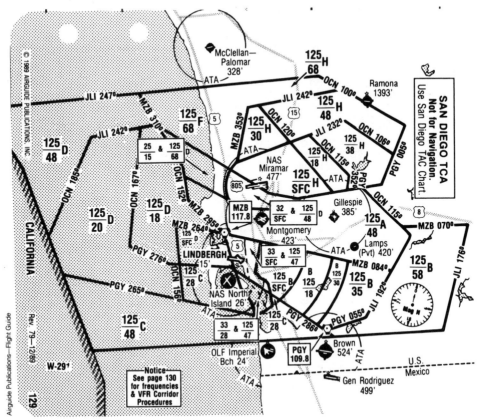

Fig. 9-25. *San Diego TCA. Top is 12,500 feet.*

Both Montgomery and Gillespie have restaurant and rental car facilities on the field.

SAN FRANCISCO

Airports:

San Francisco International (SFO/primary)
Half Moon Bay (HAF/uncontrolled)
Livermore Municipal (LVK/controlled)
Hayward Air Terminal (HWD/controlled)
Metropolitan Oakland International (OAK/controlled)
Palo Alto of Santa Clara County (PAO/controlled)
Reid Hillview of Santa Clara County (RHV/controlled)
San Carlos (SQL/controlled)
San Jose International (SJC/controlled)

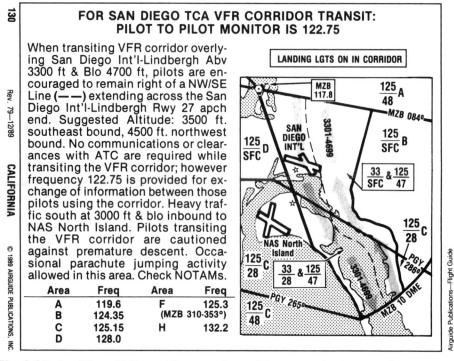

**FOR SAN DIEGO TCA VFR CORRIDOR TRANSIT:
PILOT TO PILOT MONITOR IS 122.75**

When transiting VFR corridor overlying San Diego Int'l-Lindbergh Abv 3300 ft & Blo 4700 ft, pilots are encouraged to remain right of a NW/SE Line (— —) extending across the San Diego Int'l-Lindbergh Rwy 27 apch end. Suggested Altitude: 3500 ft. southeast bound, 4500 ft. northwest bound. No communications or clearances with ATC are required while transiting the VFR corridor; however frequency 122.75 is provided for exchange of information between those pilots using the corridor. Heavy traffic south at 3000 ft & blo inbound to NAS North Island. Pilots transiting the VFR corridor are cautioned against premature descent. Occasional parachute jumping activity allowed in this area. Check NOTAMs.

Area	Freq	Area	Freq
A	119.6	F	125.3
B	124.35		(MZB 310-353°)
C	125.15	H	132.2
D	128.0		

Airguide Publications—Flight Guide

Fig. 9-26. *San Diego VFR corridor procedures. No communications or clearances are required from ATC, but pilots should self-announce on 122.75.*

VORs:

    OAK - Oakland (116.8)

    OSI   - Woodside (113.9)

    SAU - Sausalito (116.2)

    SFO - San Francisco (115.8)

    SJC - San Jose (114.1)

Top of TCA:

    8,000 feet

San Francisco is a city that really shouldn't be bypassed but, if we must, it's a simple matter to use the available VORs and the Pacific coastline or the edge of the San Francisco Bay as landmarks (FIG. 9-27). It must be kept in mind, though, that despite the 4,000- to 6,000-foot clearances under the outer rims of the TCA, there are mountains climbing to around 3,000 feet in some places. In other words, the amount of space available between the terrain and the base of the TCA overhang is not as ample as it appears. In addition, San Francisco is frequently given to attracting heavy layers of fog, the top of which may further limit the amount of space available for VFR flight. Also note that the Oakland and San Jose ARSAs underlie the San Francisco TCA, further limiting the airspace available under the TCA.

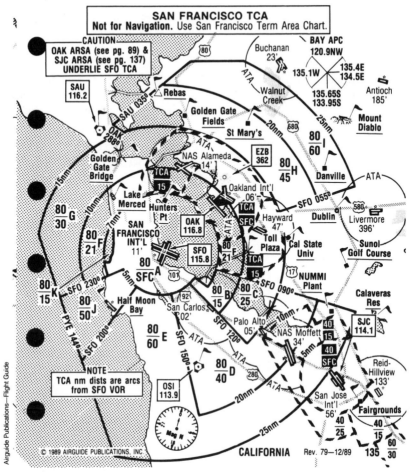

Fig. 9-27. *San Francisco TCA. Top is 8,000 feet.*

As mentioned elsewhere, the most convenient airport to downtown San Francisco is Oakland, which is easy to find and very hospitable to VFR types.

SEATTLE

Airports:
> Seattle-Tacoma International (SEA/primary)
> Boeing Field/King County International (BFI/controlled)
> Renton Municipal (RNT/controlled)
> Tacoma Narrows (TIW/controlled)

VORs:
> PAE — Paine (114.2)

SEA - Seattle (116.8)

TCM - McChord (109.6)

Top of TCA:

10,000 feet

Lying smack between the Puget Sound and the Cascade Mountains, Seattle is another city that is likely to be bypassed in only one direction—namely north-south (FIG. 9-28). The designers of the TCA obviously paid much attention to keeping VFR traffic happy. As a result, what they came up with is, in fact, a narrow north-south climb corridor with most of the airspace to either side outside TCA jurisdiction. When coming up from Olympia and wanting to go north and beyond, or vice versa, the best suggestion is to fly right over the middle of Puget Sound at an altitude below 3,000 feet. But be aware of other VFR traffic, as there may be quite a bit of it. An alternate

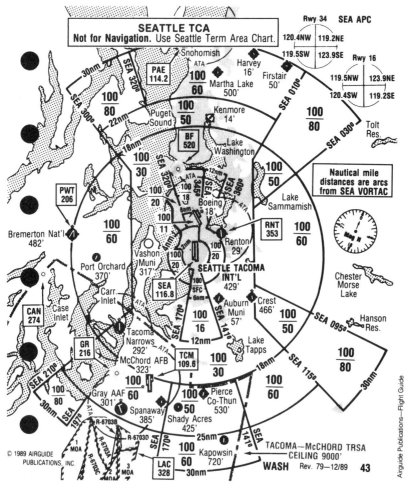

Fig. 9-28. *Seattle TCA. Top is 10,000 feet.*

132

route would be outside the TCA to the east, using radials from the Seattle VOR as well as Lake Washington for guidance.

The most convenient airport for downtown Seattle is Boeing Field, where Boeing builds all those 747s. It can be reached from either the east or west at convenient altitudes and with a minimum of circumnavigation of the more forbidding portions of the TCA. Another excellent airport is Renton, though it is a somewhat greater distance from the heart of the city.

When approaching from the south, be sure to avoid the restricted areas south of McChord AFB and Gray AAF. Also note that the Tacoma-McChord TRSA intermeshes with the Seattle TCA up to 9,000 feet. While radar service is not mandatory in a TRSA (as explained in chapter 7), it's not unreasonable to expect this TRSA to evolve into an ARSA sometime in the future, considering what has occurred with other TRSAs in the past.

WASHINGTON, D.C.

Airports:
> Washington National (DCA/primary)
> College Park (CGS/uncontrolled)
> Dulles International (IAD/controlled)
> Frederick Municipal Airport (FDK/uncontrolled)
> Freeway (W00/uncontrolled)
> Leesburg Municipal/Godfrey Field (W09/uncontrolled)
> Montgomery County (GAI/uncontrolled)
> Potomac Airfield (W28/uncontrolled)
> Washington Executive/Hyde Field (W32/uncontrolled)

VORs:
> ADW - Andrews (113.1)
> AML - Armel (113.5)
> DCA - Washington (111.0)
> FDK - Frederick (109.0)
> OTT - Nottingham (113.7)

Top of TCA:
> 7,000 feet

Washington—with its busy airline terminals and Andrews Air Force Base, which constitutes the second primary facility in the Washington TCA—is a place that must be handled with a fair amount of care (FIG. 9-29). The most intelligent way of bypassing it is to fly around the outer perimeter of the TCA at an altitude of 2,500 feet or less. Even though jet traffic is supposed to enter and depart the TCA through the top, jets are frequently observed at lower levels outside the TCA.

When flying north-south, or vice versa, using the western perimeter seems preferable, since passing by to the east puts us over Chesapeake Bay. But when staying to

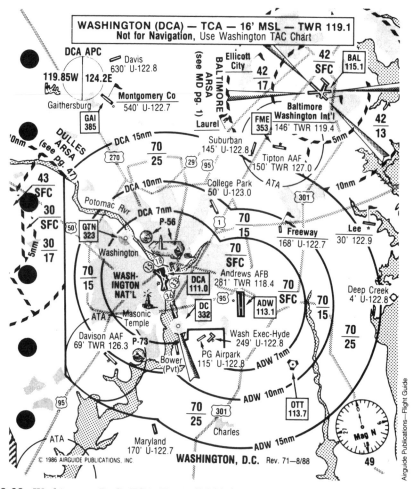

Fig. 9-29. *Washington, D.C. TCA. Top is 7,000 feet.*

the west, be sure to stay out of the Dulles ARSA. When north and east, pay attention to the Baltimore ARSA.

In order to fly to Washington, the choice of convenient airports is quite limited. Dulles is, of course, great and quite receptive to general aviation, but it's over 20 miles from downtown Washington. However, there is public transportation available. College Park, said to be the oldest airport in the country, is probably the closest to the city, but it's miserably hard to find—especially from the low altitude at which we have to be in order to stay below the floor of the overhanging TCA. And, once there, the only way to get into town is by taxi or rental car. The most convenient airport, of course, is Washington National, but landing there means dealing with the TCA and, at certain heavy-traffic hours, all arrivals—whether IFR or VFR—must have made advance reservations in order to be permitted to land.

The alternative airports (Freeway, Hyde, Prince Georges, Montgomery County, and Frederick) are some distance from Washington, D.C., but they are fair options for the general aviation pilot. As a note of interest, Frederick Municipal Airport is adjacent to the headquarters of the Aircraft Owners and Pilots Association.

As of mid-1990, approval was pending for a new TCA, which would cover Washington National, Dulles International, Baltimore-Washington, and Andrews Air Force Base. The ceiling of this new TCA is expected to be 10,000 feet msl and the highest floor 4,500 feet msl. Some 20 smaller airports will come under the TCA's underlying airspace and about 12 others will be within the 30-DME Mode-C veil.

All of the TCA charts used in Chapter 9 are from Flight Guide Airport and Frequency Manual available in three volumes: Vol. 1-11 western states, Vol. 2-15 central states, and Vol. 3-22 eastern states. Flight Guide may be obtained from your local airport dealer or Airguide Publications, P.O. Box 1288, Long Beach, CA (213)437-3210. The charts are copyrighted.

10
Summer

SUMMER IS GENERALLY THOUGHT OF AS THE TIME OF THE YEAR WHEN THE weather is best and cross-country flying is easiest. It is also the time when kids are home from school and most vacation trips are planned. But just because it is warm and the sun shines much of the time, that doesn't mean that summer flying doesn't have its problems.

The good thing about summer is that days are long and nights comparably short, thus reducing to a minimum the need to fly at night. Airplane engines can be started without difficulty and, much of the time, wind velocities are low, reducing the adverse effect of the ever-present head winds.

And then there are the negative aspects.

THUNDERSTORMS

While few and far between during winter, spring, and fall, thunderstorms tend to be produced by summer heat with depressing regularity. Early mornings may be beautiful, but as soon as the heat of the day warms the surface of the earth, vertical currents of air spawn clouds, which slowly rise to great heights until that tell-tale anvil shape forms as a strict warning to pilots to stay away. Throughout most of the country we can virtually count on finding those storms either singularly and scattered or combined into huge squall lines and weather systems (FIG. 10-1).

Fig. 10-1. *A developing thunderstorm.*

Thunderstorms vie with icing conditions for the distinction of being flying's worst enemy. Neither skill nor guts nor all the instrument proficiency in the world are of any help to the hapless pilot who accidentally or intentionally stumbles into one. It is estimated that some 50,000 thunderstorms occur each day on earth. All are caused when the weight of the air is being reduced by heat, thus, causing it to move vertically upward. There are six distinct meteorological conditions that bring about their formation. The first two are the result of air being heated by contact with warm surfaces. One type, occurring when the surface of the ground is warmed by radiation from the sun, is encountered in the temperate zone most frequently during summer afternoons in mountainous regions. These storms, usually well-defined in areas of unlimited visibility, build individually rather than in groups. The other type is the result of cool air being warmed by moving over large bodies of warmer water and occurs primarily over the sea during the winter months, especially in the coastal regions of large continents.

Another group, often referred to as *frontal storms*, is associated with line squalls and warm fronts. It is formed when warm air is lifted over cold currents. This type of thunderstorm will frequently be embedded in large areas of IFR weather and low visibilities, making it hard to see and avoid and a distinct danger to the instrument flyer.

The next two groups are caused either by converging airflows within warm currents or the interaction of cold and warm currents at different levels. They are found most often in advance of cold fronts or in the vicinity of low-pressure troughs and occur more frequently at night than during the day.

The last group is spawned by the lifting of air by upslope winds. It is found on the windward slopes of mountains, usually during windy spring afternoons.

No matter what the cause, the effect always includes vertical winds moving both up and down at velocities that frequently exceed the structural capability of any aircraft, no matter its size, as well as the ability of the pilot to maintain some measure of control. The rising air gathers moisture and is supercooled at higher altitudes, producing precipitation in the form of rain or hail. The friction between the opposing air masses results in charges of static electricity that have been estimated to reach magnitudes of 20,000,000 volts and over 200,000 amps (FIG. 10-2). The visible lightning is what happens when these huge amounts of electricity are being discharged from cloud to cloud or into the ground. Since an aircraft does not represent a body of opposing polarity or a means of discharging electricity into ground, lightning is not likely to seek it out but may strike if the aircraft happens to be in its path. There are many reports of instances of lightning striking aircraft, resulting in varying degrees of damage. Some describe damage to wings or other surfaces; and there are cases where the entire electrical system, including, of course, all avionics, were knocked out.

From the pilot's point of view, thunderstorms are usually better thought of as VFR situations, making it possible to visually avoid areas of danger without having to argue with ATC about permission to deviate from the flight-plan clearance. With the

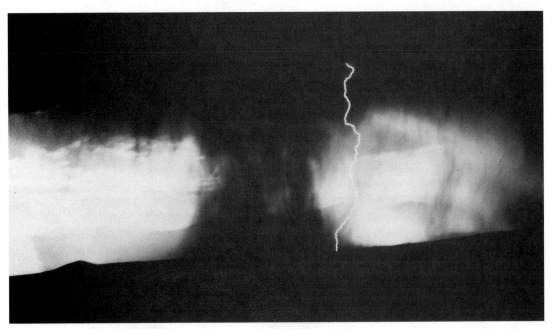

Fig. 10-2. *Visible lightning is the result of static electricity, which is estimated to reach magnitudes of more than 20 million volts and 200,000 amps.*

ever-present danger of hail, which frequently falls even from the outer clouds, the periphery of such storms should be avoided by a safe distance of some 20 miles.

The best advice is to do as much flying as possible early in the day during the thunderstorm season. It is quite rare to find one still active from the night before, and new ones haven't yet had time to build to meaningful proportions.

The two instruments other than the human eye that are useful in thunderstorm avoidance are airborne weather radar and something called a Stormscope. Weather radar paints a picture of the areas of precipitation, while the Stormscope indicates the direction and distance of lightning.

FRONTAL ACTIVITY

One of the phenomena most annoying to the VFR pilot is the tendency of warm fronts to cover huge areas of the east or midwest with low ceilings and inadequate visibility. And the worst part is that they will often sit there for days on end without any noticeable sign of movement.

While presenting no serious problem for the IFR pilot, they do make life miserable for those who must or prefer to operate VFR. If such a front is located between the departure and destination airports and if the pilot is flying an aircraft with adequate range, it is usually possible to climb to a flight level above the tops of the overcast. The tops of such fronts, more often than not, are somewhere around 10,000 to 12,000 feet and, even if there are occasional higher buildups, they can easily be circumvented. But unless the pilot is willing, able, and equipped to go IFR if the need should arise, he had better make absolutely sure that his destination is VFR and forecast to remain so. And by this we mean VFR either with no overcast or, at the very least, with a broken overcast that will permit him to descend while remaining clear of clouds.

Though the ceilings of these fronts tend to be quite low, it is sometimes possible to stay in the clear beneath the overcast and follow a river or major highway. In situations like these it is important that the pilot is proficient in navigating by pilotage alone as, for much of the time, he is likely to be beyond reception distance of nav aids. He must have the appropriate Sectional or WAC charts in the cockpit and must be experienced in relating the landmarks on the ground to what is represented on the charts.

Under these conditions the air frequently is excessively humid, with temperature and dew point being only a few degrees apart. Though the outside air temperature may be quite warm, this is the ideal recipe for the formation of carburetor ice. Always be prepared to apply carburetor heat at the first sign of an otherwise unexplained loss of engine power. When needed, carburetor heat should always be applied fully and the mixture leaned somewhat.

HAZE

Haze is one of the most annoying phenomena, and summer haze conditions have increased notably during the last 20 years in the midwest and east (FIG. 10-3). On many a summer day haze will be present in a thick layer, rising as high as 9,000 or

Fig. 10-3. *Haze is one of the most annoying phenomena.*

10,000 feet, drastically restricting lateral visibility especially when flying toward the sun.

Conditions at the airports may be barely VFR or may require requests for special VFR clearances. (Tower controllers never offer or suggest special VFR; it must be requested by the pilot.) Once airborne one has the feeling that forward visibility is zilch. Still, vertically down we can see the ground quite clearly, and above us is the sun with not a cloud anywhere. So we climb and climb, and it always looks as if the top of the haze layer is just another few hundred feet higher, only to find that when we get up there we're still in it. Finally, somewhere around 10,000 feet, we're in the clear where the lateral visibility is unlimited. Flight up there is likely to be smooth, pleasant, and cool. The bad part is that all we can see of the ground is what is directly beneath us. At a slant everything turns out to be milk soup.

While this is no great problem during the en route portion of the flight, it does prevent us often from finding our destination until we're right on top of it. If the destination airport has an associated nav aid, homing in on it even under conditions of restricted visibility is relatively easy. When it becomes difficult is when there is no such nav aid nearby and we have to depend on finding our way visually.

TURBULENCE

Summer days, especially during the afternoons, can get pretty rough at times. Even when there are no thunderstorms around, those pretty, fluffy, scattered little cumulus clouds all over the sky are the result of vertical air currents and at any level below their bases it is likely to be a pretty bumpy ride. So we climb to a higher altitude and will find that as soon as we have reached a level above the bases of those clouds the air suddenly becomes smooth.

The worst such thermal effect will be encountered on summer afternoons in mountainous areas. Here the sun heats one side of the mountain while the shadow side stays cool, causing air currents to fight one another all over the place. Other than landing and waiting for the cool of the evening, the only thing a pilot can do is to sit back and let the airplane bounce up and down as much as it wants while he tries to pretend to relax and enjoy it. If the aircraft is equipped with a wing leveler or autopilot, let it do the work. It makes the whole process a lot more pleasant. If it's a sophisticated autopilot equipped with altitude hold, disconnect the altitude-hold portion because trying to maintain a steady altitude under such conditions will put excessive strain on the servo mechanisms.

In such mountain areas there is usually little gained by climbing higher and higher in an effort to get above the turbulence. More probably than not it will extend beyond the level at which we will want to fly; unless, of course, we're flying something like a Learjet.

HEAT

So far we have talked about heat in its relation to weather and turbulence. But there is another effect of summer heat that may require certain precautions. Day in and day out, while the airplane is tied down, summer heat cooks the interior of that airplane resulting in interior temperatures that can eventually cause a variety of expensive problems.

Heat reduces the useful life of interior fabrics and plastics. In extreme cases it reduces the tensile strength of seatbelts and shoulder harnesses. And worst of all, it can play havoc with expensive avionics equipment. Today's airplanes often contain a large number of individual avionics units, all built into small containers that become miniature furnaces when the outside temperature is in the 80s or 90s and temperatures in the cabin are twice that level.

Certain precautions can be taken. Covering the instrument panel with a reflective cloth helps some. Better, still, are those commercially available covers that are designed to fit all popular models of single- and twin-engine aircraft. Next, never turn on any of those instruments until after the engine has been started and the propwash has had an opportunity to cool the airplane. Turning on a radio before the engine is started, maybe to listen to the ATIS or some such, simply adds one more shot of heat to that already present, and sooner or later this accumulation of heat will begin to break down some of the components in that radio.

Taking a few precautionary steps will help to reduce the accumulation of heat in the aircraft and, thus, its detrimental effects:

- Leave all vents open while the aircraft is tied town. It doesn't help much except when there is wind that will produce a modicum of air circulation;

- If at all possible, tie the airplane down with its nose into the prevailing wind;

- Immediately upon arriving at the airport, open all doors and windows wide while performing the preflight, storing luggage and so on;

- Start the engine before turning on any of the radios or other avionics equipment;

- When ready to taxi, turn on only one radio to obtain taxi clearance. Leave the others off until movement of the airplane has helped to further cool things down;

- Keep the number of avionics units in use to a minimum until airborne, when the airflow is able to finally produce a meaningful cooling effect; and

- In hot desert areas like Palm Springs or Las Vegas, either ask for (and be prepared to pay for) hangar space or at least park where there is shade. Many FBOs in those areas provide covered outdoor parking. Even if there is an extra charge, it's worth it. (By the way, parking an aircraft under a tree in order to obtain shade may not be a good idea. Birds tend to sit in trees, and an airplane covered with bird droppings is a mess to clean up.)

SUMMER SQUALL LINE

A flying vacation was scheduled to end early Friday morning with a final leg home, but a squall line located right on top of the route delayed departure for several hours.

The vacation had started on the previous Saturday morning when the pilot and his mother left Snyder, Texas, for Norman, Oklahoma, to take her home; then the solo pilot would fly to Tulsa, Oklahoma, that afternoon to visit his brother.

Snyder to Norman was uneventful until a very light rain shower smacked the windshield for several miles while descending for a landing. Other showers were seen to the northeast toward Tulsa, and the pilot hoped they would dissipate or move away within the next hour. Landing at Westheimer Field was an adventure, with a stiff 25-knot crosswind at a 90-degree angle to the active runway. The airport was uncontrolled, and the pilot, who learned to fly there, later wished he had landed directly into the breeze on a very long, strong taxiway. Once on the ground he got a quick lunch, and he was on his way to Tulsa.

Sure enough the rain had moved to the south, and winds moderated for an uneventful landing at Tulsa. Monday the brothers flew in the area tracing some of the

Kerr-McClellan Waterway that runs from the Tulsa Port of Catoosa toward the Mississippi River.

On his way back to Texas the pilot stopped in Norman for two days—planning to return to Snyder on a Friday morning. But the squall line had different ideas.

Thunder rumbled in about dawn, and with the cloud mass it never got all that bright when the sun came up—and it was raining heavily. No real need to "rise and shine," so he turned over and went back to sleep—after all it was vacation time. Finally, the heavy rains gave way to general showers, and he had hopes of taking off soon after lunch. Weather reports from Flight Service confirmed it was a squall line that would clear the area around noon.

After lunch, standing at his mother's back door looking west, the pilot saw bright lights under the clouds that heralded sunshine. So he gathered his bags and loaded the car—shaking off some light sprinkles of rain that lingered. A final call to Flight Service verified his suspicion that locally and along his route it was already VFR with only scattered clouds. Flight plan filed, he was on his way.

Water was still draining from the tarmac as he loaded the plane and performed a preflight check, but the sun was shining and visibility was crystal clear—save the predicted scattered cumulus clouds.

After takeoff he found the ride rather rough under the clouds, so he climbed above the scattered deck and enjoyed smooth air. To his right was a deep blue sky, underneath were the harmless clouds, and to his left were the deadly clouds. He looked back as far as he could see to the left and there was nothing but a wall of dark gray; likewise in front of the airplane to the left it was nothing but gray. The storms stretched from Central Kansas through Oklahoma and into Texas past the Dallas-Fort Worth Metroplex. Fortunately it was moving east, and the pilot was headed to southwest. Unfortunately the harmless clouds below were starting to gather and form a broken cloud deck.

Not wanting to be stuck on top he descended back to the rough but clear air. The gray wall of cumulonimbus clouds became a black slab of rain etched with lightning strikes; to the right was a patchwork quilt of cloud shadows.

Fortunately the clouds were high enough that a cruise altitude kept the airplane in reception range of VORs and other radio aids. About halfway home he made a right turn over a VOR that would take him away from the squall line directly toward home.

The clouds broke up enough that he again climbed up to smooth air for the remainder of the flight. Two rain showers were south of his course; had they been directly along the route to Snyder he could have easily deviated around them.

By keeping a respectable distance from the squall and avoiding those stray showers behind the line of thunderstorms the pilot was safely home by mid-afternoon.

11
Flight Number Four

Date: June 4, 1973.
Pilot: Male, age 51, manufacturer's representative.
License: Commercial, MEL, instrument.
Pilot-In-Command Time: 3,142 hours.
Aircraft: Cessna Skylane.
Flight: From Reading, Pennsylvania, to Santa Fe, New Mexico.
Purpose of Flight: Pleasure.

Skylane N58504 was one of over 1,000 light aircraft tied down in the grass at Reading Airport (FIG. 11-1) where, for one last time during that year's Reading Air Show, the team of military precision pilots was performing those breathtaking aerobatic gyrations that traditionally have been part of so many general aviation air shows in the United States. The pilot, having seen the performance several times before, paid little attention as, carrying his luggage, he walked through the tall grass to his airplane.

He stashed his luggage, preflighted the aircraft, removed the tiedown chains, climbed in, and then sat waiting. For anyone like him who was interested in airplanes and flying, the past three days had been fascinating and fun. He'd met old acquaintances and made new friends and had spent most of his time studying the new airplanes and avionics that manufacturers from all over the world had brought to Reading for the show.

Fig. 11-1. *Heydays of the Reading Air Show.*

Immediately after the conclusion of the current performance, he and hundreds of others would be ready to scramble for position in order to be able to take off as soon as possible.

DEPARTURE

Screech . . . screech . . . screech. . . . One after another the brightly painted military jets touched down on the long runway. The pilot started his engine and began to inch forward, but despite his preparations others managed to get into takeoff position ahead of him. Still, he was among the first 50 or so, which wasn't bad. Last-day departures from the Reading Air Show are a unique experience. Rows upon rows of light aircraft line up for takeoff, two abreast on the same runway, each moving ahead a few feet every time the one in front starts its takeoff run. There is no radio chatter. The men in the tower are silent, having turned the takeoff control over to controllers on the ground, who use flags to clear one aircraft after the other for takeoff. The routine is simple. As soon as the aircraft ahead is seen to be airborne, the next one is waved off, the understanding being that the one on the right side of the runway makes a right turnout, while the other one turns to the left.

Finally, the Skylane was first in line on the left side of the runway. The controller waved his flag. Throttle full in, accelerate, lift off. Bank slightly to the left and suddenly all those other aircraft seemed to have vanished in the vastness of the sky. Though he had seen each take off—dozens of them—none remained in sight.

He climbed to 6,500 feet and leveled off. It was late afternoon, and the sun, shining into the haze that seems to be a permanent condition on summer days in that part of the country, gave the impression that the visibility was less, in fact, than it was.

Everything was calm for the moment. The engine was purring its reassuring steady hum, and the pilot was humming a song as he often did when flying or taking a shower.

THUNDERY FORECAST

He had been flying for an hour, maybe a little less, when the sun sank behind tall cloud buildups in the distant west—the first sign that after a while things might become somewhat less tranquil. When he had checked the weather prior to his departure there had been forecasts of widely scattered thunderstorms along his route of flight westward. He now tuned to the nearest FSS to get the latest reports, and when the disembodied voice read off the current conditions at the various reporting stations ahead, there was no indication that those storms would be diminishing with the onset of night.

The darkness of night was complete by the time he was approaching the first of the storms. The sky above still shone with stars, and behind him, in the far eastern distance, a three-quarter moon hesitatingly began its nocturnal journey westward. But, straight ahead, there was a wall: Gray-black, punctuated by streaks of lightning, which intermittently illuminated the mountains of clouds reaching all the way up to jet altitudes like boiling cauldrons.

Years of flying light aircraft day and night, summer and winter, and uncounted occasions of jousting with all manner of weather and storms had taught the pilot not to let himself be intimidated too soon. He continued on course, studying the lightning patterns carefully to determine which areas would have to be avoided and where he might find a chance to penetrate. One thing was certain: this was time to fly instruments. On too many previous occasions under similar circumstances he had found that the route and altitude for which he had been cleared by ATC had led too close for comfort to one storm center or another. No, this sort of thing could better be handled VFR or not at all. If he would find that he couldn't get through to Cincinnati, which was reporting clear and where he had planned to stay overnight, he'd simply have to turn back and find some other place to stay.

Gradually it began to look as if there might be a reasonably wide space between two major areas where lightning was concentrated, which appeared less solid and free of any noticeable activity. Dropping down to about 1,000 feet above the highest obstacle in the area, he headed in that direction and tightened his seatbelt and shoulder harness in anticipation of the turbulence that, he was certain, would start to bounce him around any minute now.

And he was right. With lightning at a reasonable distance to the right and left, things began to get rough with a vengeance. The stars above disappeared behind a black curtain, as did the moon, but lights from houses and cars on the ground were proof that there was ample visibility to safely continue on his course.

In situations like this, minutes seem to stretch into hours. The airplane bounces around, wants first to climb, then drop, and all you can really do is sit there, suffer, and make sure you stay out of the clouds.

Suddenly rain hit the windshield like bullets fired from 100 machine-guns. And then it stopped. One more violent bump and, quite suddenly, it was all over. The stars began to reappear above, and far in the distance there was the tell-tale glow of the lights of a city. He looked at his watch. What had seemed like half the night had, in fact, been only 10 minutes or so.

He loosened his seatbelt, sat back, and relaxed. He tuned his nav receiver to 117.3 and watched with satisfaction as the OBI told him that those lights at the horizon ahead must be Cincinnati. He'd land at Lunken; spend the night at that corny El Rancho Motel located just off the airport, and tomorrow, after a good breakfast, he'd continue west with (he hoped) no further interference from thunderstorms or squall lines.

CLEARED TO LAND?

And then he made one of those embarrassing mistakes that even experienced pilots make from time to time. Once he spotted the rotating beacon of what he assumed to be his destination airport, he headed for it and called Lunken Tower to announce his intention to land. Everything seemed to be perfectly fine. There was the lighted runway and, turning downwind, he asked if he was cleared to land.

"Cessna Five-Zero-Four, we do not have you in sight."

How could that be? He was downwind with his landing light on and the tower clearly in view to his left. He said so.

There was a pause, then: "Cessna Five-Zero-Four. Greater Cincinnati informs us they have an unidentified Cessna downwind."

The wrong airport! How dumb can you get? He had made that typical error of once having spotted what he assumed to be his destination airport, disregarding all other indications and landmarks, and simply deciding that this must be it. Embarrassed, he admitted his mistake and accepted vectors to Lunken, remembering how he had laughed when he'd heard about an airline pilot on approach to Portland, Oregon, landing by mistake at Troutdale.

The next day dawned like a pilot's dream. It was clear and sunny with not enough wind to noticeably slow his westerly progress. The long-range tanks on his airplane made Oklahoma City the next logical stop for food and fuel, and when he checked the weather it was advertised as CAVU all the way. He took off, climbed to 8,500 and, using a reasonably economical power setting, watched the country below glide by (FIG. 11-2).

For most of the flight the forecast proved correct; but, then, when it finally did fall apart, it did so at just the wrong time and place. Why is it that if there is only one black area in the sky, it is always just exactly where we want to go? With Oklahoma City barely 50 miles away, there it sat: huge, fat, and defiant, proudly flying its immense anvil like a regimental flag, spewing a million gallons of water from its lightning-laced boiling black center. Like a renegade bull elephant, outcast by the herd, it blocked the course in solitary splendor.

There were only two choices: He would have to detour around it, either to the

Cessna Aircraft Company

Fig. 11-2. *A Cessna Skylane en route.*

right or to the left. He called the nearest FSS and asked for weather at specific locations that, according to his chart, would give him an indication of which direction might result in the lesser distance. Oklahoma City was reporting clear with towering cumulus to the east. And based on the reports from the south and north, detouring to the left seemed the better choice. Still, by the time he finally shut down the engine at Oke City he had flown a lot of extra miles and used more fuel than he had anticipated.

A LINE OF GRAY

Apparently that lonely thunderstorm was serving notice of things to come and, when he was ready to continue on his way, the forecast did acknowledge what was described as scattered thunderstorm activity fast moving in a northeasterly direction. At first everything was fine but, after he'd flown about 100 miles or so he could see them sitting there on the horizon, and there seemed to be nothing much scattered about what he saw. An apparently endless line of dark gray, like dirty snow piled high by a giant snowplow, lay diagonally across his course from southwest to northeast.

And as he came closer he soon knew that there was no alternative but to parallel the line southwestward in hopes that, sooner or later, an opening would present itself.

He was flying under the outer clouds, and soon a rather strange phenomenon made itself felt. As if drawn by a magnet, the airplane kept wanting to climb into the base of the overhanging clouds above. He trimmed the nose down and watched the airspeed creep upward, and still the airplane continued to gain altitude. More trim, more speed until, with the airspeed indicator needle high up in the yellow, he had to throttle back to keep from climbing. It was, without a doubt, the longest sustained updraft he had ever encountered and, though he was forced to continue south of his intended course, he found himself gobbling up miles at an unheard-of fuel economy.

Just as he was beginning to wonder if he'd ever be able to get back on course, there appeared a break. It wasn't really a break in the squall line but was more like a barn door—a huge gate to paradise with black clouds joining hands above. He banked to the right, dropped down to within 500 or 600 feet of the flat ground below, and, keeping a constant lookout above to make sure that there would be no horizontal lightning across the top of his path, headed into the opening while trimming the nose back up and feeding in power as the effect of the updraft began to disappear. Again, minutes

Fig. 11-3. *The lighter areas to the left of the center of the storm seem to indicate that a detour to the left is the logical choice.*

stretched into bumpy hours. Low hanging scud raced by at his right and left, but there was light ahead and it kept getting lighter (FIG. 11-3). And then there was sunlight.

Once clear of the squall line he concentrated on his nav radio because, by this time, he had no clear idea of exactly where he was (FIG. 11-4). Well, it turned out that he was somewhere southwest of Amarillo, so he adjusted his heading to one that he assumed would get him to Tucumcari and from there, in a more or less straight line, home to Santa Fe, New Mexico. But that, too, turned out to be easier planned than accomplished. True, he soon picked up the Tucumcari VOR, but between there and his destination one thunderstorm after another seemed to sprout like a field of so many mushrooms. One detour led to another and then another still until finally, with the Sandia Mountains east of Albuquerque in sight, he found that one or more of those oversized monsters had decided to squat right on top of where he knew Santa Fe to be.

MORE FUEL

By now both fuel tanks were below a quarter and, though he assumed that there would be sufficient fuel to get him home, he didn't relish the idea of trying to outfox that thunderstorm while at the same time worrying about how much flying time was left in those tanks. Las Vegas (New Mexico), some 60 miles east of Santa Fe, was in the clear, so he turned toward it, landed there, and topped off the tanks.

From the window in the Flight Service Station he could see much of the route to Santa Fe, most of it covered by a solid deck of clouds representing the outer rim of the thunderstorm. The Flight Service specialist assured him that the storm was, in fact, still west of Santa Fe, where it appeared to be stalled.

There is a four-lane divided highway (Interstate 25) leading from Las Vegas to Santa Fe, but it winds through some fairly narrow valleys, which makes following it at a low altitude somewhat scary.

Fig. 11-4. *Clear weather lies ahead after successfully circumventing the storm.*

"Looks to me like if I follow the highway I ought to be able to make it before the worst of the storm hits Santa Fe," he told the Flight Service specialist.

"I wouldn't. See those two small mountains to the left?"

"Yeah."

"When they look clear, head between them and then turn right. Along that route the terrain is much lower and you should be able to safely stay below the clouds. And if it doesn't look good when you get there, you can always turn around."

That sounded good. He thanked him, fired up his airplane, and took off, heading for the two mountains as the man had suggested. He stayed quite low, just a few hundred feet above the terrain, which in that area is about 7,000 or 8,000 feet high. Though there were clouds not too far above and he could see a few scattered showers here and there, the lateral visibility was ample, and once past those two mountains he recognized the landmarks associated with Santa Fe. He called the tower and asked for the conditions at the airport.

"Estimated ceiling 3,000 overcast, visibility two-zero. Thunderstorm west of the field."

That certainly was better than it looked.

"Santa Fe Tower, Cessna Five-Zero-Four landing Santa Fe."

"Report downwind Runway Two-Zero."

Later, in his car driving home from the airport, the storm hit Santa Fe full force, drenching everything with a thundering downpour, occasionally reducing visibility to less than a city block while hurricane-force gusts of wind were howling through the canyons between the mountains—a less-than-subtle reminder that there are times when it's preferable to be on the ground.

12
Winter

WITH WEATHER BEING ONE OF THE KEY ELEMENTS THAT AFFECTS SAFE cross-country flying, it is not surprising that winter, in those portions of the country that have a real winter, presents some quite unique problems of its own. Still, if adequate precautions are taken, there is no real reason to reduce flying activity during those months. Those of us who own our own airplanes virtually have to keep on using them in order to justify the investment.

Every phase of each and every flight requires a degree of special attention during those months when much of the country is covered by a blanket of snow. Preflight preparations must be more thorough and may have to include items that would be of little or no importance at other times. En route we are faced with weather patterns that often differ from those encountered in spring, summer, or fall. Airports may become unusable for hours, or even days, after a major storm has passed. Preparation, therefore, in the form of advance knowledge of what might be encountered is the secret of safe winter flying.

PREFLIGHT

The preflight weather check should be more thorough than usual. Not only do we need to know the expected ceiling and visibility figures for the proposed route, we have to be concerned with possible precipitation, which could be in the form of snow or freezing rain. We must inquire about the expected conditions at our destination airport. If there has been or will be a frontal passage sometime prior to our expected arrival, will the runways be sufficiently cleared of snow and ice to permit a safe landing; and, if conditions are questionable, is there an alternate airport within a reasonable distance? How about possible icing conditions en route? If such conditions are forecast, a trip that was planned to be made IFR might better be made VFR unless we are certain that we can reach ice-free altitudes before too much structural ice has accumulated (FIG. 12-1).

If your airplane is not certified for flight in icing conditions, don't ever plan a flight into known or forecast icing, or you may find yourself in the role of unpaid test pilot. If the manufacturer didn't consider icing tests worth the time and expense to convince the FAA to give the airplane an icing certification, you're not going to gain anything by doing the testing for them free. The risk just isn't worth it.

If your airplane is certified for icing, remember it's often hard for even experienced pilots to make the distinction between a trace of icing and light icing or between light and moderate, and so on. It's even harder to know when the white stuff accumulating on the wings is going to create a new airfoil, or how much weight it's adding to the machine. With respect to aircraft ice, it's better to be conservative and figure conditions are worse than they are than the other way around (TABLE 12-1).

Even if a thin layer of ice doesn't affect the airplane aerodynamically, think what a coating of ice on the windshield does to forward visibility. The defrosters in most light airplanes are really "de-misters," and the combination of cold air and airspeed may just make it impossible for the defroster to clear the windshield of ice. A 10-minute accumulation of ice could end up sticking tenaciously to the windshield for the rest of the flight. Those who have done it know that landing an airplane with visibility only out the side windows is a rather harrowing experience.

As far as the actual preflight inspection is concerned, the walk-around should

Fig. 12-1. *Climbing to VMC above.*

Table 12-1. Icing Definitions.

Icing Definitions

The present definitions of icing intensity used in aviation forecasts were established in 1968 by the Subcommittee for Aviation Meteorological Services of the Federal Coordinator for Meteorological Services and Supporting Research.

Trace of Icing

Icing becomes perceptible. The rate of accumulation is slightly greater than the rate of sublimation. It is not hazardous, even though deicing/anti-icing equipment is not utilized, unless encountered for an extended period of time—more than one hour.

Light Icing

The rate of accumulation may create a problem if the flight is prolonged in this environment more than one hour. Occasional use of deicing/anti-icing equipment is needed.

Moderate Icing

The rate of accumulation is such that even short encounters become potentially hazardous, and deicing/anti-icing equipment or diversion must be used continuously.

Severe Icing

The rate of accumulation is such that deicing/anti-icing equipment fails to reduce or control the hazard, even when used continuously. Immediate diversion is necessary.

---

include a look into the wheel fairings (on fixed-gear aircraft) to check for accumulations of mud or ice that might have frozen inside. The aircraft itself has to be completely free of snow, ice, or frost before takeoff can even be considered. If it has been tied down outside, it may be necessary to move it into a heated hangar for several hours in order to permit snow and ice to melt. But, even after it has melted off, don't attempt takeoff before it is completely dry. If the outside temperature is below freezing, all moisture will immediately freeze to the metal when the aircraft is taken out of the hangar. With space in heated hangars hard to come by during the winter, it is a good idea to call ahead, reserve space, and have the FBO move the airplane into the hangar long before the estimated time of departure.

Always check fuel-cap vents and static ports. Frozen fuel-cap vents can cause fuel tanks to collapse as fuel is drained from then. Frozen static ports can cause the altimeter and vertical speed indicator to become inoperative.

Prior to trying to start a cold aircraft, the prop should be pulled through several times (with the ignition switch in the *off* position). This will help to loosen the oil and reduce the strain on the battery which, when cold, provides less power than it does in warmer temperatures. In really cold weather it may become unavoidable to use an auxiliary power unit. The oil will simply be too thick and the battery too weak to produce the degree of rotation necessary to get the engine to fire.

All control surfaces—rudder, aileron, flaps, and trim tabs—must be checked and exercised to make sure that none of them are frozen in the hinges. Water tends to collect in those hinges and, when it freezes, it may be impossible to move those surfaces as freely as necessary. On aircraft equipped with constant-speed propellers the prop should be exercised more often than at other times. It takes a while for the oil in the mechanism to warm up sufficiently to permit the prop to operate properly. And then, when we are certain that everything is in working order, let's wait until the oil-pressure is in the green. It will take considerably longer, and on really cold days the oil temperature gauge may never register in the green until after the aircraft is airborne.

TAXI AND TAKEOFF

Prior to attempting to taxi we should examine the conditions of the taxi and runway surfaces. Patches of frozen moisture or differing amounts of snow on the ground can make taxiing difficult and may affect takeoff procedures, especially if there is a crosswind of any consequence. Brakes must be used with extreme caution. Braking with one main wheel on a patch of ice and the other on solid ground can result in an unanticipated groundloop even in a tricycle-gear aircraft. I once saw a Gulfstream II at Teterboro Airport making a complete and very slow 360 on the taxiway as a result of brake application with ice on the ground.

Ice on the ground may also make a run-up impossible. The brakes simply won't hold the aircraft in place as power is applied. It may be necessary to perform the run-up while the aircraft is still tied down. (Chocks alone are not enough. They'll slide on icy ground just as the wheels will.) In such an instance we must make sure that there is nothing behind the airplane that could be damaged as the result of the propwash and the ever-present possibility of some debris being blown by it. Alternatively, we might be able to do a cursory run-up while taxiing, or we may simply have to take off without the usual run-up and check the mags during the takeoff roll.

Taxiing itself should be done as slowly as possible and with great care, avoiding sudden turns or stops. And, especially in low-wing aircraft, attention must be paid to the piles of snow that may line the taxi and runways on both sides. Such piles of snow tend to freeze rock hard and, when hit, are easily able to dent a wingtip or break a navigation light.

If the runway is icy or slippery and there is a strong crosswind, we may find that we tend to slide across the runway during the slow initial portion of the takeoff run before sufficient speed has been attained to cause the rudder to be effective. Under such conditions it is advisable to start the takeoff run on the upwind edge of the runway. By the time we have skidded across most or all of the width of the runway we should have sufficient speed to become airborne.

EN ROUTE

Once airborne the degree of necessary vigilance depends largely on the prevailing weather. If the visibility is good and the temperature is way below the freezing point, there is little to worry about. Still, we should listen religiously to the hourly sequence reports and all other weather information that may become available over the radio. During the winter months weather systems tend to be smaller and move faster than they do at other times of the year. Knowing what the weather conditions are to the right and left of our proposed route of flight is often helpful in anticipating sudden changes.

If the temperature at the departure airport was above freezing and there was moisture, rain or drizzle, it is important to frequently move the various control surfaces (especially the trim tab) during the initial portion of the climb out. Most likely we will be climbing into colder, subfreezing temperatures and the moisture may freeze and cause trim tabs and other control surfaces to become immobile. It is extremely unpleasant to arrive at one's cruising altitude and find that it is impossible to trim the nose of the airplane down for cruise. It will, of course, fly all right but, we may have to sit there for a long period of time pushing the yoke forward with considerable muscle power.

If IFR and in clouds, attention must be paid to the leading edges of the wings. This is usually where ice will start to build up and, once it starts, it may do so with frightening rapidity. When that happens it is important to know the temperature conditions above and below. Warmer temperatures will melt it away, while colder temperatures will inhibit further buildup and allow whatever ice has accumulated to gradually dissipate. Depending on the aircraft being flown, the colder altitudes—which are usually up high (except when there is an inversion, in which case they may be below with warmer air above)—may or may not be within reach. If there is plenty of reserve power to get up at a fast enough rate to minimize additional ice buildup, fine. If that is not the case, dropping down to a lower and warmer altitude or to a level below the clouds may be the only practical alternative.

In such a situation ATC should be contacted as soon as ice starts to build in order to get clearance for a change in altitude before things become critical. If they should refuse, there may be no alternative but to tell them that descent to VFR conditions is imperative—requiring that IFR be canceled as soon as VFR conditions are reached. The controller, after all, is there to serve us, not the other way around. It's our lives that are on the line, not his. It would, therefore, be foolish to let ourselves be intimidated by him.

If we're in VFR conditions and are staying clear of clouds as we should, there is little likelihood of picking up ice in any meaningful quantity. Moisture-laden air may produce some, but it is not likely to become serious. However, knowledge of the type of precipitation that might be encountered is vital. Rain or dry snow, while reducing forward visibility, usually represent no serious problem. Freezing rain, on the other hand, represents a considerable danger and must be avoided at all costs. Wet snow likes to adhere to the airfoils and especially the windshield, which it has been known to cover to such an extent that no amount of defroster activity can effectively fight it. In such a case a quick 180 should be decided upon before all forward visibility is lost.

Throughout the en route portion of any winter cross-country flight it is a sensible precaution to constantly keep track of the runway conditions at nearby airports just in case an unscheduled landing becomes necessary. When braking action is reported to be fair or poor by a car or truck, it can be expected to be worse for an aircraft touching down at higher speeds. If a landing is indicated, ask yourself, "Are the runways long enough to permit a safe rollout with little or no braking?" As always, knowing what is available in the event of an emergency will keep such an emergency from becoming serious.

LANDING

Again, the primary fact to worry about is the condition of the runway. If it's dry and clean, luck is with us. If it is slippery, partially or wholly frozen, or covered with a thin film of snow, short-field technique is indicated in order to touch down at a sufficiently low speed to permit safe rollout without the use of brakes. What braking is done should be done gingerly so that uneven traction doesn't result in a sudden groundloop. In crosswind situations it is advisable to touch down on the upwind side of the runway to allow for a certain amount of skidding as the aircraft slows down.

If the runway is covered with several inches of snow, especially if the prevailing temperature suggests that it might be wet snow, a full-stall landing is safest. The nose-wheel must be held up as high as possible because the sudden resistance as the wheels plow through the deep snow may be more than the nosewheel can take without damage.

MISCELLANEOUS WINTER ADVICE

A sudden drop in temperature may cause the oleo struts to deflate and become ineffective. As soon as cold weather sets in they should be checked and, if necessary, reinflated before the airplane is taxied for any distance or flown. If a flight takes us from warm weather conditions to cold ones, the first landing should be made with extra care just in case the shock-absorbing action of the oleo struts has been reduced to nil.

Is the oil at the right weight for the temperatures at which we expect to operate? Winter calls for lighter weight oil. On the other hand, if we are flying from a warm climate such as in Florida or Southern California to the cold north or northeast, it is better to use the oil appropriate for the warmer regions and then to suffer the delays and expense associated with having the engine preheated before takeoff in the colder region because using too light an oil in warm weather can be more harmful to the engine than using too heavy an oil in cold weather.

Heater hoses must be checked for leaks or deterioration. Hardly anything is worse than to sit up there with one's fingers and toes slowly turning to ice. Conversely, leaks in the hoses can cause carbon monoxide to collect in the cockpit. Carbon monoxide, being colorless, odorless, and tasteless, is impossible to detect (unless we have one of those gimmicks in the cockpit that turns brown or some other color when exposed to carbon monoxide). Therefore, at least one vent should always be kept open to constantly feed fresh air into the cockpit. Ideally the cold air should be directed toward the face with the warm air blowing toward the feet.

Winter months, with their short days and long nights make it difficult to avoid flying after dark. Even if actual night flight is not anticipated, there should always be a flashlight with extra fresh batteries in the airplane. (Don't use one of those flashlights that are equipped with magnets to adhere to metal surfaces. It could result in unreliable readings of the magnetic compass.) Navigation lights and anticollision lights must be kept in working order, and the same is true of the dome light, map light, instrument lights, and so on.

In the winter, an extra thought should also be given to carrying survival equipment in the event of an emergency landing (FIG. 12-2). This is not to imply that one has to come equipped for an assault on the North Pole, but rather that the terrain and conditions along the route must be considered. What would you do, for example, if you had to land in the most remote area along your route? How far would you have to walk to come to a house or road? Is the ground dry, muddy, or snow-covered? A pair of boots, a ski parka, a hat, and a few candy bars may make the difference between a jaunt through the woods and a survival trek. Perhaps even a sleeping bag, a small tent, a camping stove, and some dehydrated food are worth taking along, depending on the route. (See Appendix D for a Private Aircraft Survival Kit.)

Fig. 12-2. *Within an hour this Piper Warrior will be negotiating the snowy mountains in the distance. The pilot should consider carrying survival equipment in case he has to make an emergency landing.*

And one final precaution: Whatever we accept as an adequate fuel reserve in the summer months should be doubled during the winter. With a considerable reduction in the number of usable airports and the rapid changes in weather and wind conditions, an adequate fuel reserve that will permit changes in plans is by far the best life saver of all.

The knowledgeable pilot who is willing to take some reasonable precautions will find winter flying in a light aircraft safe and enjoyable. And when the weather is clear, flying over the snow-covered expanse of the plains states or the intimidating peaks of the Rockies can be breathtakingly beautiful.

13
Flight Number Five

Date: December 24, 1985.
Pilot: Male, age 35, flight instructor.
License: ATP-Helicopter, Commercial-Airplane.
Pilot-In-Command Time: 3,091 hours.
Aircraft: Aerospatiale AS332L Super Puma (helicopter).
Flight: From Forus Heliport, Stavanger, Norway, to Heliport de Paris, France.
Purpose of Flight: Cross-country training.

The whole thing started as a half-serious joke.

Since the beginning of December, the pilot and several other instructors of the Norwegian offshore helicopter operator had been involved in training five Japanese Defense Force (JDF) pilots in the Super Puma (FIG. 13-1). As Christmas approached, the Japanese pilots and their two interpreters (one a Japanese former aircraft mechanic and the other a French woman who often did free-lance interpreting for Aerospatiale) found out their hotel in Stavanger planned to close down for two days over Christmas. Because they would have to move to another hotel anyway and because each pilot was to receive 100 hours flight time, someone got the idea to use the opportunity to go on a long cross-country.

The JDF pilots had military passports with visas for Norway, France, and the United Kingdom. They knew they would see much of Norway during their training,

Fig. 13-1. *An Aerospatiale AS 332L Super Puma.*

and Aberdeen, Scotland, (the closest destination in the UK) didn't seem very exciting, so Paris was suggested. The French interpreter readily endorsed the idea because she knew a reasonable hotel in Paris and could arrange to have her family travel up from southern France so they could be together over Christmas.

A quick look at the charts showed that the flight could be done with one or two refueling stops, either in Denmark or Holland, or both.

The only thing lacking was an instructor who wouldn't mind leaving home over Christmas to make the trip. The pilot volunteered, if he could take his family along. Since there were plenty of seats available in the 18-seat cabin, space didn't pose a problem.

The pilot's wife did. She didn't particularly like to fly and only did so because it's faster than other forms of transportation. She had never been in any aircraft flown by her husband, nor had she ever ridden in a helicopter. Still, the idea of spending Christmas in Paris was exciting. The temptation proved irresistible, and she agreed to go along if the pilot could promise her the flight wouldn't be too bumpy.

The chief of training approved the flight (since the JDF was paying by the flight hour, it didn't matter over what country the training took place) and suggested a mechanic go along, just in case. One was found who was willing to go, and he brought his wife, too.

The vice-president of operations approved the flight "in principle," a phrase that would take on deeper meaning only later. The plan was to fly down the 24th, spend the night in Paris, and return on the 25th because the helicopter was needed for the normal flight schedule on the 26th.

Never having flown to France before, the pilot knew that preparation was the key to making a safe journey. He talked to other pilots who had flown on "the Continent" and they assured him that it was a "piece of cake," much easier than flying offshore because one was always under radar control.

Nevertheless, the pilot instructed all the Japanese pilots to work out their own routes using IFR airways and to check their work against each other. All the pilots were instrument-rated. For his own peace of mind, the pilot did his own flight planning and used this as his "master copy" against which he compared the JDF pilots' work. Each JDF pilot would fly one leg of the trip in the right seat (captain's seat of a helicopter), while the pilot would fly the entire trip from the left seat.

The pilot also carefully checked the airport section in Jeppesen and the NOTAMs available in his company flight office to be sure the airports he planned to use had Jet A fuel and would be open during Christmas.

The most worrisome part of the journey was the last 10 miles. Paris has a heliport not far from the center of the city. It only made sense to land there instead of at Orly, Charles de Gaulle, Le Bourget, or one of the other outlying airports. The chief of training knew the chief pilot of a French helicopter operator based at Heliport de Paris, also known as Issy Les Moulineaux Aerodrome, and permission was given to refuel the helicopter there and park it overnight.

But getting to the heliport was a problem. The heliport was strictly a VFR facility, with no nav aids indicating its location. The Super Puma was equipped with a VLF/OMEGA, which the pilot knew could be as accurate as one-half mile or as inaccurate as five or six miles, not good enough when trying to find a small heliport in a big city. On the other hand, he had no qualms about relying on the VLF/OMEGA when en route and out of range of VOR stations.

From the French helicopter operator the pilot learned that the standard procedure to get into Issy Les Moulineaux Heliport in bad weather, was to shoot an ILS approach to Pontoise Airport northwest of Paris, break out below the clouds, fly in a southerly direction until picking up the Seine River, and then follow the river to the heliport. The pilot was assured that this was a perfectly safe procedure, and although he had been to the heliport once before, he had never flown to it, and he realized it wasn't going to be easy to find. But if push came to shove, he reasoned, he could always contact Orly approach and land there instead.

Two days before the flight the pilot checked the long-range forecast. There was a low pressure system over Scotland and a high over Italy. A cold front was moving northwestward over the North Sea and was expected to leave relatively good conditions in its wake, except for 20- to 25-knot winds from the south. It wasn't the greatest of forecasts, but ceilings and visibilities would be more or less VMC. En route visibility conditions didn't bother the pilot too much because they'd be going IFR anyway, and after eight years of offshore North Sea flying, IMC didn't bother him at all. It was the weather in Paris that had to be VMC. The pilot also worried that he'd have to tell his wife it could be fairly turbulent and she would decide not to go. He wanted her to go along.

The pilot checked the weather on the morning of the 23rd and again in the afternoon. The cold front was passing over Stavanger and it was raining, but it should clear by morning. A warm front was moving eastward off the Atlantic toward the Continent and wasn't expected over Paris until later in the afternoon on the 24th. The flight was a "go," but the pilot couldn't promise his wife a smooth ride all the way. The late evening forecast was more optimistic, and the pilot's wife decided to go, as long as the forecast wasn't much worse the next day.

Everything was set for an 0700 departure. With luck, they'd be in Paris by 1500, in time to do some shopping before the stores closed at 1900 on Christmas Eve.

The pilot and his family arrived at Forus Heliport at 0600, shortly before the Japanese pilots and their translators. He checked the weather again and called customs at nearby Sola Airport to find out if they had to fly there for clearance before leaving the country. Perhaps because it was Christmas Eve, the customs officer cleared them to leave directly from Forus Heliport.

The mechanic had already preflighted LNOMD and filled the tanks. With 3,900 pounds of fuel, a true airspeed of 130 knots, and a fuel burn of 1,000 pounds per hour, the pilot figured they could make it to Gronningen, Holland, a distance of 385 nautical miles, with as much as a 17-knot head wind. If they ended up with less than a 113-knot ground speed, they'd have to refuel at Esbjerg, Denmark, and again at Gronningen before continuing to Paris, a distance of 329 nautical miles.

Unfortunately, the winds were southwesterly, almost direct head winds, so the pilot figured they'd have to refuel at Esbjerg unless they did better on fuel than expected. He decided to maintain a closer-than-normal check on the fuel burn.

It took longer than expected to load the passengers and baggage, but the pilot was satisfied that they were able to lift off at 0718. It was still dark, and an overcast hid the clouds, but the pilot felt comfortable. He had planned as best he could, and they were on their way.

THE FIRST LEG

The first 44 miles to Lista were flown slightly off the coast at 1,500 feet. Abeam the Lista ADF, they altered course more to the south and flew toward Esbjerg. The pilot could have chosen a more direct route from Stavanger to Gronningen and planned to use one of the many oil platforms in the North Sea as a refueling stop, but he didn't like risking a ditching so far out to sea with his family on board. The route he chose took him no more than 30 miles from land at any one point.

About two hours after takeoff the sun came up, and through breaks in the clouds the pilots and passengers could see the coast of Denmark toward the east. The wind was more southerly than forecast, which gave them more of a head wind than expected, and they had only been able to average 105 knots on this leg. Using the information from the VLF/ OMEGA and a nav computer, the pilot figured they would make nearly 120 knots en route to Gronningen and with the fuel remaining they could safely do it. He decided to bypass Esbjerg and turned right 25 degrees toward Holland.

Fifteen minutes later he was regretting his decision. Instead of holding at 180 degrees, the wind seemed to have followed the helicopter in the turn and was still dead on the nose. Groundspeed fluctuated between 105 and 110 knots. There was still enough fuel, but they'd cut into the 30-minute reserve, and the pilot knew some of that was unusable. Gronningen was reporting CAVOK ("ceiling and visibility okay" which is European for CAVU), so weather wasn't a problem.

Soon the coast of Holland was in sight, and the specter of running out of fuel over water was gone. The remaining 20 miles to Gronningen seemed twice as long. At last, the airport appeared. The Japanese pilot in the right seat made the landing, and as they taxied toward the terminal, the "LOW FUEL" warning light came on.

The good-natured Dutch customs and immigration official had no problem with a Norwegian-registered aircraft and its Japanese, American, French, and Norwegian crew and passengers. However, the Shell fuel truck driver was another matter; he wouldn't accept any of the credit cards the aircraft or pilot carried. After some discussion, he finally agreed to accept the Japanese translator's American Express card (for almost 2,500 liters of jet fuel).

NOTAM PROBLEMS

The pilot's problems had only just begun. In flight operations, he learned that Gronningen would be closed on the 25th. This came as a total surprise to him because he had checked the airport information in Jeppesen and the NOTAMs listed in his company operations, and neither had said anything about the airport being closed for Christmas. His mistake was that he had not checked international airport NOTAMs, which his company didn't list since most of its flights were in Norway.

The original plan was to return to Norway on the 25th, so the pilot found a chart and began looking for an alternate return route and checking it against the NOTAMs. What he learned was that different European countries celebrate Christmas at different times. Some countries close down their airports on the 24th (Christmas Eve), some close them down on the 25th (Christmas Day), some close them down on the 26th (Boxing Day), and some use a combination of the above. The bottom line was that the earliest they'd be able to return was on the 26th, using their original route.

Complicating matters was the weather, which was forecast to deteriorate over Paris sooner than expected. The pilot realized they'd have to navigate from Pontoise to Issy Les Moulineaux below the clouds, and he wanted to do that in daylight. If they were going to continue, they had to go soon.

It was time for a command decision. If they continued to Paris, they were committed to returning to Norway a day late. The prudent, respectable decision was to scrap the rest of the trip and turn back that day. That would have spoiled the exciting adventure for everyone. What the hell, the pilot figured, he'd just tell the company he didn't find out he couldn't return on the 25th until *after* they had arrived in Paris, and take whatever consequences that caused when he returned.

They took off from Gronningen at 1221, expecting to make the 329-nautical-mile trip to Heliport de Paris in about three hours. The pilot had filed for FL80 (8,000 feet pressure altitude) in an attempt to reduce the effect of unfavorable winds. They received FL50, and the winds weren't too bad; but the temperature was below freezing, and they were flying in thin haze. Soon the pilot noticed the torque readings on both engines increasing and felt the telltale increase in vibrations that indicated the rotor blades were icing up. His only choice was to descend.

They leveled off first at 4,000 feet to no avail and had to go down to 3,000. The ice melted away, but the wind was up to 40 knots, right on the nose. As they flew southwestward toward Paris and the approaching warm front, patchy, scattered clouds appeared below them and quickly gathered into a solid layer. For the second time that day, the pilot began to worry seriously about fuel.

Calculations showed they could make it to the heliport and the alternate, Orly, but would have precious little as a reserve for holding or delays. Each forecast showed successively lower ceilings in the Paris area, and it just didn't make sense to the pilot to try to scud run an unknown area as fuel ran out. He would have liked at least another 1,000 pounds to play with and that meant another refueling stop. But where?

He hadn't planned on refueling after Gronningen and was completely unprepared. The IFR chart showed airports all over the place, but not all of them had Jet A fuel. The only thing the pilot could do was find an airport on the chart, then laboriously look it up in the airport section of the Jeppesen manual. He wanted to find an airport close to their route so as to waste as little time as possible, but it had to have the right fuel and be open. As Christmas Eve progressed, more and more airports were closing below them.

Compounding the problem were the Japanese pilots. They were flying the machine while the pilot did the radio work, changed frequencies, maintained the flight log, kept an eye on the instruments to be sure nothing went wrong, and now looked for another airport. Every time a controller gave the crew a new heading or instruction, the pilot had to repeat the instruction to the interpreter, who sat in a jump seat between the pilots, and the interpreter repeated the instruction to the Japanese pilot, who usually asked for confirmation from the interpreter before turning toward the new heading or whatever. It made crew coordination very cumbersome and often caused errors. The pilot found he had to cross-check repeatedly to make sure what he said actually got done.

After a frantic half hour, the pilot found an airport close to their route that, according to Jeppesen, was open and had the fuel they needed. The French ATC controller confirmed that fuel was available there, gave the crew a revised clearance, and eventually cleared them for an ILS approach to Lille, France (FIG. 13-2).

They broke out some 300 feet above minimums. The tower instructed them to land on an intersecting runway closer to the general aviation terminal. From the air-

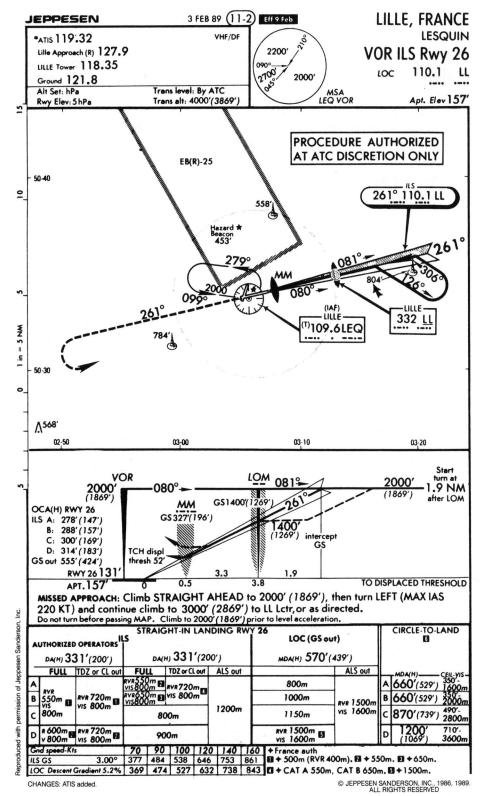

Fig. 13-2. *VOR ILS approach at Lille, France.*

port diagram the pilot knew the other runway was to the right, but he couldn't see it. Figuring his Japanese counterpart couldn't see it either and may not have understood the instructions as well, the pilot took the controls and flew in what he hoped was the right direction.

They soon saw the runway and a helipad right next to the threshold, so the pilot gave the controls back to the Japanese pilot so he could make the landing on the pad. For whatever reason, the JDF pilot landed on the runway past the pad. As they turned around to taxi back down toward the pad, the tower asked them to clear the runway because another aircraft was on final. The pilot looked up to see a Falconjet fast approaching them, wheels down. The Japanese pilot didn't react, so the pilot quickly took the controls again and hovered off the runway toward the general aviation terminal.

The general aviation terminal was a disappointment to the pilot and passengers alike. It was after two o'clock and everyone was hungry; but there were no facilities except for one toilet, a cigarette machine, and some hard chairs. To make matters worse, they had to obtain customs clearance to enter France, and the customs officials were at the main terminal.

Again there was a problem with paying for the fuel. The ELF fuel truck driver would only take an ELF credit card, so the Japanese interpreter couldn't use his American Express card again. Fortunately, the driver agreed to accept a personal check from the French interpreter, and she had enough in her French bank account to pay for 1,000 liters of Jet A.

It seemed like forever before the customs official arrived, and as always he had forms to fill out. Fortunately, the pilot had the forethought to make several copies of his passenger manifest before leaving Norway, and this saved some time. The ICAO flight plan was also in French but followed a standard format. Calling it in took longer than normal because the pilot didn't speak French and had to use the French interpreter. The meteorologist told them ceilings at the Paris airports got lower with each report (the heliport itself didn't report weather); the warm front had obviously reached the area. Outside, daylight was fading.

At last they took off at 1705 for the final leg of the flight. The pilot expected the flight to take about one hour fifteen minutes, and with luck the ladies might still get some shopping in before the stores closed at 1900.

They climbed to 3,000 feet again, and broke through the solid overcast at 2,500 feet. The sun was setting with brilliant hues of orange, pink, and purple, but the pilot had little time to enjoy it. He had been up since 0530, after a restless night and less than six hours sleep. He had already flown over six hours on what was turning out to be one of the most stressful flights of his flying career. Having his family in the back only raised the stakes.

LANGUAGE PROBLEMS

The pilot had decided before leaving Norway to use the French interpreter on the leg into France. She proved invaluable in helping the English-speaking pilot understand the French controllers, as well as doing her primary job of translating English to Japanese. The pilot kept telling the controllers they were going to "Moulinex Heliport" instead of "Moulineaux," which amused the interpreter. Moulinex makes food processors.

During the first legs of the flight, the pilot realized his JDF copilots/students had a basic misunderstanding of the instruction "track to such-and-such a beacon or VOR," or perhaps the instruction wasn't being translated properly. Whatever the case, the result was the same: The JDF pilots would home toward the nav aid instead of tracking toward it. No amount of correction or explanation seemed to work, and the pilot's only recourse was to maintain a constant check of the nav instruments.

The French controllers directed LNOMD toward Pontoise. The pilot had studied the Pontoise ILS 05 approach plate (FIG. 13-3) before the flight, and he studied it again while he set up the radios and instruments. Then he briefed the JDF pilot as best he could through the interpreter. They received radar vectors from approach control, which complicated matters, because the French interpreter sometimes had to clarify to the pilot what the controller had said and then relay the instruction to the JDF pilot who was flying. Before he expected it, the controller cleared them for a straight-in approach.

The pilot looked at the CDI, confirming they were on an intercept angle to the localizer and above the glide slope. The VOR located on the airport was tuned to the number one receiver, and the ILS was tuned to number two. An Outer Marker identified the final approach fix. As they passed the Outer Marker, they still had not intercepted the localizer.

The pilot knew they were close to it because of the VOR pointer; he knew the ceiling was reported at 600 feet agl (decision height was 545 feet msl, 220 feet agl) and the visibility was six kilometers; he knew they were close to the airport; he knew if they didn't descend soon they'd never catch the glide slope and may have to go missed approach; and he knew it was getting darker by the minute. He decided to do something he normally never would have accepted. He told the JDF pilot to start descent.

When the JDF pilot didn't respond quickly enough, the pilot pushed the collective down for him. They passed the Outer Marker above glide-slope intercept altitude and on an intercept to the localizer. The light faded as they descended further into the overcast. Finally, the CDI started to move toward the center, but the glide slope never appeared. They turned to the final approach course of 048 degrees and descended through 1,100, 1,000, and 900 feet msl, still apparently well above the glide slope. At 850 feet, the clouds began to thin out and lights were visible on the surface. At 800 feet, the pilot could make out ground features. He had the JDF pilot level out at 750 feet msl, while he looked for Pontoise Airport and the Seine River.

Southwest of Pontoise Airport is another smaller airport, and to the south of Pontoise is a heliport. Both are marked on the approach chart, and both are right of the localizer course. Flying at 100 knots, the helicopter passed over a small, dimly lit area that the pilot figured was the small airport. That satisfied him that they were on the

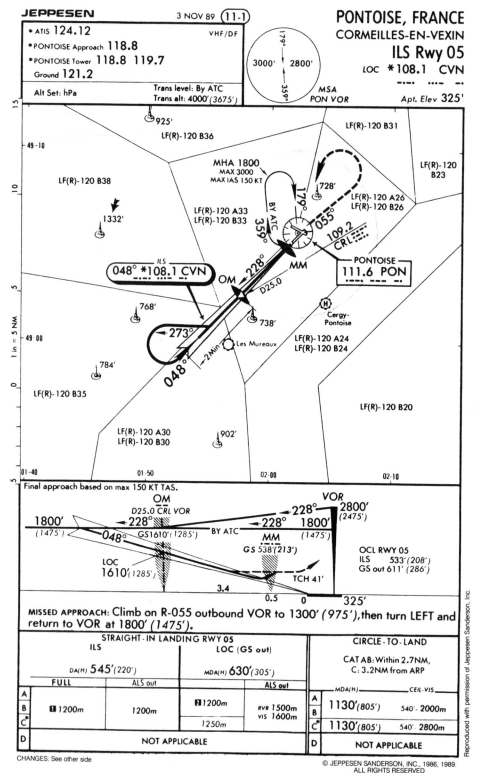

Fig. 13-3. *ILS approach at Pontoise, France.*

right track, and they continued on a course of 048 degrees, looking for approach lights of Pontoise Airport. The pilot could only assume that they had descended above the normal glide slope the whole time and had luckily broken out of the clouds.

WHERE'S PONTOISE?

After one minute, the pilot began to get worried. Where were the approach lights? He should have seen them by now. Less than 30 seconds later, he was really worried. Something definitely was wrong. The only things in front of them were farms and small villages.

He checked his navigation instruments. The VOR needle pointed ominously to the tail of the aircraft, meaning they had passed the VOR at Pontoise. The VLF/OMEGA indicated they were northeast of the field. The pilot wasn't sure how they had managed to miss the airport, but he knew it was behind them. He took the controls, did a 180 to get them headed toward the VOR again, and gave control back to the JDF pilot.

Then the pilot noticed his most dangerous mistake. His CDI control switch was set to receiver number one instead of number two. That meant they had flown the ILS approach using the signals from the VOR. He had meant to flick the switch from the number one radio to the number two when they were inbound on the procedure turn, but they had received radar vectors to final and he had forgotten. It was a stupid mistake caused by stress and fatigue. But it was unforgivable and could have cost them all their lives, and the pilot knew it. The pilot thought about his family in the back, a newspaper headline about a helicopter crash in France, and an accident report concluding that the cause had been "pilot error." He felt the need to apologize to someone for his mistake, but there was no one he could to talk to.

Besides, he didn't have time to dwell on past mistakes and their possible consequences. They were approaching Pontoise again, and the pilot still didn't see it. If he couldn't find the airport, how was he ever going to find the Seine and Issy Les Moulineaux Heliport?

It was then that serendipity saved the flight.

At the general aviation terminal in Lille, the French interpreter had met a French businessman who was on his way to Paris for Christmas. He had planned to take the train from Lille, a trip of several hours, but when he learned that a helicopter was going that direction, he asked if he could ride along. There were extra seats in the aircraft, and weight was no problem, so the pilot agreed. It wouldn't make any difference to him, and besides, it was Christmas. It wasn't until weeks later that the pilot realized he should have had his new passenger fill out a standard passenger ticket, absolving the company of liability in case of an accident, but he had never even thought of it at the time.

Shortly after they had made the 180-degree turn, the French businessman squeezed behind the French interpreter in the cockpit. He was also a private pilot and knew Paris well. As the VOR pointer began to fluctuate, he pointed out Pontoise to the pilot. It was the same airfield they had flown over before—the one the pilot had mistaken for the small airport indicated on the approach chart—and it was still unlit, no approach lights, no runway lights. The French pilot explained later he had seen Pontoise the first time they had flown over it and wondered why they hadn't turned south toward the Seine.

There was no time for discussion. The tower operator at Pontoise didn't seem to care that LNOMD had passed over the field once without a word and was now passing over the field again from the opposite direction. There was no other traffic. The French pilot picked out the Seine and started giving directions.

By now it was definitely dark. The ceiling was solid at 800 feet msl, and the tops of some apartments on the higher hills along the Seine disappeared into the overcast. The pilot had a detailed map of the area, he had the VLF/OMEGA programmed to the heliport, and he had plotted bearings from two NDBs to help locate Issy Les Moulineaux; but it was the French pilot who helped him navigate the most. At least, they didn't have to worry about fuel.

The pilot soon learned that following the Seine at night at low altitude was more difficult than he had thought it would be. The river twists and curves and turns back on itself constantly. Flying a precise track over the river would have meant continuous banking, which would have made it extremely uncomfortable for the passengers and was unnecessary, as long as one could determine the general direction of the river. The pilot was having trouble keeping track of the river, but fortunately the French pilot seemed to know the general direction of it.

About halfway between Pontoise and the heliport, the pilot switched to the heliport frequency. The heliport didn't have a tower, but in a small terminal building with large windows overlooking the area sat a girl who gave the wind as southerly and told them there was no other traffic. The pilot knew it was just a matter of time before they found the heliport.

ENGINE PROBLEMS

Then, without warning, the red "ALARM" light flashed on. The pilot checked the master warning panel, saw the red "DIFF ENG" light, and knew immediately they had an engine problem. He checked the Ng and T4 gauges and determined that the number one engine had decelerated to ground idle. It hadn't quit completely, but neither was it providing any power to the main transmission. The pilot couldn't believe his eyes.

The problem was not inherently dangerous because they were in level flight and the other engine easily took over the load. The landing would require both engines, however, and fortunately the pilot could use the emergency position of the fuel control lever to get power from the malfunctioned engine. If the engine failed altogether, they would have problems because the heliport didn't have a runway and a single-engine running landing requires a runway. A single-engine landing to a helipad is easier in a Super Puma than most twin-engine helicopters, but the pilot was in no mood to tax his skills to that degree on this flight unless he had to. He was already stressed enough.

The JDF pilot flying at the time was the one who knew the least English but the one the pilot considered to be the best "stick." Two weeks earlier they had flown VFR up the coast of Norway below a 400-foot ceiling, and the JDF pilot had been completely at ease. The pilot had no worries about letting the JDF pilot do the flying (with instructions from the French pilot through the French interpreter).

On the other hand, not two days before in the simulator, the pilot had given this same JDF pilot the same emergency they were now experiencing, and he had crashed on landing, which was completely unnecessary. The pilot felt he had no choice but to handle the emergency himself while he let the JDF pilot fly.

He used the emergency checklist, even though he knew the procedure by heart, having done it so many times in the simulator. After his mistake with the CDI switch, the pilot wasn't taking any chances. Soon, the engine was delivering flight power again, and the only thing the pilot had to remember was to pull back the fuel control lever after landing, but before lowering the collective all the way, or the rotors would overspeed and cause considerable damage to themselves and the transmission.

The French pilot was calling out landmarks all the time—there's this, there's that, there's the Eiffel Tower—but after the engine problem, the pilot was somewhat disoriented and never even saw the famous landmark until the next day. He knew from studying the map that the heliport was close to the Seine and just south of a highway, the Peripherique, that roughly describes an oval around the center of Paris. If he could find the intersection of the Peripherique and the Seine, he felt he could find the heliport. But just following the Seine was proving hard enough.

The pilot knew they were getting close to Issy Les Moulineaux, but before he really started worrying about missing it, the girl sitting in the terminal building radioed, "LNOMD, I have you in sight. You are on a right downwind for the heliport. Wind from the south at five knots."

They were right over the Seine at the time, and this observation from the girl in the heliport didn't make sense to the pilot. They were supposed to be flying in a generally southerly direction toward the heliport, but she said they were on downwind with a southerly wind and that meant they were heading north. The pilot checked the compass and it confirmed they really were heading north. For a moment he thought they might have had a compass failure, but this was very unlikely, and he had to accept the extent of his own disorientation caused by the serpentine route of the Seine and his loss of position sense when he took care of the engine. With the lights of downtown Paris quickly approaching them, the pilot didn't have much choice but to take the girl in the heliport at her word. They were on downwind for landing, and the heliport was somewhere out there to their right.

The heavy Christmas Eve traffic made the Peripherique easy to pick out about one mile distant. On the east side of the river, a large power plant with stacks about 150 feet high spewed out a cloud of thick whitish smoke, and the helicopter was headed right for the cloud. The pilot thought the JDF pilot would surely alter his course a few degrees left to avoid the cloud. After all, they were VFR under an 800-foot ceiling above one of the biggest cities in the world, at night, and with their landing spot not yet in sight.

But no. He flew right into it. They were IMC for only a few moments but for the second time in about five minutes—the pilot couldn't believe this was happening to him. He took the controls and said very loudly and distinctly, "I HAVE CONTROL." It was the one English phrase the pilot personally had made sure all the JDF pilots understood.

There was no time for a complete landing checklist and passenger briefing—the mechanics of having the JDF pilot do a complete "challenge-and-response" checklist escaped the pilot anyway. He lowered the gear and switched on the "SEAT BELT" and "NO SMOKING" signs.

The Peripherique appeared below the nose of the aircraft, and the pilot figured that was good enough for a base leg and turned right 90 degrees. If he had been sitting on the right side of the cockpit, he might have seen the heliport on base, but from the left seat he could only guess where it was. He figured there wasn't any point asking the JDF pilot if he saw it. There just wasn't time to explain the whole thing through the interpreter. The pilot continued on base for a few seconds and turned onto final.

Compared to everything else lit up in Paris, the heliport looked smaller than a postage stamp. It is actually the site of the first airfield in Paris and had been frequented by many well-known French aviators. At the age of 19, Igor Sikorsky, father of the modern helicopter, had met Louis Bleriot and Ferdinand Ferber there. But today Issy Les Moulineaux Aerodrome is only a shadow of its former glory, not much bigger than a football field.

But it did have helipad lights. There were eight lights that outlined a square. This the pilot was used to. All helipads on the North Sea platforms are outlined in similar lights. The pilot felt at home as he made his approach.

ONE FINAL HAZARD

Prudence and the engine-on manual control dictated an approach to a hover instead of directly to the ground. The pilot stopped over the lights and looked down, intending to descend straight onto the lighted pad. To his surprise, he saw that the lights were mounted on three-foot poles, not the kind of thing you land a helicopter on. The helipad, an unlit asphalt pad, was behind them. The lighted square was apparently some sort of visual approach aid to the pad.

Thankful to the gods watching over them that a single-engine approach to a spot hadn't been necessary (or he would have landed on the poles for sure), the pilot turned the helicopter 90 degrees, hovered left until they were over the asphalt, and then slowly lowered the collective lever until the wheels were on the ground. He let go of the collective and took hold of the cyclic with his left hand, reached up with his right hand to the fuel control lever, and brought the malfunctioning engine back to ground idle. It responded as advertised, and the rest of the shutdown was uneventful.

At 1835 the passengers piled out of the cabin. The pilot opened his door and climbed to the ground, his legs shaking. His wife, who had been through her own ordeal, was the last one out. She carried their two-and-a-half-year-old son, their youngest, who 10 minutes earlier had thrown up on her. She was also tired and hungry but glad to have survived her first trip in a helicopter and to be in Paris at last. "Why didn't you tell us when we were going to land?" she asked the pilot before kissing him on the cheek.

"I didn't have time," he answered softly. "You won't believe all that happened." It was a long time before he got the courage to tell her everything.

ANALYSIS

What is intriguing about this flight is that for every good thing that happened, something bad occurred; for every bit of good luck the pilot had, a bit of bad made the situation a little worse; and for every right decision the pilot made, a poor decision somehow nullified it. In the end, the good things and the bad things seemed to just balance out, or perhaps, the good were ahead by one. If just one more bad thing had happened, one more mistake been made, it's quite likely there would have been an accident.

The pilot thought he had prepared sufficiently for the flight and had checked everything he needed to check. But he should have checked international NOTAMs at an airport (instead of only at the company heliport) and called ahead to each airport where he expected to land. Had he done that, he would have learned of the problems with closing times and fuel availability over the Christmas holidays. The whole trip might have been scrubbed before takeoff, or perhaps rescheduled to a more appropriate time.

Paying for the fuel was something the pilot had not even worried about. He assumed the fuel credit cards carried in the helicopter would be accepted at any airport, but this was not the case. It was fortunate the Japanese interpreter had an American Express card and the French interpreter had enough money in her checking account, but it was the pilot's responsibility in the first place.

The weather almost got the better of the pilot. Even though he updated the weather constantly, the front that moved faster than forecast over France and the delay of the extra fuel stop at Lille resulted in a lower ceiling and visibility over Paris than the pilot had originally planned for. The pilot was well experienced with IFR and accustomed to using minimums of 200 feet and one-half mile visibility when flying offshore, so the 800- to 900-foot ceilings that were forecast over Paris didn't seem that difficult to him. But flying 500 feet agl over a city is a lot different than flying 500 feet over water. The pilot should have required higher weather minima for himself, especially considering he was unfamiliar with the route and destination.

Perhaps the most important factor influencing the entire flight was that the pilot had a near-fatal case of "get-there-itis." It wasn't that he wanted to get to Paris so much for himself (after all, he had been there before), but rather that he wanted to get there for his passengers (FIG. 13-4). This intense desire to complete the flight clouded his normally conservative judgment.

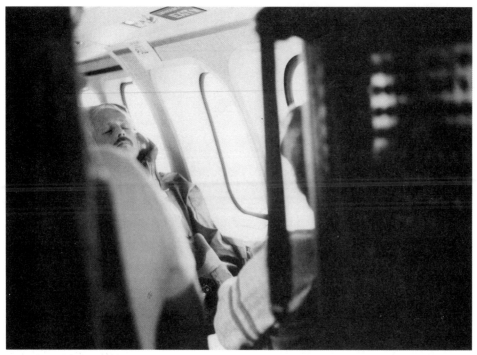

Fig. 13-4. *Too much concern for the desires of one's passengers can often lead a pilot to make decisions he normally wouldn't make.*

Symptomatic of his "can-do" attitude was the "go" decision he made at Gronningen, despite the fact that he knew he'd have to stay an extra night in Paris if they continued. The pilot just couldn't stand the thought of being the "bad guy" by making the decision to return and, instead, took the risk of incurring a reprimand from the company for returning the aircraft a day later than planned. His willingness to make such a decision should have set off numerous alarms in his head, alerting him to the fact that he was allowing outside factors to influence his judgment.

Psychologists have found, not surprisingly, that many pilots often exhibit this "serve other people" personality type. Medevac, corporate, and search-and-rescue pilots are particularly susceptible to allowing outside elements (the sick baby, the important meeting, the sinking boat) affect their decision-making in the air. These pilots must continually remind themselves that these outside factors have no relation at all to the elements that the pilot should be basing his decisions upon, i.e., the weather, the fuel on board, obstacle clearance, etc. The weather won't miraculously improve because the baby is dying, the fuel burn won't be less than normal because the CEO's meeting is crucial, and the mountains won't part just because the boat's crew is drowning.

Private pilots, too, can easily find themselves unduly influenced by any number of outside factors: vacation time running out, credit card charges mounting, kids getting sick in the back. Anything that takes one's mind away from the principle task at hand—flying—is an outside factor. As important as outside factors may be or seem to be, they must be considered secondary to the factors that have direct influence upon the safe conduct of the flight.

Outside factors, like the primary factors, tend to increase a pilot's stress level. Stress improves performance to a degree, but past a certain point, everyone starts to make mistakes when they are stressed. The pilot's most glaring error on this particular flight, failing to check the CDI switch so that they ended up flying the ILS approach on VOR indications, was the result of a culmination of numerous events that had increased his level of stress (FIG. 13-5). Apprehension, expectation, the desire to find the heliport before dark, the close turn onto final by ATC, the difficulty in understanding the French controllers, the constant requirement to double-check the Japanese pilots' flying, the problems with fuel, and the fear of making mistakes with his family on board, all combined to make the forgetting of one switch almost inevitable. If they had crashed, the human factors specialist on the accident investigation team would have had a field day.

The specialist would have also cited supervisory error as a contributing factor, arguing that the flight should have never been allowed to go in the first place. It's easy to think of a cross-country trip mainly in terms of distance and aircraft capability: If

Fig. 13-5. *In the stress of the moment, the pilot forgot to set his CDI control switch (the rotating knob under the HSI) to nav receiver number two.*

the aircraft has the range, the trip is possible. Theoretically, this may be true, but practically it may not be. In this day and age, much more must also be considered. A trip from Stavanger to Paris by helicopter would have been difficult enough for two qualified pilots who had never flown the route or been to the destination before. At least, they could have shared the workload. The burden of having to do virtually everything alone, being an instructor, and being unfamiliar with flying internationally was really too much for one pilot. Having to go through an interpreter to give instructions to the Japanese pilots made it all the more difficult.

To the pilot's credit, he managed to cope with an awful lot going against him. He didn't "break" even after realizing his error with the switch and still maintained a professional attitude when dealing with the engine malfunction. That he didn't land on top of the light posts at the Paris heliport showed that he still had at least a few wits about him even though, by this point, he was very close to his wits end.

Four lessons stand out from this flight.

First, you can never plan too much, especially when you're going to a destination you haven't been to before. Call ahead to your destination and refueling stops to confirm they have what you need and will be open when you get there.

Second, know thyself. Aviation safety experts tell us that 70−80% of all accidents are caused by human factors. Try to mentally remove yourself from the situation and examine it objectively. Are you allowing "outside factors" to cause you to make decisions you wouldn't ordinarily make?

Third, know your own capabilities. Legal minimums are just that, minimums. Just because a flight can be done legally doesn't necessarily mean it can be done safely. Stack the odds in your favor by carrying more fuel than legally required and making your personal weather minima higher than those set by the FARs, particularly when you're going somewhere for the first time. Remember that airline and commuter pilots have to be checked out over every single route they fly. That's one reason the airlines have an overall better safety record than general aviation.

And finally, what Yogi Berra said about baseball is true about flying, "It ain't over 'til it's over." Even after the most harrowing of flights, you can't let your guard down for a second until you're walking away from your parked aircraft.

POSTSCRIPT

Strange as it may seem, the return trip to Norway generated more attention in the company than the trip down.

On Christmas Day, while everyone else toured the "City of Lights," the pilot and mechanic returned to the heliport to try to find out what was wrong with the engine. When they started it up again, it worked perfectly. Try as they might, they couldn't duplicate the malfunction. Obviously, there had been a problem before, but unless it manifested itself again, it was hard for the mechanic to figure out what to fix or replace. Both he and the pilot suspected the fault was in the electronic fuel control unit, but as long as it was working okay on the 25th, they really couldn't justify the expense of changing it in Paris.

The mechanic shrugged his shoulders and suggested they just fly the thing home and keep a close watch on the engine. The pilot accepted this because, one, the malfunction was something he knew he could live with and still keep flying (he had already done it once!) and, two, the mechanic would be flying with him in the back. Mechanics sometimes try to snowjob pilots, but not when they're going to be riding along in the same aircraft.

(As it eventually turned out, the identical engine malfunction occurred again about three weeks later during a flight to an offshore oil platform. The crew brought LNOMD back to land without problem. The occurrence of the malfunction twice within one month was enough to justify changing the fuel control unit.)

The morning of the 26th dawned clear, crisp, and cool. They took off from Heliport de Paris heading south, passed safely by the smokestacks that had looked so ominous two days before, and turned northward to the Pontoise VOR.

There was a scattered layer of white, fluffy cumulus between 3,000 and 4,000 feet and a 30-knot tail wind at their flight level at 5,000 feet. The air was smooth, ATC cleared LNOMD as requested, and the required airports were open. The pilot felt good: The weather was better, they had flown this way before, and he wasn't tired. After a sleepless night on the 24th, when his mind had insisted on replaying the flight to Paris all night long, the pilot had finally slept well on the 25th. The odds were in their favor again.

About 30 minutes out of Gronningen, the controller radioed, "LNOMD, do you know fuel is not available at Gronningen today?"

"Roger," the pilot replied. "We made arrangements with the fuel operator on the 24th and he said he would take care of us today."

"Oscar Mike Delta, that's not the information we have. According to Gronningen tower, they have no fuel service today."

"Could you check that for us, please? I even put a note in our flight plan to notify the Shell operator for us."

"Standby, Mike Delta."

While they waited, the pilot thought, Here we go again!, and began to go through the Jeppesen airport section to find another place to refuel. With considerably less trouble than the previous flight, he found a Dutch Air Force Base, and ATC confirmed they had Jet A fuel and would allow them to buy some. The pilot was about to ask for a revised clearance, when the controller said, "LNOMD, Gronningen confirms that they will have fuel available for you." One crisis resolved.

Unfortunately, a more serious one was waiting in the wings.

Fifteen minutes out of Gronningen, the "CHIP DET" light illuminated. This warning light is connected to a magnetic plug in the oil sump of the main gear box. Its purpose is to detect the presence of metallic particles in the transmission oil, a possible indication of a gear box failure. A helicopter can fly without a lot of things, but an operating gear box is not one of them, so pilots and mechanics take chip warning lights seriously.

On the other hand, normal wear of the gears in the transmission often produces minute slivers of metal. These slivers collect on the magnetic plug over time, and when there are enough of them, the collection of metallic fuzz can cause the "CHIP DET" light to illuminate. Since this is considered normal, some helicopters are equipped with a "fuzz burner," essentially a switch that sends a shot of electricity to burn the metallic fuzz off the magnetic plug. If the light stays on after activating the fuzz burner once, the pilot knows that the particle on the plug is more than just fuzz and there's a good chance the main gear box is deteriorating. If the light goes out, the pilot can continue the flight unless and until the light comes on again.

The pilot hit the "fuzz burner" switch and the light went out. So far so good, he thought. If the light stayed off, they were all right.

But no. About two minutes from the runway at Gronningen, the light came on again. They landed and taxied to the terminal.

Despite the seriousness of the indication, the decision was an easy one to make. Maintenance procedures prescribed that the magnetic plug be checked and cleaned. The mechanic pulled off the plug and found a chip of indefinite size: It could be either normal wear or something more serious. The pilot ran up the helicopter to test the system, and the light remained off.

The passengers boarded, and they taxied to the runway for takeoff; but before they got there, the chip light came on again. Again the decision was easy: Taxi back and shut down. This time the mechanic found a collection of small metallic flakes on the plug as well as a few small slivers on the oil filter screens. The light stayed off during the second run-up.

The passengers boarded a second time, but LNOMD didn't even make it out of the parking spot before the chip light came on again. They disembarked and the mechanic checked the plug and strainers; more chips were found on both. Now the gear box oil had to be completely changed.

Fortunately, the mechanic had the forethought to have brought along enough oil to do the job. He went to work, and about two hours later the helicopter was ready for a 30-minute test flight. The pilot went out with a JDF pilot and translator and hovered over a taxiway for 30 minutes, much to the delight and interest of the local residents of Gronningen, who had come to the airport restaurant for their Boxing Day dinner.

The chip light remained off during the test flight, and this bothered both the pilot and the mechanic. Enough chips had already been found to make them wary of the gearbox. They had a three-and-one-half-hour flight ahead of them, most of it over water, and it would be dark soon. Neither treasured the thought of the light coming on again halfway into the flight. They also had an engine that, although working normally for them today, had malfunctioned earlier. Things just didn't seem quite right.

As it turned out, the magnetic plug made the decision for them. The mechanic pulled the plug and found another good-sized chip that had fastened itself in such a way that it hadn't made the electrical connection that causes the warning light to come on. When the mechanic nudged the chip just a little, the "CHIP DET" light illuminated. That was enough for the pilot. He wasn't taking this helicopter anywhere until the main gear box was changed. The mechanic agreed.

They had kept their company continually informed of the chip problem from their first landing at Gronningen that day, so it didn't come as any great surprise to them that the transmission had to be changed. Arrangements were made to have a Sikorsky S-61N flown down the next day with a new transmission, the necessary tools, and a couple more mechanics.

The crew and passengers of LNOMD spent a second unscheduled night, this time in Gronningen. By now everyone had run out of clean clothes, but at least the hotel had a swimming pool and good food.

They returned to Norway on the 27th of December in an S-61N. The Sikorsky didn't have the range of the Super Puma, so they had to refuel at Esbjerg, Denmark. The pilot sat in the cabin with his family, the JDF pilots, and the interpreters. He was disappointed he couldn't complete the flight in his own aircraft but also relieved to be out of the hot seat for awhile.

A week later the vice-president of operations called the pilot to his office. "Who authorized the training flight to Paris?" he asked the pilot.

"I thought you did," the pilot answered.

"No, I didn't."

"But you said you approved the trip in principle."

"Yes, I approved it in principle, but only if it could be done without problems. I didn't approve that particular flight."

"But there was no way we could have predicted the chip warning light or the engine problem. They could have happened at any time. Even on an offshore flight."

"That's not the point. The point is I didn't approve that particular flight. Understand?"

"No."

"Well, that doesn't matter. Just remember I only approved the flight in principle, but not that particular flight."

"I understand," the pilot answered, but he really didn't. He thought, Well, who did approve the flight then?

"And one last thing," the vice-president of operations said. "There won't be any more training flights outside Norway. Not without my specific approval for each flight."

The pilot nodded. "Okay."

"And I'm not going to approve any more. Understand?"

The pilot nodded. Now he did understand. The vice-president of operations was afraid of getting a black eye for the expenses incurred because the transmission had to be changed in Gronningen. He must have figured he could distance himself from the flight by hanging onto his "in principle approval" and making a retroactive policy decision. The logic didn't seem all that good to the pilot, but if the V-P thought it would work and no one else got in trouble, the pilot wasn't about to complain. The trip had caused him enough stress already.

It worked.

14
The High Price of Fuel

IN THE OLD DAYS WHEN FUEL WAS CHEAP AND PLENTIFUL MOST OF US simply bored holes in the sky using a power setting that we assumed to be an approximation of about 75 percent. This made us feel that we were getting to our destination in a hurry, and we didn't worry much about the fact that we might have saved a few dollars by using our fuel more sparingly.

Those days are gone forever and, with avgas today more than two dollars a gallon, pilots will simply have to learn to conserve. To achieve maximum fuel economy, careful consideration must be given not only to the percent of power but, also, to mixture control; to the relationship between manifold pressure and rpm; to the altitude at which to cruise; and, of course, to the wind.

Let's look at mixture first.

FUEL/AIR MIXTURE

The word *mixture*, in this context, refers to the blend of air and vaporized gasoline that is burned in the engine, making it go. The perfect mixture for this purpose is a proportion of 15.2 pounds of air to each one pound of fuel. When used in this proportion the entire mixture is completely consumed, leaving only so-called pure combustion products, namely carbon dioxide and water. While this is considered the perfect proportion, it is not necessarily ideal for the engine. Mixtures as rich as nine to one and as lean as 20 to one are capable of combustion, though they leave all manner of what are referred to as "products of disassociation," of which carbon monoxide is probably the best known.

As is obvious by the terms used, rich mixtures contain excessive amounts of fuel, while lean ones are composed of too much air. Though nonideal in theory, either may be selected to achieve a desired result. Thus rich mixtures help to keep the engine cool while producing maximum power as may be needed during takeoff, and it is a common belief that rich mixtures are kind to the engine, while lean ones are not. As a result, many pilots habitually will not start to lean the mixture until climbing to an altitude above 5,000 feet msl. That is nonsense (FIG. 14-1).

Mixture control should be determined by the percent of power, not the altitude. Aircraft engines, both carburetor and fuel-injection types, are designed to be operated at full-rich mixture when using 75 percent of power or more. They are equipped with automatic enrichment valves that enrich the mixture at full throttle and at idle, and lean it somewhat during all other power settings. At idle this action of the enrichment valve tends to help minimize the detrimental effects on combustion of unscavenged exhaust gases, while at full throttle it keeps the engine temperature at a reasonable level and protects it from possible damage due to detonation.

This automatic system works fine at sea level under standard-temperature conditions, but it reacts neither to changes in air temperature nor density, leaving the necessary adjustments to the pilot. It is important to emphasize that the enrichment valve and, in turn, its cooling effect on the engine are functioning only at full throttle (or at

Fig. 14-1. *A well-planned climb to cruise altitude can save fuel and reduce costs.*

idle). Thus, pilots who think that they are babying their engines by reducing the throttle settings slightly after liftoff are, in fact, accomplishing the opposite. As a general rule, the exhaust-gas temperature during climb out at full power should stay some 200 degrees on the rich side of peak. But as soon as the power setting is reduced to below 75 percent, regardless of whether this is during climb, cruise, or descent, the mixture should be leaned to an exhaust-gas temperature reading in accordance with the manufacturer's instructions.

The exhaust-gas temperature is the heat generated by the exhaust gases as they are expelled through the exhaust manifold. It is highest when the mixture is ideal (or very close to ideal), which is referred to as *peak EGT*. Whenever the mixture is either enriched or leaned beyond peak, the temperature drops. Thus we talk about operating at a certain number of degrees on the rich or lean side of peak EGT. For operation at below 75 percent of power, different manufacturers spell out varying EGT settings for the different engines. Some may be flown at peak, others recommend 25 degrees on the rich side, and some even permit operation at 25 degrees on the lean side.

In order to control the mixture with any degree of precision, it is necessary that the aircraft be equipped with an exhaust-gas temperature gauge. Such gauges consist of probes that read the temperatures in the exhaust manifold(s) and display this reading in the cockpit. The cheaper types of EGT gauges have only one probe installed in the exhaust manifold of the cylinder, which habitually runs at the highest temperature. The more expensive models (also referred to as engine analyzers) have a probe for each cylinder, permitting the pilot to monitor not only the exhaust-gas temperature produced by the mixture he is using but, also, the relationship between the cylinders. Since a sudden change in this relationship is usually an indication of impending engine trouble, these units are a valuable safety device.

In aircraft not equipped with any kind of EGT gauge, the only thing the pilot can do when leaning the mixture is to pull out the mixture control knob slowly until the engine starts to run rough (engine rpm start to decrease), and then advance it just enough to restore smooth operation. While this was adequate when fuel consumption was of no great consequence, these days the relatively small cost of an EGT gauge will soon be amortized by fuel savings resulting from the more precise means of controlling the mixture. Aircraft with fixed-pitch propellers and no EGT gauge should *not* be enriched until maximum rpm is reached. Though maximum rpm does represent the best power it, in fact, increases the speed by only approximately two percent for a fuel-consumption penalty in the neighborhood of 14 percent.

Once a desired mixture has been set, it remains at that proportion only as long as there are no appreciable changes in rpm, manifold pressure, density altitude, or temperature. Changes in any of these will affect the mixture one way or the other, though these changes may be frequently too minor to justify adjustment.

To achieve the greatest fuel economy during cruise, the engine should be run at the very leanest setting permitted by the manufacturer's recommendations. (Many pilots who own their own aircraft and are, therefore, intimately familiar with their engines will habitually operate 10 to 20 degrees leaner than is recommended by the manufacturer, but this is a decision that can only be made by the individual and is not to be recommended as a general rule.) If atmospheric conditions during a portion of a flight require the use of carburetor heat, the mixture should be readjusted. Carburetor heat automatically enriches the mixture, but since this enrichment has no positive effect on the carburetor-ice-melting capability, it is wasteful. In fact, to a small degree, it reduces the effect of the carburetor heat by causing the engine to run cooler.

The effect of mixture control on fuel economy is considerably more dramatic than many of us may realize. For example, if an aircraft were flown full rich at 7,500 feet (admittedly a stupid thing to do) it would consume *twice* the fuel that would be used if it were operated at peak EGT, doubling the fuel bill and cutting the range in half.

RPM

Another important money-saver is the correct relationship between rpm and manifold pressure in aircraft equipped with variable-pitch (constant-speed) propellers. The effect of the rpm control is similar to that of the gearshift in an automobile. When operating at flat pitch (high rpm), it works like the low gear in a car. It takes many small bites out of the air while revolving at very high speed. Meeting a minimum of air resistance per revolution, it results in less strain on the engine and is, therefore, ideal for takeoff and climb out. In less flat pitch (lower rpm) it resembles high gear. Each revolution takes a larger bite of the air, requiring fewer revolutions to achieve a comparable amount of forward motion. This is ideal during cruise, when velocity has been established and moving more air per revolution does not strain the engine. (Using this type of low-rpm setting during takeoff and climb out would be comparable to trying to drive a car up a steep hill in high gear, resulting in excessive strain on the engine.)

MANIFOLD PRESSURE

The manifold-pressure control controls the amount of the fuel-air mixture that is being fed to the engine and, in turn, the amount of power produced by it. The term *manifold pressure* refers to the amount of air pressure in the intake manifold. It is directly related to the atmospheric pressure displayed in the adjustment window of the altimeter when at sea level. At any altitude above sea level it is related to the actual pressure, which decreases with altitude. (An atmospheric pressure of 29.92 at sea level is comparable to about 25.00 at 5,000 feet.) Since the pressure in the intake manifold is supplied by the outside air it can never exceed the actual atmospheric pressure at any given altitude (except in turbocharged engines) and, as a result, the available manifold pressure drops with increases in altitude.

Rampant in pilot circles is some kind of fairytale that claims that it is poor practice to fly with an rpm/MP combination in which the rpm is the same or higher in terms of hundreds of revolutions than the manifold pressure in terms of inches of mercury (in hg). Since hundreds of revolutions and inches of mercury have absolutely nothing to do with one another, this is patent nonsense. Granted, when carried to extremes such as setting up a combination of 1,700 rpm versus 28 inches of manifold pressure, the result could easily ruin an engine in a matter of minutes. But when used with common sense and, of course, within the limits of the manufacturer's recommendations, flying with the lowest permissible rpm will produce considerable savings in a variety of ways. It is an obvious fact that the faster the engine turns, the more fuel it consumes since each and every revolution requires the burning of a given amount of fuel. Logically, therefore, fuel can be saved by reducing the rpm and increasing the MP to the allowable maximum for a power setting that results in the desired percent of power. As an example, for some of its 260-hp engines, Continental recommends a fuel-economy power setting of 1,900 rpm and 22 inches MP.

There is an important fringe benefit to be gained by habitually using the lowest possible rpm setting. Engine tachometers read the total number of revolutions, not the actual hours of engine operation. They are set to convert this reading into hours based on what is assumed to be the average rpm. In most Cessnas, for instance, this setting assumes an average rpm of 2,566. A bit of fancy arithmetic quickly shows that if the engine is operated at 1,900 rpm instead of at 2,566, one hour on the tach will actually represent one hour and 21.03 minutes of flying. This means that a 2,000-hour TBO would be increased to 2,701 flight hours, or a decrease of 35.05 percent of the cost of a major overhaul.

But a word of caution: The successive order of adjusting rpm and MP when changing from climb to cruise or from cruise to descent is important. After climbing at, say, 2,500 rpm and 25 inches of MP, when it comes to changing to a cruise setting of 1,900 rpm and 22 inches, never reduce the rpm first as it would result in a dangerous setting of 1,900 rpm and 25 inches for a brief moment. The never-to-be-forgotten rule of thumb is: *When reducing power—first MP, then rpm. When increasing power—first rpm, then MP.* This, of course, is also the primary reason for always changing to high rpm before landing. Just imagine a 1,900 rpm setting just before touchdown followed by a decision to go around. Shoving the throttle full in would result in a combination of 1,900 rpm and as much as 29 inches of MP, which could produce catastrophic engine failure within less than a minute.

SPEED/ALTITUDE

The third and fourth considerations that affect fuel consumption are speed and altitude. While speed, in general, is the result of a given percent of power, this is not true during the descent phase of any flight. During the descent a percentage of the speed is the result of gravity, and gravity is free. Therefore, from the point of view of economy, it makes sense to throttle back and either maintain cruising speed or even reduce it to a level below that used in cruise. As a result the aircraft will fly a longer period of time propelled partially at no cost to the pilot. For this same reason it is sensible to set up a long, gradual descent when circumstances and ATC permit. Granted, a few minutes are lost in a slow descent; but this loss of time is quite out of proportion to the gain in fuel economy.

Aside from this, the speed and, in turn, the power setting used during the cruise portion of the flight control the amount of fuel being burned. Although the actual mph or knots depend on the aircraft and altitude, there are three basic speeds to be remembered—variations of which will normally be used in every cross-country flight.

Maximum cruise speed for most aircraft and engines is considered to be 75 percent of power at the altitude at which this percentage coincides with full throttle. It is the speed that will get us to our destination fastest; but since it requires high fuel flow it creates a reduction in range.

Best range speed is the one that will get us the farthest using the least fuel. In most aircraft this is approximately 40 percent above the best-angle-of-climb speed but is rarely indicated in manufacturers performance charts because it might make the aircraft seem slower than the manufacturer would like customers to think it is. It falls generally around 45 percent of power and, since true airspeed increases with altitude in relation to indicated airspeed, the ideal altitude at which to achieve the absolute maximum range for the amount of fuel consumed is the altitude at which 45 percent coincides with full throttle. Except for aircraft equipped with oxygen, this is usually too high for comfort (and probably illegal). A more reasonable altitude of 10,000 or 12,000 feet will produce only a slight increase in fuel consumption and attendant reduction in range in return for greater comfort. When selecting a cruising speed it should be kept in mind that the added power and fuel flow needed to achieve even a slight increase in speed are quite out of proportion to the amount of speed actually being gained. As an example: 55 percent of power will result in 10 to 15 percent less speed than 75 percent but at a fuel savings of between 25 and 30 percent.

And then there is *best endurance speed*. This is the speed at which we can stay in the air for the longest possible time on a given amount of fuel, regardless of the distance covered. It falls somewhat below the best rate of climb speed and should be used to conserve fuel during delays, such as being held by ATC in a holding pattern or when arriving at the destination VFR on top and learning that it will take another hour before the airport is expected to clear to VFR (or special VFR) conditions.

WINDS

The advantages of flying at high altitudes relative to fuel consumption may, especially when flying in a westerly direction, be negated by the wind. In order to achieve best economy, both head-wind and tail-wind components should always be taken into consideration. With a tail wind of any consequence it is more economical to reduce power and to maintain the ground speed that would have been flown without wind. In doing this the aircraft is exposed for a longer period of time to the free speed increase produced by the wind. Conversely, it is a good idea to increase the indicated airspeed when flying into a head wind, thus minimizing the length of time in which the airplane is exposed to its detrimental effect. As a rule of thumb, these increases and decreases in speed should be held to approximately 25 percent of the head- or tail-wind component. If, on the other hand, the winds are in excess of 15 to 20 percent of the aircraft's true airspeed, it is usually better to adjust altitude in order to avoid head winds or to take advantage of tail winds—meaning, of course, that we search out the stronger winds if they blow from the rear and try to get below or above them if they blow on our nose. At those velocities the economical advantages of flying high into a head wind would be canceled out, as would the economical disadvantages of flying low, if that is where the tail wind is to be found.

Pilots using intelligent fuel-saving techniques, such as careful mixture control and the best combination of rpm and MP, who take advantage of the appropriate altitudes and winds and who, when possible, fly a straight line instead of zigzagging all over the sky, will find that they can easily reduce the cost of operating the airplane by 25 percent or more without any reduction in the actual flying activity.

AUTOGAS

Some aircraft owners can tally up additional fuel savings by using automotive fuel. A wide range of STCs are available through the Experimental Aircraft Association in Oshkosh, Wisconsin. With the STC an operator can legally use the less expensive fuel meant for cars in his aircraft. However, it may be hard to find the fuel in a convenient place to refuel the plane.

Contracts with fuel companies, FBOs, governmental agencies, and the like that control an airport can prohibit the dispensing of nonaviation fuel on an airport; therefore a pilot would be wise to examine availability and potential savings before acquiring the STC.

15
The Mathematics of
Cross-Country Flight

WE WALK AROUND THE AIRPLANE TO MAKE SURE THAT NOTHING IS hanging or dripping, climb in, fire up the engine, take off, and climb to an altitude that for one reason or another strikes us as a good level at which to fly; then, when approaching our destination, we throttle back, descend, land, shut down the engine, lock the door, fasten tiedown chains, and walk away. That, in telegraph style, is the profile of the average flight. And, admittedly, that is what most of us do most of the time without ever bothering to figure out scientifically if the speeds and altitudes we have selected are actually the most efficient or economical.

There are some fairly simple mathematical formulae that will give us answers to many of the often used flight-related questions. But the cockpit of the airplane is not a good place in which to try and figure out all that. A better idea is to use some spare time on a rainy or foggy day to arrive at the appropriate figures for the airplane we either own or most frequently rent. All that is needed are the mathematical equations described in this chapter and the various tables. Enter the performance parameters for your airplane into the empty boxes in those tables, and then use any simple electronic pocket computer to perform the computations. It can, of course, also be done without such a computer, but then it takes a lot longer.

In the examples shown here we have used a 1974 Cessna Skyhawk and a 1976 Bellanca Super Viking and the figures given by the manufacturers in the respective owners' manuals.

ALTITUDE VERSUS SPEED VERSUS FUEL

It certainly is no secret that it is cheaper to fly slowly than quickly and that fuel economy increases with altitude. But how much? And is it worth it? In order to find out whether the savings in fuel is worth the extra time spent, the computation looks like this:

Divide the distance by the speed in order to determine the time aloft. Then multiply the result by the fuel flow per hour to arrive at the amount of fuel that will be burned.

Now, using this formula, let's examine how the 1974 Skyhawk and 1976 Super Viking will do, using different altitudes and speeds in order to cover a distance of 500 nm under no-wind conditions. (It makes no difference whether the various parameters are figured in nm or sm or km as long as the speed figures used are comparable: knots/mph/kph. Similarly the fuel figures can be in gallons or litres or pounds as long as the same unit is used for fuel flow.)

All figures shown below assume proper leaning at all power settings below 75 percent.

The compilation of figures above seems to make several interesting points:

1. With the Skyhawk, the slowest speed appears to be the most economical, regardless of the altitude used, with the higher altitudes being a trifle more economical than the lower ones.
2. With the faster Super Viking the most economical speed seems to be between 53 and 56 percent of power, depending on the altitude, with the highest altitude again producing the greatest savings.
3. The difference in percentages in terms of time aloft versus fuel consumed, in the case of the Skyhawk, amounts to a 24-percent difference in time between the slowest and fastest speed, for a fuel saving of 21.4 percent.
4. In the case of the Super Viking the percentages work out to an 11.4-percent time difference between the most expensive and least expensive speeds, while the difference in fuel consumed is 20.2 percent.
5. It would, therefore, seem that using economical power settings is more meaningful in high-performance aircraft than it is the slower types. It also appears that by flying a high-performance single at a miserly power setting we still fly 17.4 percent faster than we would in the slower aircraft at top speed at a fuel-consumption difference of only 2.9 percent. (To figure the percentages for your own aircraft, use the formula shown in TABLE 15-1.)

Table 15-1. Altitude/Speed/Fuel.

Distance   :   Speed   =   Hours   ×   PPH   =   Fuel used (lbs)

[ ]   :   [ ]   =   [ ]   ×   [ ]   =   [ ]

:   =   ×   =

In terms of percentages:

Higher total time or fuel	−	Lower total time or fuel	=	Sum	:	Higher total time or fuel	%	Result in time or fuel
[ ]	−	[ ]	=	[ ]	:	[ ]	%	[ ]

Note: If the calculator does not have a % button, use the : button and move the decimal point two spaces to the right to get the correct percentage figure.

SPEED VERSUS FUEL WITH HEAD OR TAIL WINDS

The generally accepted rule is to increase speed by 25 percent of the head-wind component when flying into a head wind and to reduce it by 25 percent of the tail-wind component when taking advantage of favorable winds. Let's look at it mathematically and see how it works out for our Skyhawk and Super Viking:

The formula calls for dividing the distance to be flown by the true airspeed minus the head-wind component to arrive at time en route. Multiply the result by the fuel flow in units per hour to find how much fuel will be burned.

As the figures indicate, the Skyhawk, when fighting a head wind, does best at the third fastest speed, yet the best economy with the Super Viking is obtained at the third slowest speed (TABLES 15-2 and 15-3). By taking advantage of a comparable tail wind, the Skyhawk does best at its slowest speed, but the Super Viking saves the most fuel at its second slowest speed. It must be remembered that different wind components will produce different results. And, obviously, the effect of the wind, whatever its velocity, is greater on the slower aircraft than it is on the faster one—representing a greater percentage of the TAS of the slower aircraft.

SELECTING THE BEST ALTITUDE AT NO WIND, STANDARD TEMPERATURE

So far we have talked of cruise situations ignoring the effects of climb and descent. If we want to do it right, these, too, will have to be cranked into our computations. This requires performing a number of consecutive series of equations.

Climb

Here the formula looks like this: *Divide the altitude differential by the rate of climb in fpm to arrive at the number of minutes spent in climb. Multiply that figure by*

Table 15-2. Skyhawk.

% Power	distance	:Knots	= Time en route	× PPH	= Fuel used (lbs)	
@ 2,500 feet msl						
87 %	500 nm	: 121	= 4.1 hours	× 58	= 238	(40.46)
78 %	500 nm	: 116	= 4.3 hours	× 52	= 224	(38.08)
70 %	500 nm	: 111	= 4.5 hours	× 46	= 207	(35.19)
63 %	500 nm	: 106	= 4.7 hours	× 43	= 202	(34.34)
57 %	500 nm	: 101	= 5 hours	× 40	= 200	(34.00)
51 %	500 nm	: 95	= 5.3 hours	× 37	= 196	(33.32)
@ 5,000 feet msl						
81 %	500 nm	: 120	= 4.2 hours	× 53	= 223	(37.91)
73 %	500 nm	: 116	= 4.3 hours	× 49	= 211	(35.87)
66 %	500 nm	: 111	= 4.5 hours	× 44	= 198	(33.66)
60 %	500 nm	: 105	= 4.8 hours	× 41	= 197	(33.49)
54 %	500 nm	: 99	= 5.1 hours	× 38	= 194	(32.98)
48 %	500 nm	: 93	= 5.4 hours	× 36	= 194	(32.98)
@ 10,000 feet msl						
72 %	500 nm	: 120	= 4.2 hours	× 47	= 197	(33.49)
66 %	500 nm	: 114	= 4.4 hours	× 44	= 194	(32.98)
59 %	500 nm	: 108	= 4.6 hours	× 41	= 189	(32.13)
54 %	500 nm	: 102	= 4.9 hours	× 38	= 186	(31.62)
48 %	500 nm	: 96	= 5.2 hours	× 36	= 187	(31.79)

the speed and divide by 60 to find out how far the airplane will travel during the climb. (No allowance is made for the slant angle of the flight path of the aircraft, as its effect on the distance traveled is too minimal to be of consequence.)

Cruise

Take the total distance from departure to destination airport; deduct the distances covered during climb and descent; and divide the result by the cruising speed plus or minus wind components, if any, to find the time spent in cruise. Multiply this figure by the fuel flow per hour to find the amount of fuel burned during the cruise portion of the flight.

Descent

Divide the distance from the point at which descent will be started to the destination by the speed to be maintained during the descent to find the time spent in hours. To

Table 15-3. Super Viking.

@ 2,500 feet msl

78 %	500 nm	: 159 = 3.1 hours	× 98 = 304	(51.68)
73 %	500 nm	: 155 = 3.2 hours	× 92 = 294	(49.98)
68 %	500 nm	: 150 = 3.3 hours	× 86 = 284	(48.28)
61 %	500 nm	: 143 = 3.5 hours	× 77 = 270	(45.90)
54 %	500 nm	: 134 = 3.7 hours	× 68 = 252	(42.84)
47 %	500 nm	: 119 = 4.2 hours	× 62 = 260	(44.20)
41 %	500 nm	: 109 = 4.6 hours	× 57 = 262	(44.54)

@ 5,000 feet msl

79 %	500 nm	: 163 = 3.1 hours	× 99 = 307	(52.19)
75 %	500 nm	: 160 = 3.1 hours	× 94 = 291	(49.47)
72 %	500 nm	: 157 = 3.2 hours	× 90 = 288	(48.96)
67 %	500 nm	: 153 = 3.3 hours	× 85 = 281	(47.77)
60 %	500 nm	: 144 = 3.5 hours	× 75 = 263	(44.71)
53 %	500 nm	: 133 = 3.8 hours	× 66 = 251	(42.67)
46 %	500 nm	: 116 = 4.3 hours	× 60 = 258	(43.86)
42 %	500 nm	: 96 = 5.1 hours	× 55 = 281	(47.77)

@ 10,000 feet msl

67 %	500 nm	: 159 = 3.1 hours	× 83 = 257	(43.69)
63 %	500 nm	: 153 = 3.3 hours	× 77 = 254	(43.18)
60 %	500 nm	: 150 = 3.3 hours	× 76 = 251	(42.67)
56 %	500 nm	: 142 = 3.5 hours	× 70 = 245	(41.65)
49 %	500 nm	: 123 = 4.1 hours	× 63 = 258	(43.86)
46 %	500 nm	: 104 = 4.8 hours	× 60 = 288	(48.96)

Note: Time-en-route figures are rounded out to the nearest decimal. Fuel figures are rounded to the closest full figure. Dollar figures are based on a fuel cost of $ 0.17 per pound or approximately $1.00 per gallon.

determine the necessary fpm figure, divide by 60. (See section, "Climb and Descent: Rate and Distance.")

To figure the amount of fuel burned during the climb and descent portions, *multiply time spent during these phases of the flight (in hours) by the fuel flow as shown in the owner's manual for the approximate power setting to be used.* Use the highest power setting listed for the climb portion and the lowest one for the descent.

Totals

Add the time to climb, time in cruise, and time to descend to arrive at the total time from liftoff to landing. Also, add the fuel used during the three stages to determine the amount of fuel burned.

Table 15-4. Speed/Fuel with Head Wind.

Distance : (TAS minus head wind component) = Hours × PPH = Fuel used

☐ : ☐ = ☐ × ☐ = ☐

Speed/fuel with tail wind

Distance : (TAS plus tail wind component)   = Hours × PPH = Fuel used

☐ : ☐ = ☐ × ☐ = ☐

In order to determine how this formula affects our two airplanes, here are examples of flights covering a total distance of 500 nm with the cruise portions being flown at 2,500 feet, 5,000 feet, and 10,000 feet, and no allowances made for wind. Wind components would simply have to be added to or deducted from the various speeds.

As it turns out, a study of the results shows that it really doesn't make a great deal of difference at what altitude we cruise. What we save at altitude we seem to use up during climb. In other words, the advantage of flying at higher altitudes can only be realized if we are talking about a rather long distance to be flown or if the winds aloft are more favorable than those down low.

CLIMB AND DESCENT: RATE AND DISTANCE

In practice, most of us pay little attention to how much distance is covered during climbs or descents or to the fpm figure needed in order to achieve a desired altitude differential in a given distance. Much of the time knowing these figures is of little importance, but there are instances when they can come in handy.

Let's say that we are flying toward a mountain range that requires an altitude gain of 7,000 feet. And then let's assume that the rate of climb that we can comfortably expect to average is 400 fpm at an average TAS of 110 knots. How far from the mountain range will we have to commence our climb?

To find the answer we have to *divide the altitude differential in feet by the rate of climb in fpm to find the number of minutes we will be spending in climb. That figure must then be divided by 60 and the result multiplied by the TAS (or, if known, the ground speed), and the resultant figure is the distance from the mountain range at which we must start to climb in order to make it* (see TABLE 15-9).

Conversely, we might want to know what rate of climb we must make good at a given speed in order to reach the needed altitude within the distance available to us. To work this out requires two steps. *First we divide the available distance by the speed of the airplane (ground speed, if known). Then we multiply the result by 60 to find the number of minutes available for the climb and then divide the altitude differential by this figure to arrive at the needed fpm* (see TABLE 15-10).

Table 15-5. Head Wind and Tail Wind.

% Power	distance	:TAS minus head wind	= Hours	× PPH	= Fuel	used ($)
		Skyhawk				
81%	500 nm	: (120−25=) 95	= 5.3	× 53	= 281	(47.75)
73%	500 nm	: (116−25=) 91	= 5.5	× 49	= 270	(45.90)
66%	500 nm	: (111−25=) 86	= 5.8	× 44	= 255	(43.35)
60%	500 nm	: (105−25=) 80	= 6.3	× 41	= 258	(43.86)
54%	500 nm	: (99−25=) 74	= 6.8	× 38	= 258	(43.86)
48%	500 nm	: (93−25=) 68	= 7.4	× 36	= 266	(45.22)
		Super Viking				
79%	500 nm	: (163−25=) 138	= 3.6	× 99	= 356	(60.52)
75%	500 nm	: (160−25=) 135	= 3.7	× 94	= 348	(59.16)
72%	500 nm	: (157−25=) 132	= 3.8	× 99	= 342	(58.14)
67%	500 nm	: (153−25=) 128	= 3.9	× 85	= 332	(56.44)
60%	500 nm	: (144−25=) 119	= 4.2	× 75	= 315	(53.55)
53%	500 nm	: (133−25=) 108	= 4.6	× 66	= 304	(51.68)
46%	500 nm	: (116−25=) 91	= 5.5	× 60	= 330	(56.10)
42%	500 nm	: (98−25=) 73	= 6.8	× 55	= 374	(63.58)
		Skyhawk				
81%	500 nm	: (120+25=) 145	= 3.4	× 53	= 180	(30.60)
73%	500 nm	: (116+25=) 141	= 3.5	× 49	= 172	(29.24)
66%	500 nm	: (111+25=) 136	= 3.7	× 44	= 163	(27.71)
60%	500 nm	: (105+25=) 130	= 3.8	× 41	= 156	(26.52)
54%	500 nm	: (99+25=) 124	= 4.0	× 38	= 152	(25.84)
48%	500 nm	: (93+25=) 118	= 4.2	× 36	= 151	(25.67)
		Super Viking				
79%	500 nm	: (163+25=) 188	= 2.7	× 99	= 267	(45.39)
75%	500 nm	: (160+25=) 185	= 2.7	× 94	= 254	(43.18)
72%	500 nm	: (157+25=) 182	= 2.7	× 90	= 243	(41.31)
67%	500 nm	: (153+25=) 178	= 2.8	× 85	= 238	(40.46)
60%	500 nm	: (144+25=) 169	= 3.0	× 75	= 225	(38.25)
53%	500 nm	: (133+25=) 158	= 3.2	× 66	= 211	(35.87)
46%	500 nm	: (116+25=) 141	= 3.5	× 60	= 210	(35.70)
42%	500 nm	: (98+25=) 123	= 4.1	× 55	= 226	(38.42)

As an example, let's assume that by checking our charts we find that we are 20 nm from the 7,000-foot mountain range. We are flying at 1,000 feet and want to clear the range by an equal amount—meaning that we'll have to gain 7,000 feet in that distance (see TABLE 15-11).

Table 15-6. Selecting Best Altitude (No Wind, Standard Temperature).

1. Altitude
   differential : FPM = Minutes × Knots : 60 = Distance covered in climb

   $$\boxed{\qquad} : \boxed{\quad} = \boxed{\quad} \times \boxed{\quad} \ = \ \boxed{\qquad}$$

2. Total   _ Distance covered in   Time in   Fuel consumed
   distance   climb and descent   : Speed = cruise   × PPH =   in cruise

   $$\boxed{\quad} - \boxed{\qquad} : \boxed{\quad} = \boxed{\quad} \times \boxed{\quad} = \boxed{\quad}$$

3. Distance covered   Time of descent   Time of descent
   during descent   : Speed =   in hours   × 60 =   in minutes

   $$\boxed{\qquad} : \boxed{\quad} = \boxed{\qquad} \times 60 = \boxed{\qquad}$$

4. Time to climb + Time in cruise + Time to descend = Total time

   $$\boxed{\qquad} + \boxed{\qquad} + \boxed{\qquad} = \boxed{\quad}$$

5. Fuel to climb = Fuel in cruise + Fuel to descend = Total fuel

   $$\boxed{\qquad} + \boxed{\qquad} + \boxed{\qquad} = \boxed{\quad}$$

Table 15-7. Skyhawk—2,000; 5,000; 10,000 Feet MSL Cruise (Takeoff at Sea Level).

Altitude differential	: FPM	=	Minutes	× Knots : 60	=	Distance covered in climb	(Fuel used)
2,500 ft	: 645	=	39.6	× 1.3	=	5.1 nm	3.77 lbs
5,000 ft	: 540	=	41	× 1.3	=	12.1 nm	8.99 lbs
10,000 ft	: 437	=	41	× 1.2	=	27.5 nm	22.16 lbs

Total distance	_ Distance covered in climb and descent	: Knots	=	Time in cruise	× PPH	=	Fuel consumed in cruise
500 nm	− (5 + 8 =) 13 = 487	: 101	=	4.8	× 39.6	=	190 lbs
500 nm	− (12 + 17 =) 29 = 471	: 105	=	4.5	× 41	=	185 lbs
500 nm	− (28 + 35 =) 63 = 437	: 108	=	4.0	× 41	=	164 lbs

Distance covered during descent	: Knots	=	Time of descent in hours	× 60 =	Time of descent in minutes	(Fuel used)
8 nm	: 101	=	0.08	× 60 =	4.8	2.96 lbs
17 nm	: 105	=	0.16	× 60 =	9.7	5.82 lbs
35 nm	: 108	=	0.32	× 60 =	19.4	11.6 lbs

Time to climb	+	Time in cruise	+	Time to descend	=	Total time
0.065 hrs	+	4.8 hrs.	+	0.08 hrs	=	4.95 hrs (4:57)
0.155 hrs	+	4.5 hrs.	+	0.16 hrs	=	4.82 hrs (4:49)
0.382 hrs	+	4.0 hrs.	+	0.32 hrs	=	4.70 hrs (4:42)

Fuel to climb	+	Fuel in cruise	+	Fuel to descend	=	Total fuel	
3.77 lbs	+	190 lbs	+	2.96 lbs	=	196.73 lbs	($33.44)
8.99 lbs	+	185 lbs	+	5.82 lbs	=	199.81 lbs	($33.97)
22.16 lbs	+	164 lbs	+	11.6 lbs	=	197.76 lbs	($33.62)

Table 15-8. Super Viking—2,000; 5,000;
10,000 Feet MSL Cruise (Takeoff at Sea Level).

Altitude differential	: FPM	= Minutes	× Knots : 60	= Distance covered in climb	(Fuel used)
2,500 ft	: 950 =	2.6	× 1.6	= 4.16 nm	4.29 lbs
5,000 ft	: 800 =	6.3	× 1.6	= 10.08 nm	10.4 lbs
10,000 ft	: 580 =	17.2	× 1.6	= 27.52 nm	28.4 lbs

Total distance	− Distance covered in climb and descent	: Knots	= Time in cruise	× PPH =	Fuel consumed in cruise
500 nm	− 12 = 488	: 119	= 4.1	× 62 =	254 lbs
500 nm	− 27 = 473	: 133	= 3.6	× 66 =	238 lbs
500 nm	− 62 = 438	: 142	= 3.1	× 70 =	217 lbs

Distance covered during descent	: Knots	= Time of descent in hours	× 60 =	Time of descent in minutes	(Fuel used)
7.84 nm	: 119 =	0.07	× 60 =	4.2	3.85 lbs
19.92 nm	: 130 =	0.15	× 60 =	9.0	8.25 lbs
34.48 nm	: 135 =	0.25	× 60 =	15.6	14.3 lbs

Time to climb	+ Time in cruise	+ Time to descend	= Total time	
0.04 hrs	+ 4.1 hrs	+ 0.07 hrs	= 4.21 hrs	(4:13)
0.11 hrs	+ 3.6 hrs	+ 0.15 hrs	= 3.86 hrs	(3:52)
0.29 hrs	+ 3.1 hrs	+ 0.25 hrs	= 3.64 hrs	(3:38)

Fuel to climb	+ Fuel in cruise	+ Fuel to descend	= Total fuel	
4.29 lbs	+ 254 lbs	+ 3.85 lbs	= 262.14 lbs	($44.56)
10.4 lbs	+ 238 lbs	+ 8.25 lbs	= 256.65 lbs	($43.63)
28.4 lbs	+ 217 lbs	+ 14.3 lbs	= 259.70 lbs	($44.15)

Table 15-9. Distance Covered During Climb or Descent.

Altitude differential in feet	: FPM	= Minutes in climb or descent	: 60	= Hours	× Knots	= Distance
	:	=	: 60	=	×	=

Altitude differential in feet	: FPM	= Minutes in climb or descent	: 60	= Hours	× Knots	= Distance
7,000	: 400	= 17.5	: 60	= .29	× 110	= 31.9 nm

Table 15-10. Rate of Climb or Descent to Achieve Given Altitude Differential within a Fixed Distance.

1. Distance : Speed = Hours × 60 = Minutes

[   ] : [   ] = [   ] × 60 = [   ]

2. Altitude : Minutes = FPM required
   differential

[   ] : [   ] = [   ]

Table 15-11. Example.

1. Distance : Speed = Hours × 60 = Minutes

[20 nm] : [110] = [.18] × 60 = [10.9]

2. Altitude : Minutes = FPM required
   differential

[7,000] : [10.9] = [642.2]

Table 15-12. Example.

1. Distance : Speed = Hours × 60 = Minutes

[200] : [130] = [1.54] × 60 = [92.4]

2. Altitude : Minutes = FPM required
   differential

[7,000] : [92.4] = [75.76]

If, as in the previous example, the best we can get from our airplane is a rate of climb of 400 fpm, we will obviously have to fly S-turns in order to increase the actual distance flown by 11.9 nm.

This formula is also especially useful in figuring long, slow descents, which are effective fuel savers. For argument's sake we might want to start a descent from an 8,500-foot cruise to the 1,500-foot pattern altitude at our destination airport some 200 nm before we get there. What will the fpm rate be to achieve this right on the button?

Let's assume we have been cruising at 130 knots and, for reasons of economy, we will throttle back and maintain that speed all the way down to pattern altitude (see TABLE 15-12).

In other words, assuming that weather conditions permit such a gradual descent (and we are VFR because ATC would rarely, if ever, clear an aircraft for such a long descent), we would spend slightly over one-and-a-half hours at cruise speed using a very minimum of fuel because, even at a shallow descent angle of slightly less than 76 fpm, gravity would be giving us a meaningful free shove.

There are a number of other flight-related mathematical formulae, but most are too complicated to be of practical use in everyday flight operations. Some of the more expensive electronic computers are designed specifically for use in aviation. They contain a wide variety of predesigned programs that automatically perform the series of calculations necessary to obtain the desired results. While very useful for the pilot flying such sophisticated equipment as turboprops or jets—which require computations for accelerate-stop distances, balanced field length, takeoff speed and similar parameters under prevailing weight, wind, and runway-surface conditions—it is doubtful that these instruments are worth their fairly considerable cost to the average general-aviation pilot flying a single or light twin.

The advantage of playing these numbers games with the performance figures applicable to our aircraft or the type of aircraft we habitually rent is knowing what this aircraft will actually do under varying conditions—knowledge that can greatly improve the efficiency and economy of the airplane.

16
Flight Number Six

Date: July 31, 1968.
Pilot: Male, age 25, student.
License: Commercial, SEL, instrument.
Pilot-In-Command Time: 418 hours.
Aircraft: Waco (Italian-built single engine retractable, low wing).
Flight: From Rockford, Illinois, to Santa Barbara, California.

There were three of them in the airplane: the pilot; his father, who was also a pilot; and a passenger, a friend who had never before been in a light airplane. The airplane was fully IFR-equipped, with dual navcoms, ADF, glide slope, marker beacon, and autopilot. Gear and flaps were electric. The tanks held 55 gallons of fuel, 50 of them usable, and the 220-hp Franklin engine was known to burn some 12.5 gph at 75 percent of power, producing a TAS of 148 knots at sea level. The N-number was 972WA.

The three had spent the last two days at the fly-in of the Experimental Aircraft Association, which takes place each year around the end of July or the beginning of August in Rockford, Illinois, in those days, and now in Oshkosh, Wisconsin. They were on their way home.

It was a beautiful VFR day and, after extricating themselves from the incredible traffic congestion that always is part and parcel of those EAA fly-ins, they had leveled off at 10,500 feet above the layer of summer haze heading west and planned to stop somewhere in the vicinity of Kansas City for fuel and lunch. The upper winds at their altitude had been forecast to be less than 15 knots, and the air was smooth as the pilot engaged the autopilot to sit back and enjoy the flight.

They had been on their way for about an hour when the father, occupying the copilot seat, remarked to his son, "We don't seem to be getting anywhere very fast. I guess you've noticed."

"I have. Maybe we'd be better off lower down, especially now that the haze seems to have dissipated."

"Why don't you call somebody and find out."

The son tuned in the nearest FSS and asked about the upper wind reports for three, six, and nine.

"Two Whiskey Alpha, the forecast upper winds at three thousand two four zero at two zero, at six thousand two six zero at two five, at niner thousand two seven zero at three zero."

"Thank you, Two Whiskey Alpha." He put the mike on its hook. "At that rate, we might as well stay where we are. No wonder the haze has disappeared with those winds. Maybe that front they talked about earlier is moving faster than was expected."

AIRBORNE ODOR

It wasn't until some time after they had crossed the Mississippi that they began to notice it. The father mentioned it first.

"What's that funny smell? You notice it?"

"I don't know."

"If we were lower I'd say someone must be crop dusting with nitrogen fertilizer. It smells something like that. But way up here?"

"Anybody drop a cigarette onto the rug or something?"

Nobody had, but the smell continued to get stronger and more annoying.

"This is ridiculous. Open that little side window and see if that does anything."

It did. Instead of making it better it made it worse. The pilot put his face close to the open window to determine whether the smell was coming from the outside.

"Doesn't seem to come from out there."

"Better close it. It's making it still worse."

The father was the first to put his handkerchief to his face in an effort to filter the air he was breathing.

"I'd say we better find a place to land, and I mean right now, before we all pass out."

And by now it was clear to all of them that he wasn't kidding.

The pilot throttled back, pulled the nose up to slow the aircraft to gear-down speed, dropped the gear and part flaps and, descending at better than 2,000 fpm, headed for a narrow little landing strip that he had noticed just moments earlier. It took less than five minutes to get down at that rate of descent, but to the three in the airplane it seemed a lot longer. All of them were now pressing handkerchiefs against their noses and mouths despite the fact that it didn't seem to do much good.

The touchdown was firm and the landing roll short, and as soon as the airplane had come to a stop off the runway they all piled out in great haste. None of them had dared mention it, but the fear of some hidden smoldering fire somewhere in the airplane had begun to affect all of them.

It was good to be able to breathe again. Then, with the airplane sitting there peacefully as if nothing were wrong, they all stood around eyeing it with suspicion.

"Well, apparently it isn't going to blow up on us, so maybe we better start looking and find out what's been doing that."

They gingerly opened the cowling. Nothing. Everything looked the way it was supposed to, and nothing appeared to be smelling of something it shouldn't. Inside the cabin the smell continued to linger, but with the door open it wasn't too bad any longer. One of them crawled inside and peered under the instrument panel. There, too, everything was the way it was supposed to be.

"Let's try the back."

They pulled the luggage from behind the back seats and unfastened the panel that closes off the tailcone.

"Look at that!"

HOT CELLS

There, bathed in a cloud of foul-smelling smoke, sat the battery with a hole in its side the size of a fist.

"The damn thing has simply melted."

"Now what?"

"Damn if I know. Let's air this thing out for a while."

They sat in the grass and looked at one another and then at the airplane.

"Where are we anyway?"

"Beats me."

They looked around. Not a soul. The shack at the far end of the runway was obviously deserted, and a lonely Piper Cub minus prop and half its horizontal tail, covered with a thick layer of dust, was the only other occupant.

"Welcome to 'Noplace International,' " someone said in an attempt at humor, but nobody laughed.

"I'm still wondering, now what?" It was the passenger who so far had said little.

"Well, I guess all we can do once that thing has stopped stinking up the airplane is to disconnect what's left of that battery and then fly to Kansas City and have them install a new one."

"It's Sunday."

"Obviously. Things like this never happen except on Sundays."

"If we do that my guess is Fairfax Airport is better than Municipal. That's where most of the little airplanes are, and they're more likely to have a mechanic on duty on a Sunday."

"Fine with me. Fairfax it is."

"They've got a tower."

"I know."

"And we're not going to have any radio."

"I know, but we've got a telephone. At least I hope we do." He pointed to the lonely phone booth near the deserted shed.

At the end of a couple of hours or so, with the smell having dissipated and the battery cables disconnected, they reloaded the luggage. Fairfax Tower had been alerted to the impending arrival of a silent aircraft operating under conditions of total electrical failure and had instructed the pilot to make a low pass by the tower and watch for a green light.

Neither of the two pilots had propped an airplane in years, and the passenger, of course, hadn't even known that an airplane could be flown without a battery. In addition, they weren't completely certain that they would be able to get that 220-hp engine started by propping it, but they were sure going to try.

"Contact!"

Plup, plup, plup. Nothing.

"Switch off!"

Then . . .

"Contact!"

This time she caught.

Everyone got back into his seat, strapped himself in, and they taxied to the end of the runway, performed the usual run-up and magneto check, and took off.

The father dug out the Kansas City Sectional and studied it.

"Between that Interstate down there and the Kansas River we ought to be able to find Kansas City all right," he said, looking at the dead navigation radios.

"Assuming that the fuel holds out."

With the gear down, the airspeed had dropped by better than 20 knots, while the electric fuel gauges motionlessly leaned against the EMPTY peg.

"Any idea how much we've got?"

"We've got fuel. I looked in the tanks. But how much? I haven't got the foggiest."

Neither pilot said so but both silently wished that they had paid closer attention to the fuel consumption earlier, when the gauges were still doing their thing.

"Better keep an eye out for places to land, just in case."

"I know. There's Marshall and Higginsville and East Kansas City and then, of course, there's always the Interstate."

"That would give a bunch of Sunday drivers something to tell their grandchildren about."

"I'm going to run one side dry and then fly the rest of the way on the other, I hope."

"Okay."

By the time they finally passed north of East Kansas City Airport they had been flying on the second tank for quite a while.

"Keep your fingers crossed."

"I have been."

GREEN LIGHT

They descended straight toward Fairfax Tower, and the controller responded with a green light almost immediately. The pilot flew a tight pattern, grateful that the extended gear helped to slow the plane down. He would have liked to use full flaps but they, too, were electric. So, he better do it right the first time because he had serious doubts that there would be enough fuel for a go-around.

Thump. The airplane was on the ground, slowed, turned off the active and toward the ramp. It took a bit of doing to find an FBO with a mechanic on duty, but eventually one was located at a Beech dealership. Pretty soon helpful souls were crawling all over the airplane. One, a bystander with nothing else to do, looked into the tanks.

"What'd you fly on? Fumes?"

The bottoms of both tanks looked bone dry.

It turned out that what apparently had happened was that sometime during the flight the voltage regulator had become stuck in the full-charge position. This resulted in a continuous overcharge of the battery, eventually causing it to boil and finally to melt.

"The needle must have been way up on CHARGE for a long time. Didn't anybody notice?"

Apparently no one had.

It took several hours to install a new battery and to locate and then install a replacement voltage regulator, but eventually everything was back in working order and, with 54.6 gallons of fuel pumped into the 55-gallon-capacity tanks, the three and their revitalized airplane were back in the air and on their way to California.

ANALYSIS

They had been lucky, probably luckier than they deserved to be considering the degree of inattention that had marked the early portion of their flight. First, there was the problem of the malfunctioning voltage regulator. While few of us are likely to remember to include a check of the CHARGE/DISCHARGE indicator when we scan the instruments, a constant high-charge readout should have been noticed, especially with two pilots occupying the front seats. Had it been spotted in time, the main switch could have been cut and a landing made in time to save the battery and possibly even repair the ailing voltage regulator. This not only would have precluded getting into what might have been a dangerous situation, it would also have saved them the better portion of $100.

Second, there was the fuel situation. As long as everything is working perfectly it doesn't make too much difference whether or not the pilot is constantly aware of exactly how much fuel is being burned and how much is left in the tanks (as long as the next planned fuel stop is within range). But then, when suddenly something does go wrong, this information can provide the means of avoiding disaster. There is really no good excuse for sitting up there fat and happy without paying attention to the various indicators that relate to the different parameters of flight. In this case, of course, it all worked out but, judging by those four-tenths of a gallon that were apparently left in the tanks, an additional knot of head wind or a delay in getting clearance to land could easily have resulted in a bent airplane or worse.

Actually, in this case, because the pilot did not know how much fuel was on board, he would have been smarter to pick a closer airport. If an airport with a mechanic on duty could not be found in the direction where they were heading, they probably should have tried for one east of their position to take advantage of the fairly strong tail wind. This, it would seem, never occurred to them—bent, as they were, on continuing toward their destination.

It is quite possible, of course, that with two experienced pilots on board, each subconsciously figured that the other was helping to keep track of everything and, as a result, neither proved to be as vigilant as either might have been had he been alone. There simply is no such thing as two pilots flying an airplane unless a clearly defined pilot/copilot division of duties has been arranged in advance.

One thing is certain. The more we fly, the more casual we tend to become. We should, therefore, always remember that a minor mechanical in-flight malfunction can lead to catastrophic results unless we are constantly aware of the performance of the aircraft systems and instruments, the fuel situation, current position, ground speed, and anything else that would become instantly vital in the event that something does go wrong. The sum total of such information makes it possible to make the right decision unhesitatingly when we are faced with an untoward occurrence.

17
Instruments
and Equipment

TODAY THE PILOT WHO IS PLANNING TO EQUIP HIS AIRPLANE WITH ALL the latest goodies designed to make cross-country flying easier and more enjoyable is faced with a bewildering array of avionics, instruments, and equipment. While it is beyond the scope of this book to explain and analyze each and every one of those in complete detail, let's just take a quick look at what is available and at the function that each performs or is designed to perform.

THE BASIC PANEL

In years past we thought nothing of flying airplanes equipped only with an altimeter, airspeed and vertical speed indicators, a magnetic compass, a needle-and-ball turn-and-bank instrument, and a fuel gauge. Period. We stayed out of clouds because controlling an airplane by those instruments alone, though not impossible, is rather difficult. We used a combination of whatever charts were available and visual landmarks to navigate strictly by pilotage.

Today we would have a hard time finding an airplane that doesn't have, in addition to the above, a directional gyro, an artificial horizon, and at least one navcom radio. The directional gyro permits us to hold headings with greater precision and to make turns involving a predetermined number of degrees. The artificial horizon helps us to keep our wings level under conditions of restricted visibility or when flying in IFR conditions. The navcom radio makes it possible to utilize the various electronic nav aids when navigating and the com portion is the price of admission to controlled airports and, of course, a means of obtaining weather and other information while in flight.

NAV AND COM RADIOS

Nav and com radios come in a profusion of different models, though the basic function of all is identical; namely to receive signals from ground-based nav aids and display the information obtained from those signals in one form or another in the cockpit and to facilitate communication by voice with ground stations and occasionally other aircraft.

Some units, known as *navcoms*, include both functions in one box that either contains two complete and separate units, referred to as one-plus-one systems, or they share the receiver function, in which case they are known as one-and-a-half systems. Some of the lower-priced models also include the omni-bearing indicator/selector (OBI/OBS) in the same panel-mounted box, while with most of the more expensive equipment, the OBI/OBS is a separate unit.

In still more expensive installations the nav and com functions are performed entirely separately, with control heads and readouts mounted in the instrument panel and the actual heart of the equipment frequently remote-mounted elsewhere in the aircraft.

The categories of equipment break down as follows:

Navcoms

A combination of navigation and communication functions in one box (FIG. 17-1).

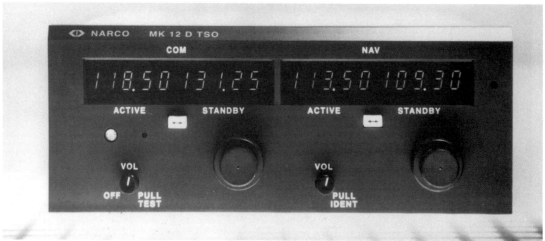

Fig. 17-1. *A typical navcom radio.*

Fig. 17-2. *A digital communications transceiver.*

Fig. 17-3. *A digital navigation receiver.*

VHF Transceivers

Communication receivers and transmitters combined in one unit (FIG. 17-2).

Nav Receivers

Radios designed to accept signals from ground-based nav aids and feed the obtained information into a cockpit display (FIG. 17-3).

Omni-Bearing Indicator/Selector

Cockpit instruments that display the position of the aircraft relative to a ground-based nav aid by visual means. All OBI/OBS readouts looked pretty much alike until several manufacturers, such as Collins, Bendix, and others, marketed entirely new designs intended to make their use in precision navigation easier. Here we have a quick comparison:

Figure 17-4 shows the traditional face of an OBI. The course-deviation-indicator needle (CDI) shows the position of the aircraft in relation to a given VOR radial or bearing. The omni-bearing selector knob (OBS) is used to select a radial or bearing, and the selector knob (OBS) is used to select a radial or bearing, and the TO/FROM indicator (also known as ambiguity meter) shows whether it is a radial from or a bearing to the station. In this instance the readout indicates that the position of the aircraft is to the right of the 90-degree bearing to the station.

Figure 17-5 illustrates a slightly different version of the same instrument. Here the swinging CDI is replaced by a horizontally moving vertical bar. As shown, the aircraft is located to the right of the 35-degree radial from the station.

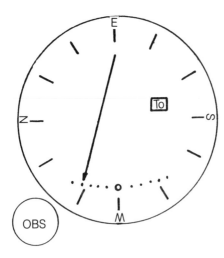

Fig. 17-4. *The traditional face of an omni-bearing indicator (OBI).*

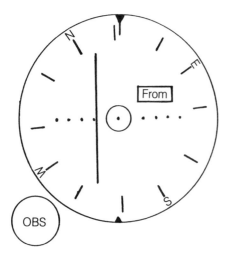

Fig. 17-5. *Modern version of an OBI.*

Figure 17-6 shows the CDI replaced by a system of lighted electronic bars combined with a digital display of the selected radial or bearing. The number of lighted bars indicates the distance of the aircraft from the selected radial or bearing. In our example the pilot is to the right of the 90-degree bearing to the station and must correct to the left to get back on course.

Figures 17-7 and 17-8 do not show a replacement for the OBI but, rather, an additional display capability, which was originated by Collins in its Micro Line. Here, depending on whether the pilot moves the knob to TO, FREQ, or FROM, the display will show the bearing to the selected station on which the aircraft is at this particular moment, or the frequency to which the unit is tuned, or the radial from the station that coincides with the present position of the aircraft. This type of display is extremely useful, especially when the aircraft is close to a station in IFR conditions because,

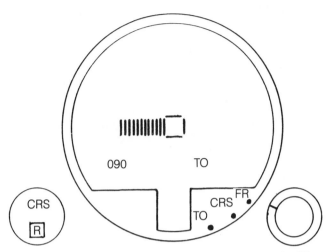

Fig. 17-6. *The face of an omni-bearing indicator designed by Bendix/King for its 2000-avionics series.*

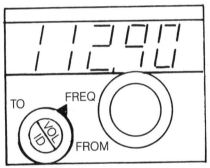

Fig. 17-7. *The face of a Collins Micro Line navigation receiver showing the tuned frequency.*

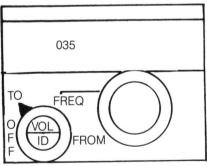

Fig. 17-8. *Collins' nav receiver showing an airplane's current bearing TO the tuned station.*

while the conventional CDI tends to become erratic and hard to read, this readout constantly tells us exactly where we are relative to the station.

TRANSPONDER

Transponders are instruments that are designed to accept interrogation from ground-based radar and, by replying automatically to this interrogation, to enhance the display on the ATC radar scope that represents the aircraft in flight or on the ground. It simplifies the life of the controller but does nothing directly for the pilot except to assure reliable radar contact when that is desirable. With much of the airspace these days being restricted to transponder-equipped aircraft, transponders have become a virtual necessity for cross-country flight (FIG. 17-9).

ENCODING ALTIMETER

Encoding altimeters are an increasingly important adjunct to the transponder. The transponder tells the controller where the aircraft is laterally. When an encoding altimeter is combined with it, it tells the controller at what altitude the aircraft is flying. Again, these systems are of no direct value to the pilot, but they are mandatory equipment in ever-greater portions of today's airspace (FIG. 17-10).

GLIDE-SLOPE AND MARKER-BEACON RECEIVERS

These are instruments for the IFR pilot and are rarely used by anyone flying VFR. The glide-slope receiver is usually combined with the OBI as shown in FIGS. 17-11 and 17-12. In FIG. 17-11 the aircraft is below glide slope and slightly to the left of the localizer centerline. In FIG. 17-12 it is above the glide slope and to the right of the localizer. In other words, the pilot always flies *toward* the needle or bar in order to get back on course and glide slope.

The marker-beacon receiver is simply a light and/or audio signal in the cockpit that is activated when the aircraft passes over the outer, middle, or inner marker, thus giving the pilot precise position indication while on final approach.

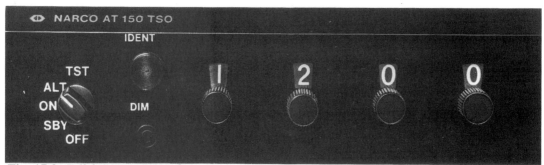

Fig. 17-9. *Full feature transponder.*

Bendix / King

KEA 129 Encoding Altimeter
To 20,000 feet.   TSO′d.

KEA 130 Encoding Altimeter
To 35,000 feet.   TSO′d.

Fig. 17-10. *Encoding altimeters.*

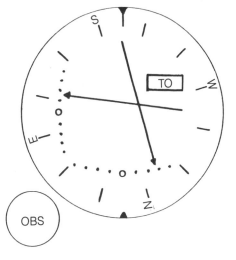

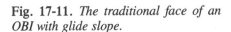

Fig. 17-11. *The traditional face of an OBI with glide slope.*

AUDIO PANELS

These are simply an array of switches that simplify the pilot's tasks when select-ing one or another com or nav radio. Quite a few of the available models incorporate the marker-beacon receiver function (FIG. 17-13).

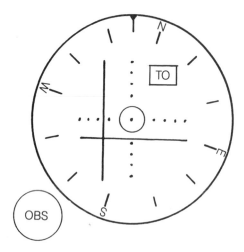

Fig. 17-12. *Modern look of an OBI with glide slope.*

KMA 24 Audio Control Console (actual size)

KMA 24 (International) with HF and AUTO (actual size)

Fig. 17-13. *Many audio panels include a marker beacon receiver.*

AUTOMATIC DIRECTION FINDER (ADF)

The ADF is one of the older navigation instruments. While navcoms and nav receivers operate in the VHF frequency range, the ADF responds to the higher frequency range used by nondirectional beacons (NDB) and by standard broadcast stations. Most units can be tuned to frequencies ranging from 190 to 1,799 kHz. They are equipped with a tuner, a cockpit readout, and voice-reception capability. When tuned to a transmitting station such as an NDB or a standard broadcast station, the

Fig. 17-14. *An automatic direction finder (ADF).*

needle of the cockpit readout will point to the station showing the direction to which the nose of the aircraft must be turned in order to fly to the station. Depending on prevailing atmospheric conditions the ADF is capable of receiving signals from much greater distances than the VHF nav radios; but at certain times, especially at dawn and dusk, the signal being received may be unreliable.

Except for instrument pilots who must fly to or from airports with only ADF approaches, this equipment is not too important for navigation within the continental U.S. (though nice to have). But as soon as we fly beyond our borders into Mexico, South or Central America, or the more remote regions of northern Canada, ADF becomes a *must* because in many of those areas it will be the only navigation aid capable of interacting with ground-based stations (FIG. 17-14).

RADIO MAGNETIC INDICATOR (RMI)

Like ADF, the RMI has been around for a long time. It takes its input from both the VHF nav radios and the ADF and provides the pilot with two simultaneous indications. The fat needle points to the station to which the ADF is tuned, while the skinny one points to the tuned-in VOR. In virtually all RMIs the compass card is actuated by a slaving mechanism, thus always showing the correct magnetic heading without the need for the pilot to make manual adjustments.

DISTANCE MEASURING EQUIPMENT (DME)

DME does just what its name implies: It measures the distance of the aircraft from a given VOR (with DME capability) or VORTAC. Conversely, by computing the rapidity with which this distance decreases or increases, it figures out and displays the actual ground speed in knots (FIG. 17-15).

AUTOPILOT

An autopilot or, at least, a simple wing leveler is a great convenience to anyone spending much time in cross-country flight. By eliminating the constant need to make minor heading corrections, it helps to make prolonged flight a relaxing and enjoyable experience. For the man or woman who flies much of the time single-pilot IFR, an autopilot is a virtual necessity. It simply isn't practical and it is, in fact, unsafe to get

KN 62A DME   Distance/Groundspeed/TTS (GS/T mode)

KN 62A DME   Distance/Frequency (FREQ mode)

Fig. 17-15. *Distance measuring equipment (DME).*

into tight hard-IFR situations and try to control the airplane, usually in turbulence, while at the same time communicating with ATC, studying approach plates, and so on (FIG. 17-16).

Autopilots come in a bewildering variety of degrees of sophistication. The simplest keep the wings level, period. The next step up is a means of coupling the autopilot to the VHF nav receiver, causing it to automatically fly the airplane along a radial or bearing and to make the adjustments necessitated by crosswinds. Or we can include a heading hold, which is controlled by a "bug" on the directional gyro. And from there up we have our choice of all manner of options until we reach the level of the so-called "integrated flight-control systems."

FLIGHT DIRECTOR

Contrary to a popular misconception, flight directors are not autopilots. In simple terms, a flight director is a computer that simultaneously accepts information from all nav and air-data instruments and translates this information into a single readout or pictorial display that tells the pilot what action to take in order to achieve the desired result. In most installations flight directors are then coupled to an autopilot, which accepts their instructions and flies the aircraft accordingly. That, then, is an integrated flight-control

KG 258

Artificial Horizon

KAP 100

Single-Axis Autopilot with panel-mounted computer, mode controller and annunicator. Manual electric trim option available.

KC 190

Digital Computer, mode controller, annunicator

KG 107

Directional Gyro

Fig. 17-16. *A single-axis autopilot.*

system. Though flight directors are occasionally found in high-performance singles, they are primarily an instrument for the sophisticated corporate turboprop or jet.

HORIZONTAL SITUATION INDICATOR (HSI)

An HSI is a highly sophisticated cockpit display that more or less combines the functions of an OBI (usually with glide slope) and an RMI in a single unit. It displays VOR or localizer, ADF, and glide-slope indications in a somewhat different form, so pilots new to the display may find that it takes a bit of time to get used to it. But after a while it can prove to be an extremely useful addition, performing, to a certain extent, like a simplified flight director. HSIs are part of all flight-director systems (FIG. 17-17).

Fig. 17-17. *Horizontal situation indicator (HSI).*

AIRBORNE WEATHER RADAR

The sole practical purpose of airborne weather radar is to point out areas of precipitation, which usually coincide with areas of the greatest turbulence in storms. While it is of little practical value for the VFR flyer, it offers a great advantage to the man who flies instruments with considerable regularity. Reading the weather-radar display takes considerable practice but, once mastered, radar makes flights possible that would be impossible otherwise.

STORMSCOPE

This instrument is designed to perform a function similar to that of airborne weather radar, but it works differently. While weather radar reads precipitation, the Stormscope tells the pilot where there is lightning and approximately how far away that lightning is in relation to the position of the airplane. Since lightning, like precipitation, is likely to occur in the most active and turbulent portions of a storm, this instrument, too, can prove useful in guiding us away from the danger portions of thunderstorms.

HF RADIOS

HF transceivers have a reception and transmitting distance of several thousand miles and are, therefore, necessary in order to maintain communication capability during transoceanic flights. Since they are of little use at other times, they can be rented by pilots planning such a flight as a one-time undertaking.

AREA NAVIGATION SYSTEMS

Fifteen years ago, pilots were content to fly from VOR to VOR, sometimes tuning in an NDB for both course guidance and background music. Loran-C was a bulky, expensive marine navigation system suitable only to large boats. For aviators, the most promising system for air navigation was something called RNAV.

RNAV, which stands for "Random NAVigation," makes it possible to navigate from point to point instead of from nav aid to nav aid. Strictly speaking, the terms *RNAV* and *Area Navigation* apply to any system that allows point-to-point navigation, such as Loran-C, VLF/Omega, inertial navigation systems (INS), DECCA, and NAVSTAR/GPS. However, common usage in the United States has come to limit the term *RNAV* to apply only to those systems that use VOR and DME signals to determine "pseudo-VORTAC" positions.

In essence, all area navigation systems potentially can do the same things, but they do it in different ways, with different accuracy, with different advantages and disadvantages, and for different prices.

At present (1990), only RNAV (the VOR kind) and Loran-C are within the price range of most private pilots. Fortunately, the accuracy of both systems can rival the higher-priced RNAV varieties, and there are a number of exciting recent developments, particularly with Loran-C-type area navigation systems, which may change the way most pilots navigate.

RNAV

Until it was eclipsed in recent years by Loran-C, RNAV was the darling of inexpensive area navigation systems. It still has a few advantages over Loran-C, so don't discount it yet if you're considering buying an area nav system (FIG. 17-18).

What RNAV does is electronically relocate any VOR with DME capability or VOR-TAC from its actual location to any other location within the reception distance of the nav aid. It thereby simplifies off-airways precision navigation, whether VFR or IFR.

In fact, the FAA has established RNAV routes and approaches to many airports. You may legally fly these routes and approaches IFR if you have an RNAV approved for IFR. You can also use your RNAV to fly direct between any two points. When you file your flight plan, you simply add "/R" behind your aircraft designator, and this tells ATC you have random navigation capability.

There are two advantages of RNAV over Loran-C. The first is the above-mentioned IFR approval. Only a few Loran-Cs have been approved for en route IFR and none for approaches. The other is the "Mid-Continent Gap," a region roughly covering the Mountain Time Zone and southern Texas, which has poor Loran-C coverage. (Since Loran-C was originally a marine navigation system, it was designed to give good reception along the coasts.) The Government has promised to fill in this reception gap in the near future, but who knows when it will actually be done.

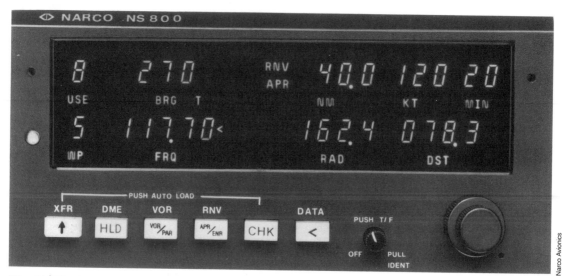

Fig. 17-18. *Area navigation unit, or RNAV, which uses VOR and DME signals.*

Loran-C

Despite the above-mentioned disadvantages, Loran-C has tickled the fancy of the general aviation community. It has become so popular because it does the same job as RNAV (except for the approved IFR) and it does it better, easier, and cheaper (FIGS. 17-19, 17-20, 17-21 and 17-22).

A Loran transmitting chain has one master and three secondary stations. For a Loran-C receiver to work, it must receive the master and at least two of the secondaries. It then calculates its position by measuring the differences between the reception of transmissions from the master and the secondaries. By also looking at where it has been, the aircraft heading, and the true airspeed, it can figure out average ground speed and wind.

So how can it be used by the cross-country pilot? Armed with long/lat coordinates you are in business. A variety of sources, such as Flight Guide, Jeppesen, airport/facilities directories, and more, contain that information. It would be a pilot's preference to find the source that best suits his needs and budget.

Let's take a typical Point A to Point B trip; Point A is your home airport, and you have business at Point B. On the ramp at the airport, your plane's Loran-C automatically displays "A" coordinates as you find and key in the "B" coordinates. In a matter of seconds the unit shows the direction and how far you will fly. After takeoff you will also have a variety of time computations available, and your flight will be guided by a course indicator like the familiar nav needle.

With your business out of the way at "B" you plan on returning home, but a call to the office reveals a regular customer at Point "C" needs to see you that afternoon. Simple enough because you have traveled to "C" several times before and you have

Fig. 17-19. *Loran-C navigation system, which uses a credit-card-size Jeppesen NavData database card to provide access to airports, VORs, NDBs, and intersections in the United States.*

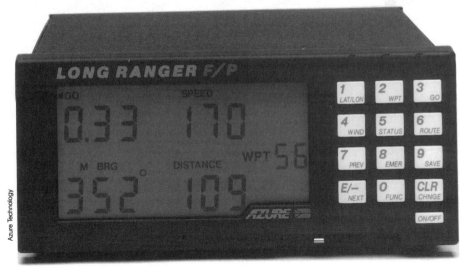

Fig. 17-20. *Loran-C navigation system, which can be both installed in the aircraft's instrument panel and easily removed.*

stored the information in the Loran unit. On the way to "C" thunderstorms move in and you have to head home after all. Again, "A" coordinates have been stored, and you just call them up and head for home.

During each flight you have flown the shortest route, saving time, fuel, and wear and tear on the airplane. It was done with one radio; not a couple of nav receivers and a DME or even an ADF—they would have required more busy work. And with less busy work a pilot can fly cross-country more easily and, ultimately, safely.

Lorans are available in a wide price range, with numerous options from which to

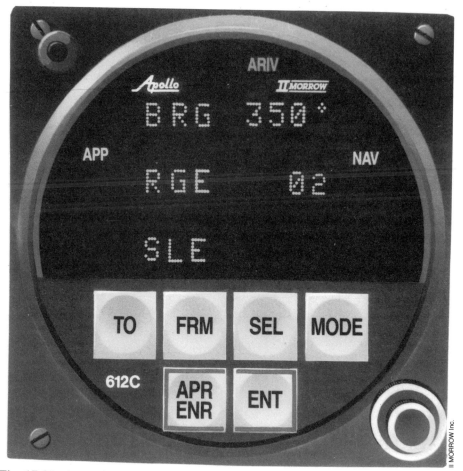

Fig. 17-21. *A round Loran-C designed to fit in a 3" diameter panel mount. Built-in database warns the pilot before penetrating special use airspace.*

choose. Needless to say, it pays to do some homework and decide beforehand what features you want and then shop around.

Two features that are considered absolute "musts" by many pilots are a database and automatic triad ability. Databases store waypoints for you—typically airports, VORs, and intersections. The least expensive units have about 6,000 waypoints in the databases; higher priced models have over 14,000.

Automatic triad ability means that the Loran itself picks the best secondary stations it needs to navigate. Some cheap Lorans require the pilot to select the secondaries. Such systems are suitable for slow boats, but not for airplanes, especially single-pilot airplanes in bad weather.

There are over 20 different Loran-C receivers on the market, some of which are

Fig. 17-22. *Altitude encoder, which interfaces with a Loran-C to provide "3-dimensional navigation."*

portable or even hand-held (FIG. 17-23). These models may be particularly attractive to pilots who rent airplanes and wish to take along their own area navigation system.

Moving Maps

Combining databases, a map display, and Loran signals seems almost inevitable in this age of computers. Since the first moving-map display for general aviation, Eventide's Argus, became available in 1988, numerous other moving maps have come onto the market, including one designed to work with a laptop computer.

Moving maps were pioneered in the 1950s for military aircraft, but their cost was such that only the military could afford them. Today, the cost of moving maps has come down to the range of many general aviation pilots.

The main purpose of a moving map is to give you a picture of the navigational landscape as you fly over it. ARSAs, TCAs, ATAs, prohibited and restricted areas, VORs, airports, and airways are all depicted on the map, which automatically updates its display as you fly (FIGS. 17-24 and 17-25).

The value of moving maps is the increased situational awareness and the other

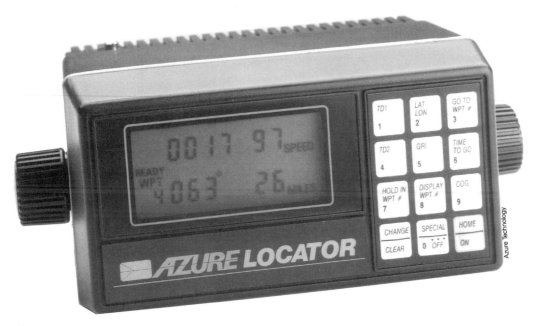

Fig. 17-23. *A fully portable Loran-C navigation system for pilots who rent airplanes, own one or more airplanes, fly nonelectrical airplanes, or have a limited budget.*

information that they provide the pilot. Navigation, flying through complex controlled airspace, and flight planning become almost simple; getting lost, virtually impossible.

An interesting, and less expensive, variation of a dedicated moving map is called LapMap. LapMap is a software program that allows you to use virtually any IBM-PC compatible laptop computer with a Loran-C receiver. The LapMap functions like any other moving-map display, updating itself from the aircraft's Loran. The computer can also be used for other tasks, including flight planning, DUAT weather access, and general business and personal uses. The disadvantage of LapMap is that you have this hunk of equipment on your lap or on the seat beside you. The advantages are its price, the size of its screen, and its portability.

Hand-Held Transceivers

Looking like walkie-talkies, hand-held transceivers are actually portable, battery-operated VHF navcoms (FIG. 17-26). In recent years, they have become important pieces of cockpit equipment, and many pilots won't fly IFR without one. Nonowner pilots find them particularly nice to have when renting an airplane.

The purpose of a hand-held transceiver is as a backup for panel-mounted radios. Two-way communication failure procedures are specified in *AIM*, but that doesn't make "silent running" particularly enjoyable IFR. And the com failure procedures

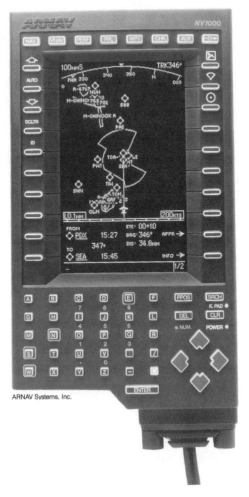

Fig. 17-24. *Loran-C-based navigation management system includes a moving map display and uses a Jeppesen Nav-Data database card.*

assume your navigation equipment is still working. With a complete electrical failure, navigation becomes rather difficult when you're IMC. A portable transceiver allows you to communicate with ATC as well as navigate using VORs.

"Glass Cockpits"

As most pilots know, the newest airliners, corporate jets, and helicopters now come equipped with cathode-ray tubes instead of electromechanical flight and system instruments. These so-called "glass cockpits" have been the envy of general aviation pilots for years, but the price has always kept them away. If all goes well, they probably won't have to wait much longer to equip their aircraft with this high-tech wizardry.

One company, Waypoint Electronics of Corona, California, is working on prototypes of a Flight Management System (FMS), an Engine Indication/Caution Advisory

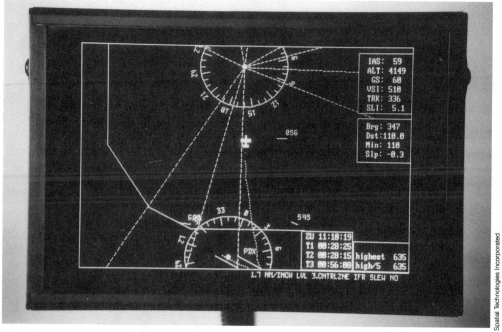

Fig. 17-25. *Multifunction display of the Spatial Dynamic Imaging (SDI) Navigation and Flight Management System in moving map mode. SDI interfaces with Loran-C, Omega/VLF, GPS, a database with over 100,000 waypoints, and add-on Air Data and Flight Dynamics Systems. The pilot can view his real-time position in relation to terrain, man-made obstructions, course lines, airways, geography, nav aids, and airports.*

System (EICAS), and an Electronic Flight Instrument System (EFIS), all aimed at the low-budget end of the market.

Reduced weight, redundancy, and the ability to display information in different formats are the main advantages of "glass cockpit" equipment. Price has not been their strong suit in the past. Doubtless the development of lower-priced systems will catch the interest of other manufacturers, and we'll soon see numerous products of this type on the market.

LONG-RANGE TANKS

While any aircraft is theoretically suitable for cross-country flight, those that have a no-reserve range of 500 nm or less are, at best, impractical and, at worst, an invitation to danger. The greatest safety feature for cross-country operations, aside from a proficient pilot and a well-maintained aircraft, is an ample fuel supply. As long as there is plenty of fuel on board, unforeseen complications can be dealt with safely and efficiently. Some light aircraft come with either "standard" or "long-range" tanks, and the extra fuel capacity is always worth the few extra dollars invested.

Fig. 17-26. *Hand-held transceiver with 760 communication, 200 navigation, and 20 memory channels.*

Sporty's Pilot Shop

EXHAUST-GAS-TEMPERATURE GAUGE

EGTs and the more sophisticated engine analyzers, are described in detail in chapter 14, "The High Price of Fuel." It can be a single-probe installation or an engine analyzer designed for a twin with six-cylinder engines.

OXYGEN

Oxygen is discussed in chapter 18, "Tackling the Mountains." While permanent oxygen installations may not be worth their cost to the pilot who spends most of his flying hours away from high mountain terrain, a portable auxiliary unit should be standard equipment on any airplane used with any frequency for extended cross-country flights.

ANGLE-OF-ATTACK INDICATORS

Considering their usefulness and the increase in flying safety that they provide, it seems strange how seldom we come across such an installation in a light aircraft. The function of angle-of-attack indicators is described in some detail in chapter 18.

ELECTRONIC FUEL-CONTROL SYSTEMS

Unlike fuel gauges, these systems read the exact fuel flow at a point where the fuel enters the carburetor or injection system. This information is transmitted to a computer, which has previously been told the amount of fuel on board at the time of engine start-up. The computer automatically deducts the fuel being used from the original amount, and a cockpit display shows the pilot: a) the amount of fuel remaining, b) the current rate of fuel flow, and c) the length of time the pilot can continue to fly at the current rate of fuel consumption with the amount of fuel remaining in the tanks. Though not exactly cheap, it is a useful instrument for the pilot who spends several hundred hours a year flying long distances.

FLASHLIGHT

Even though no night flying may be anticipated, no cross-country flight of any distance should be undertaken without a flashlight and extra fresh batteries on board. Only too often does it simply seem to make sense to continue to fly for an extra hour or so after sunset in order to reach a desired destination. Yet once the sun goes down, reading charts and otherwise finding things in the cockpit becomes quite difficult without a flashlight, since the available lighting in most light aircraft leaves much to be desired.

18
Tackling the
Mountains

PILOTS WHOSE FLYING EXPERIENCE IS LIMITED TO THE PLAINS STATES OR to those parts of the country where rolling hills rarely rise more than a few thousand feet above sea level only too frequently get into trouble when they are, for the first time, confronted by real mountains such as the Rockies. There is something awe-inspiring about just looking at those Sectional charts, which are printed mostly in varying shades of brown. One's mind tends to try to visualize the towering peaks and rock-rimmed canyons which, when actually encountered, will strain the capabilities of both pilot and airplane (FIG. 18-1).

Considerations come to mind that have never before seemed important. What is the service ceiling of the airplane, and how long will it take to climb to those rarefied altitudes? How high will we have to be prepared to fly in order to clear the terrain? Will oxygen be needed? What are the special considerations with respect to takeoffs and landings at airports the elevation of which may be as high as 6,000, 7,000 feet or more? And what about the weather? Is it similar to that to which we are accustomed? And which is better, VFR or IFR?

The fact is that mountain flying is different and more demanding. It requires an understanding of the performance parameters of the airplane, expert chart reading, and precise navigation often without the assistance of electronic nav aids. Above all it

Fig. 18-1. *A mountainous encounter.*

requires preparation unless one wants to join those too many aircraft that have disappeared, some without ever being found.

Let's take it one item at a time.

AIRCRAFT

As far as the aircraft is concerned, three parameters are of primary importance: *Range, service ceiling, and rate of climb.*

Flying the Rockies frequently involves covering long distances where no adequate airports are available for refueling. In addition, especially on westerly flights, the headwinds can often reach velocities that can seriously reduce the normal range. Therefore, caution dictates that whatever we normally consider an adequate fuel reserve should be increased by 100 percent or at least by one hour.

The service ceiling is the altitude at which an aircraft, at gross, will still climb 100 fpm at full power (FIG. 18-2). Many light aircraft have a service ceiling that is below the highest terrain in places like Colorado, Utah, and parts of California. But in practice, given enough time, an airplane will climb considerably higher than its service ceiling because by the time it has reached that altitude much fuel has been burned

Fig. 18-2. How high will we have to be prepared to fly in order to clear the terrain?

and, even if it was at gross at takeoff, it will be quite a bit lighter. (As an example, I once coaxed a Piper Comanche to 22,600 feet, at which time it was still climbing at 10 fpm.) In fact, an airplane will continue to climb at a constantly decreasing rate until the combination of full power, the appropriately lean mixture, and an attitude similar to best-angle-of-climb will result in level flight.

The rate of climb suddenly becomes a major factor (FIG. 18-3). When taking off from, say, Denver and flying west toward that 14,000-foot-high wall of mountains, it is important to know if the airplane can gain the necessary 8,000 or 9,000 feet in the available distance or if we have to fly S-turns or even 360s in order to get up high enough to be safe.

Pilots flying light twins should also keep in mind the single-engine ceiling. Most light twins cannot maintain an adequate altitude to clear the terrain in this part of the country in the event of an engine-out situation. If this happens, the only alternative may be a controlled single-engine glide toward whatever lower terrain may be available.

TAKEOFFS AND LANDINGS

Trying to get down to or up from a high-altitude airport on a warm summer day is something that must be experienced to be believed (FIG. 18-4). In order to become

Fig. 18-3. *The rate of climb suddenly becomes a major factor.*

Fig. 18-4. *Trying to get up from a high-altitude airport on a hot summer day is something that must be experienced to be believed.*

familiar with the effects of density altitude, pilots would do well to make their first such landing and takeoff at a large airport such as Denver's Stapleton Field (elevation 5,330 feet) or at Albuquerque's Sunport (elevation 5,352). Because of the length of their runways one may not notice the much higher-than-normal TAS and ground speed during the landing. But what is educational is to attempt a takeoff there on a hot summer afternoon. It takes forever for the airplane to reach liftoff speed and then, when it is barely airborne, it simply refuses to climb for what seems an inordinately long period of time. But it's good practice because it helps to instill respect for the effects of density altitude, which inanimate charts and figures never seem to generate.

It must be understood that while density altitude affects the TAS and ground speed, it does not affect IAS and altimeter readings. No matter what the density altitude, the altimeter of an aircraft on the ground at a 6,000-foot-high airport will read 6,000 feet when adjusted to prevailing atmospheric conditions. But if the temperature is, say, 90 °F, the density altitude (the altitude that affects the performance of the aircraft and engine) is 9,200 feet. According to a generally accepted rule of thumb, the takeoff and landing distance for a nonturbocharged piston aircraft increases by 25 percent for each 1,000-foot increase in density altitude. Thus, a Cessna Skylane, which has a 50-foot-obstacle-clearance distance of 1,350 feet at sea level at standard temperature conditions (59 °F), will require 3,105 feet under the conditions described above.

Pilots having heard of density altitude, but unfamiliar with it in practice, frequently feel that they should take off or land at a higher IAS than they would at sea level. This is a misconception. The IAS is not affected by density altitude, only TAS and ground speed are. Thus, if the normal indicated liftoff speed is, say, 60 or 65 knots, it remains at that figure regardless of the altitude or temperature. Actual liftoff or landing speed in terms of TAS and ground speed, on the other hand, will be much higher. Similarly, the indicated stall speed remains unchanged despite the fact that the aircraft will actually stall at a higher TAS or ground speed.

After liftoff it is a good idea to keep the nose low and keep flying in a straight line until added speed has been gained. An attempt at a steep climb out or sharp turn shortly after breaking ground can result in a stall at too low an altitude to effect recovery.

When wishing to leave a really high airport—especially one with a runway of only average length—on a hot day, it may be necessary to take on only enough fuel to get to the nearest airport at a lower elevation and, in the case of passengers, it may become necessary to fly out one at a time. (An example of this kind of airport is Leadville, Colorado. Its elevation is 9,927, and the runway is only 4,800 feet long. On a 90-degree day it has a density altitude of around 13,000 feet.) Ideally, one should plan departures from high altitude airports, even those not as extreme as Leadville, for the very early morning hours when the air is still cool and smooth.

Mixture control is important. Many of us are so used to always using full rich mixture for takeoff that it never occurs to us to lean the mixture just because this time the takeoff is at a higher altitude. The recommended technique is to go through the usual runup, then stand on the brakes and advance the throttle to full power in order to activate the effect of the enrichment valve. Then lean the mixture. If the airplane is equipped with an EGT gauge, lean to peak, and then enrich to about 100 or 150 degrees on the rich side of peak. Then reduce throttle, release the brakes, and start the takeoff. If there is no EGT gauge in the airplane, apply full throttle, lean until the engine sputters, then enrich until the engine runs smooth again and possibly just a tiny bit more. In airplanes with a fixed-pitch propeller, the best idea is to enrich until maximum rpm is achieved. Then use that setting for takeoff.

Leaning of the mixture during takeoff from airports with a high density altitude is vitally important because, when operating too rich, the sparkplugs may foul within a minute or two, causing the engine to lose power and possibly quit altogether before a safe altitude has been reached. But even if the sparkplugs don't foul, the engine, when operated too rich, cannot develop its full potential power and may actually be unable to produce sufficient acceleration to permit liftoff.

INSTRUMENTS

In addition to the usual navcom equipment, a number of other instruments take on increased importance when flying the third of the country consisting of the Rocky Mountains, the Sierra Nevada, the Trinity Alps, the Cascades, and related mountain ranges. With VORs being few and far between here by comparison to other parts of the country, an ADF is often helpful. Virtually every little village and hamlet has a standard broadcast station that can be used for navigation by an ADF-equipped aircraft.

An EGT gauge, though useful regardless of where we fly, takes on added importance as has already been emphasized earlier in this chapter. Not only does it help to achieve the right mixture both for takeoff and to cruise while using the least amount of fuel, it also helps to set up the appropriate mixture prior to landing at airports with high elevations. During the descent phase a mixture setting of roughly 100 degrees on the rich side of peak is a good precaution—just in case we find that we have to go around, needing all the power we can get.

One instrument that despite its high degree of usefulness, is rarely found on light general aviation aircraft is an angle-of-attack indicator. It simply consists of a probe, similar to the stall-warning probe, plus a cockpit readout with a moving needle that indicates whether the attitude of the aircraft is within safe limits for climb, cruise, or descent relative to the airspeed. It gives the pilot ample advance warning when a high angle of attack puts the aircraft close to its stall. Mountain flying often involves receiving misleading cues from sloping terrain and horizons consisting of high ridges. A pilot flying toward such a ridge can easily be seduced into thinking that he is climbing at a much shallower angle than is actually the case. Once one gets used to using an angle-of-attack indicator, simply flying its needle becomes so easy that we may wonder how we ever managed to get along without it. These indicators, by the way, are not affected by density altitude and produce reliable readings regardless of altitude or atmospheric conditions. They are not particularly expensive, and pilots who do a fair amount of cross-country flying would be well advised to consider investing in one.

OXYGEN

And then there is oxygen. Regardless of the legalities involved, long periods of time spent at a high altitude will result in severe headaches and may often lead to a gradual loss of efficiency caused by a reduction in the ability to make instant decisions and then act upon them quickly. Though we may carefully plan our route through the mountains to avoid the need to climb above 12,500 feet, weather or wind conditions may force us to higher altitudes. Narrow cloud banks obscuring mountain ridges, uncomfortable turbulence, or simple but continued updrafts are but a few of the reasons that may cause us to want or have to climb to, say, 15,000 or 16,000 feet. When that happens we have no way of knowing how long we may have to stay up there, and a portable oxygen unit, even if used only intermittently, becomes a vital safety feature.

Pilots planning to fly the mountains IFR will find that it is impossible to do so without oxygen. In many areas the MEAs are 15,000 or 16,000 feet for considerable distances, and when the MEA is for some reason not available, the IFR pilot may find himself cleared to even higher cruising levels. Attempting such a flight without oxygen is not only illegal, it is also dangerous and just plain stupid.

IFR VERSUS VFR

The choice between IFR and VFR depends on personal preference and, of course, the weather. IFR, assuming the aircraft has oxygen on board, simply means that we can climb to an altitude at which obstacles are no longer a consideration and cruise at that altitude until it is time for the approach to our destination. The trouble is that if the weather is actually IFR, and it often is at altitude with VFR conditions below, we have no way of knowing what is beneath us in case an emergency develops and we have to somehow find a way down. Even without such an emergency, a pilot planning an IFR approach to an airport surrounded by all kinds of high-altitude rocks better be prepared and able to fly such an approach with great precision in order to be certain that he keeps a safe distance from invisible obstacles. Quite honestly, except for the highly proficient, making a nonprecision approach (such as a VOR or ADF approach) to an airport located in a valley between high mountain peaks in actual IFR conditions can be a somewhat hair-raising experience.

Most pilots who operate habitually in the mountains prefer to do so VFR. When VFR one can stay lower and be aware of the surrounding terrain and of acceptable places to land—just in case. Many of the VFR charts include safe VFR routes through mountain passes (lines consisting of strings of blue diamonds) when it becomes necessary to stay low for whatever reason. In addition, flying the mountains is such a visually exciting experience that it seems a shame to miss all that by sitting way up there like a miniature airliner.

A word of warning! The very beauty of the country below may cause us to wish to drop down and do a bit of aerial sightseeing. Except for pilots with intimate knowledge of the terrain this can be a very bad idea. Granted, it's an exciting experience to be down low and look up at the towering cliffs, but many an airplane, when suddenly confronted by rapidly rising terrain, may be unable to climb fast enough to clear whatever is ahead and may not actually be in a position to do a last-minute 180. If the thought of studying the Indian pueblos and cliff dwellings (FIGS. 18-5 and 18-6), the goosenecks of the San Juan River, the breathtaking peaks at Monument Valley (FIG. 18-7), or the depths of Canyon de Chelly from a low-flying airplane turns you on, park your own airplane and make use of the expert services of the various operators who specialize in flying sightseers. Those pilots know the country, and they fly the kind of STOL aircraft that can deal with whatever situations may arise. It may cost a few extra dollars, but at least you'll live to remember the experience for years to come.

WEATHER

Weather in the mountains varies from that in other parts of the country. Visibilities are often enormous, with anywhere from 50 to 100 miles being not at all unusual. Haze and fog are rarities, and all that pollution that envelops much of the rest of the country is absent. The result is that one has to relearn one's ability to judge distances. Some major mountain or other easily definable landmark will seem quite close. But if we fly and fly and keep on flying for what seems to be forever, it's still some distance away. The trick is not to trust one's eyes until one has gotten used to it. Instead, check the location of the landmark on the chart and relate it to the known (we hope) position of the airplane. Then, at least, we won't be surprised when something that looked like it was 10 minutes away turns out in actuality to take an hour.

In contrast to the flatlands, where weather systems tend to be large and slow-moving in the summer and small but fast-moving in the winter, the exact opposite is true in the Rocky Mountain states. Here, summer usually brings relatively small and fast-

Fig. 18-5. *The Acoma Pueblo, commonly referred to as Sky City, built atop a mesa. The vertical cliffs make it virtually inaccessible.*

Fig. 18-6. *Ancient Indian cliff dwellings at Puye Cliffs.*

Fig. 18-7. *Monument Valley as seen from a low-flying airplane.*

moving systems during the summer months, while winter and early spring may produce large areas of clouds and precipitation that often hang around for the better part of a day or even longer.

The small and fast-moving summer storms frequently develop in areas where there are no reporting stations and may, therefore, remain unannounced in sequence reports. The safest way to deal with them is to fly around them rather than over or under. Overflying a cloud deck of any consequence can easily prove to be a sucker trap. The tops may look as if they are low enough, but once one gets up there they often continue to rise along the route until they may effectively exceed the climb capability of the airplane. Then the only way out is to turn back, assuming they have not also risen behind the airplane, or to file instruments. Simple punching through, hoping against hope that we'll soon come out in the clear on the other end, is not only illegal, but foolish. Remember, you can't go down. The lower clouds could easily be full of rocks.

Underflying, on the other hand, unless the ridges ahead are visible and clear of clouds, can easily turn into a dead end. Clouds have a way of clinging to the mountain tops and higher ridges so it may not be possible to find a pass to get through. When approaching such a pass, which appears clear even though the higher mountains on either side are obscured, it is acceptable to fly up close to it to get an idea of the conditions beyond. But actually flying through the pass, we should make sure that the next one—the one leading out of the valley toward which we are headed—is also clear (unless there is an airport in that valley where we could land if things turn sour).

Thunderstorms tend to build with great regularity during the afternoon hours of summer and fall days. They rarely combine into squall lines. Instead, they rise to impressive heights in solitary splendor. True to the character of all thunderstorms, they contain vicious winds, rain, and hail and are to be avoided at all costs. But, being clearly defined, they are easily circumvented—assuming, of course, that there is sufficient fuel in the tanks to permit such detours.

WIND

Mountain winds are greatly affected by terrain configuration, both with reference to velocity and to direction (FIG. 18-8). When air moves across mountain ranges at any appreciable speed it usually remains quite smooth on the upwind side, though the velocity will increase at a steady rate as the air is pushed higher and higher. By the time it reaches the ridge, it may have achieved nearly double its initial velocity. When flying within the wind toward a ridge, we are likely to experience strong and continued updrafts that may cause the aircraft to climb several thousand feet without any added power.

Once past the ridge, the air will tumble down like a giant waterfall, producing considerable turbulence and downdrafts. When the airplane reaches this point it is a good idea to increase power if some reserve is still available and to try and stay as high as possible to minimize the effects of the downdrafts and turbulence. It is frequently

Fig. 18-8. *Mountain winds are greatly affected by terrain.*

suggested that one fly away from such a ridge at a 45-degree angle, but my personal experience is that this only tends to prolong the time spent exposed to the unpleasant effects of the winds on the lee side of the ridge.

Mountain passes and narrow valleys may produce a venturi effect, increasing the speed of the wind to such a degree that a slow aircraft may not be able to make any acceptable headway when flying in the opposite direction. The only available alternative may prove to be to try and climb to a level above the surrounding mountain tops where the venturi effect is minimized.

When approaching a ridge from the downwind side, then, it is a good idea to do so at a 45-degree angle. We are faced with having to fight the turbulence and downdrafts while trying to climb to a level above the top of the ridge or, if already up there, to maintain our altitude. Though flying at such an angle will increase the time of exposure to the negative effects of the wind, it permits us an easy out if we should find that we can't make the ridge. When downdrafts prevent us from reaching or staying at a safe altitude, we can then simply make a 90-degree turn away from the ridge which, under those wind conditions, is easier than having to make a complete 180.

When caught in what appears to be a prolonged downdraft, don't pull up the nose. If anything, push it down to gain speed and climb capability (relative to the descending air) and minimize the amount of time spent in the downdraft. But don't overdo it. This is no time to exceed the maneuvering speed (green arc) or rough-air-penetration speed.

When flying along a valley where the wind is blowing at more or less right angles, always fly on the downwind side of the valley (the upwind side of the mountains) because the continuous updraft will result in what amounts to a nearly free ride. We may find that we can throttle back and trim the nose down and still maintain altitude as well as speed. This also simplifies the problem in the event that we have to turn back for one reason or another. We would be turning toward the center of the valley and, at the same time, into the wind, reducing the turning radius of the aircraft, which may prove important if the valley in question is narrow.

During the hot summer months it is a good idea to plan all one's flying for the morning hours, the earlier the better. First of all, at that time no thunderstorms have started to form, while those from last night will have dissipated. In addition, the thermal activity and related turbulence are at a minimum. Later in the day, especially during the early afternoon, mountain flying can easily get so rough that it becomes a tiring chore for the pilot and passengers alike. (By the way, when taking passengers who are unfamiliar with travel in light aircraft, be sure to have some "barfbags" on board. Unfortunately, they may prove necessary.)

NIGHT FLYING

Night flying in the mountains is only for experienced mountain fliers. Nothing is quite as black as a moonless night in that clear hazeless air over those endless stretches of uninhabited rocks. The mountains themselves are hard to see and, unless we are at an altitude that is safely above the highest obstacle anywhere in the vicinity, the mountain ahead may come into view too late for us to take effective evasive action.

If such flying is necessary and if, for one reason or another, it is impossible to fly at a safe altitude above the highest peaks in the area, use a VFR chart and find VOR radials or bearings that run along lower terrain and safely bypass any of the high peaks. Then fly conscientiously along that radial or bearing, keeping the needle perfectly centered. It works, but it is not a comfortable experience. If at all possible, waiting until morning must be considered a much better idea.

CHARTS

Regardless of whether operating IFR or VFR, always have VFR charts (preferably Sectionals) in the cockpit of the aircraft. In case some unforeseen situation develops, it is absolutely necessary to be able to determine the topography below. In such a situation the low-altitude radio-facility charts are simply no use at all.

SUMMARY

Flying the mountains can be breathtakingly beautiful, but it must not be taken lightly. Sloppy flying technique, slipshod preplanning, or inadequate maintenance of the aircraft or its systems and instruments can easily turn a first mountain flight into the last. Pilots who habitually operate in this area have learned to have respect for the terrain, weather, and wind. They fly safely year in and year out and, assuming adequate precaution, there is no reason for us not to join them.

TWENTY MOUNTAIN-FLYING TIPS FROM YOUR FRIENDLY FAA

1. Plan an en route stop at one of the foothill airports prior to entering mountainous terrain.
2. Consult a local accident-prevention counselor for advice on routing, etc.
3. Check the weather over your entire route. Do not attempt the flight if winds aloft near the mountain tops exceed 40% of the aircraft's stall speed. If weather is marginal, delay the trip.
4. Plan trips during the early morning or late afternoon hours.
5. Use current charts, preferably Sectionals or state air navigation charts. Radio navigation may prove difficult due to high terrain.
6. Route your trips over valleys wherever possible.
7. Learn as much as possible about your intended destination airport.
8. Carry enough fuel to make your trip with ample reserve.
9. Know your aircraft's performance and limitations.
10. Make proper corrections for pressure and temperature effects on takeoff and rate of climb.
11. Check weight and balance of loaded aircraft before takeoff.
12. Your normal horizon is near the base of the mountains.
13. Beware of rapidly rising terrain and dead ends in valleys and canyons.
14. Downdrafts and turbulence occur on the lee side of mountains and ridges.
15. Approach a ridge at an angle so you can turn away if you encounter a downdraft.
16. Maintain flying speed in downdrafts.
17. Carry survival equipment. Even summer nights are cold in the higher altitudes.
18. Be prepared for downdrafts and turbulence on final approach.
19. Use power on approaches.
20. FILE A FLIGHT PLAN.

19
Flight Number Seven

Date: July 21, 1977.
Pilot: Male, age 27, journalist.
License: Commercial, SEL, instrument.
Pilot-In-Command Time: 1,076 hours.
Aircraft: Beechcraft Sundowner C23.
Flight: From Anchorage to Barrow, Alaska.
Purpose of Flight: Pleasure.

The trip began in late June, when the pilot and three passengers lifted off early in the morning from Merrill Field in Anchorage. They flew northward along the Susitna River past Talkeetna, followed Windy Pass through the Alaska Range (dominated by 20,320-foot-high Mount McKinley), overflew Nenana near Fairbanks, and after four hours of flight time, stopped for lunch and refueling in Bettles. An hour later, they lifted off under clear skies for Wiley Post-Will Rogers Memorial Airport in Barrow. They took Anatuvuk Pass through the Brooks Range and flew the last 250 nm straight to Barrow over relatively flat tundra. Their route roughly paralleled the Alaska pipeline on its way from Valdez to Prudhoe Bay, but most of the time they were too far west to see it. Total flight time from Anchorage to Barrow was exactly seven hours.

They planned to stay on the North Slope for four weeks and visit some of the native villages within a 150-mile radius of Barrow. A friend in Barrow put them up while they were there. In the villages, they planned to stay in camping tents.

At 71°17'12″ North, Barrow is the northernmost town in Alaska, the United States, and the Western Hemisphere (FIG. 19-1). The weather in Barrow, like the rest of the North Slope, is greatly influenced by the polar ice pack in the Chukchi and Beaufort Seas. Most years, the ice pack moves off the coast of Barrow by the middle of June, permitting ships to bring supplies to the town and the oil facilities in Prudhoe Bay. In 1977 the ice was slow to move away from the coast. When the pilot and passengers of N2045L arrived on June 29th, the ice still hugged the shore line and stretched as far as the eye could see to the north.

Despite earlier assurances that a local charter operator would sell them AVGAS, this turned out to be incorrect because, as the operator explained, he would get into trouble with the FAA and his insurance company if he sold fuel to anyone. The pilot's only recourse was to buy his own fuel directly from the supplier who was located, not at the airfield, but by the town's boat docks about a mile away.

The supplier told the pilot he had to provide his own container, pump, and transportation to the airfield. Fortunately, the pilot's friend had a pump, needed to buy a fuel drum for later use, and could borrow a pick-up truck. The fuel supplier mentioned he did have a few "previously owned" 50-gallon drums for sale. Unfortunately, the selection was not very good. All the drums were dented, rusty, and contaminated. The pilot chose the barrel with the least rust and fewest dents, emptied it of as much of its foul-smelling contents as he could, and had it filled with 96-octane AVGAS.

The pilot knew the best way to filter the fuel was through a shammy, but he didn't have one. Nor were there any on sale at the small store in Barrow, so he phoned the airplane's owner, who bought one in Anchorage and had it air-freighted to Barrow the next day.

After a few attempts, the pilot and his friend became adept at priming the pump and filtering the fuel through the shammy. The shammy worked extremely well, catching all the water, paint chips, and other bits of dirt and crud the pump coughed up from the drum. The pilot was fairly satisfied the fuel he pumped into the Sundowner was as pure as any of the blue-colored AVGAS it had ever received. Just in case it wasn't, he made his first flight after refueling from the barrel in the traffic pattern at Barrow. The engine ran smoothly.

SOFT FIELD OPERATIONS

They soon started flying to the scattered outlying villages on the west side of the North Slope. Several trips were made to Nuiqsut, Wainwright, and Atksook. The 4,600-foot gravel strip at Nuiqsut gave the pilot his first real lesson in soft field operations. Although the runway surface was firm enough for the small Beechcraft, the parking area at its southern end was sandy and soft. Rolling out from his first landing there, the pilot cautiously allowed his taxi speed to drop too low as he did a 180-degree turn to park the airplane. All three tires dug into the sand.

No amount of rocking or pushing helped. Even a careful application of full power failed to move the airplane. Finally, the pilot had to seek assistance in the village. The

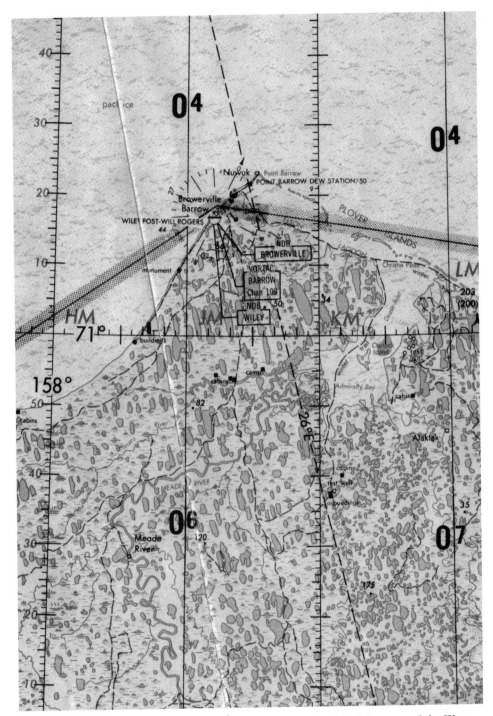

Fig. 19-1. *Barrow is the northernmost town in Alaska, the United States, and the Western Hemisphere.*

only powered vehicle in Nuiqsut, besides snow mobiles, was a six-wheeled all-terrain vehicle, which turned out to be perfect. In seconds, the airplane was back on the firm surface at the end of the runway. The pilot decided to park the airplane on the runway from then on. There wasn't any other traffic to interfere with anyway.

Prior to leaving Anchorage, the Sundowner's owner had shown the pilot a small tool kit he always carried with him when flying in the bush. The kit included a metal file, which the owner said the pilot should use to smooth out the nicks the propeller would invariably incur from landing on gravel strips. The pilot soon learned that a nicked propeller cost him 100 to 200 rpm at takeoff power and 4-5 knots in cruise. He made it a habit to file out all the nicks before taking off.

After three weeks, the pilot was starting to feel like a genuine bush pilot (although he was realistic enough to know he wasn't). He was able to recognize some of the more prominent land features around the Barrow area—Teshekpuk Lake, Admiralty Bay, the Meade River, and others—and this made navigation easier. Although the tundra is dotted with thousands of shallow lakes, the area is geographically classified as a desert because it gets so little rainfall. Most of the time, the lakes are frozen. When they do thaw in the summer, the water doesn't drain away because of the permafrost under the surface. Permafrost, as the term implies, never thaws.

After the first few days, they were very fortunate with the weather. The day after they arrived, rain and snowstorms moved in for three days and made flying impossible. A high pressure system and southerly winds finally forced the ice pack northward, and the weather was good VFR the rest of the time.

The only restrictions to visibility were low clouds that appeared when the sun was low on the northern horizon at "night." Luckily, these were thin and patchy and dissipated early in the day. The rest of the day the weather was CAVU and cold. Although the sun shone for 24 hours every day, a persistent 10- to 15-knot wind made down parkas a constant requirement. In the clear, unpolluted Arctic air, the visibility really was unlimited.

On July 18th, the pilot returned to Anchorage to pick up his Barrow friend's brother, sister-in-law, and two small children.

On July 21st, they took off from Merrill Field for Barrow, with stops in Nenana and Bettles for fuel. In Bettles, the pilot learned there was a slight chance of fog at Barrow. While flying in and out of Barrow, he had often seen the fog lay just off the coast during the middle day and sometimes slide in over land during the cooler evening hours. He wasn't too concerned about it moving in over the airport before they arrived at 1900. Besides, since he had planned on taking full fuel at Bettles anyway, there wasn't much else he could do about the fog. By the time they were within range of the Barrow Flight Service Station and would be able to get the actual weather, they would be out of range of any alternates that had fuel. It was simply a calculated risk that had to be taken if one wanted to fly to Barrow in a light airplane.

THE FOG ROLLS IN

They took off and flew northward. One hundred miles from Barrow, the northern horizon was a solid white line, but it was impossible to tell if it were low clouds or the polar ice cap. A few minutes later Flight Service told them the fog was over land, but the runways were still in the clear. Thirty miles from Barrow, small puffs of fog hung low over the ground and gradually coalesced into a solid layer with tops about 500 feet. From 3,000 feet and 10 miles out, the pilot realized Point Barrow peninsula was totally obscured.

The Flight Service Station reported a ceiling of 150 to 200 feet and visibility one mile at the airport. The ILS to runway 06, the approach with the lowest landing minima, had a decision height of 200 feet. That was going to make it a very interesting approach.

As they flew over the NDB at the field, the pilot saw that the Chukchi Sea west of the airport was in the clear. Barrow is on a section of land that forms an almost perfect right angle pointing to the north. On the eastern side of the right angle is the Beaufort Sea; on the western side is the Chukchi Sea. The airport is on the western side of the point of land. The northeasterly wind had blown the fog from the ice cap over the town and the airport, but the topography of the area had kept the fog from forming to the west over the Chukchi Sea.

The day he had flown touch-and-goes in the traffic pattern to check out the purity of his fuel, the pilot had also flown a practice ILS to runway 06. He noticed that the final approach course was clear of obstacles all the way to the runway threshold. Runway 06 at Barrow begins about a mile from the edge of a low cliff. Field elevation is 44 feet. He had decided he could use that approach down to 150 feet if he ever got caught by weather. He didn't relish the idea of busting minima, but it was better than running out of gas over the tundra.

Most of the time when an airport has a 200-foot ceiling and less than a mile of visibility, it makes sense to fly an instrument approach. But there are times when it doesn't. This was one of them. The entire course-reversal procedure was in the clear, but if the pilot flew down the glide slope he'd enter the clouds at 500 feet and might not see the runway at decision height.

The pilot flew west over the water, descended to 200 feet in good VMC, and turned back toward the airport. He saw the cliff as soon as he turned toward the airport and knew he was home free.

He descended to 150 feet just as they flew over the cliff and under the fog bank. The approach lights immediately appeared below them and seconds later he saw the runway. The final approach angle was flatter than normal, but the landing uneventful. After slightly more than seven hours of flight time in bright sunshine, fog-enshrouded Barrow seemed almost like another world. The pilot decided he'd had enough flying for the day.

ANALYSIS

Flying is risky, which means that the only way you can be sure you'll never have problems is to not fly. We make decisions based on the best available information, on our experience, and on probabilities. Sometimes the probability is 99 percent that the weather will hold; usually it's less. But even if the probability is 99 percent there's still that 1 percent. If you fly often enough, you'll hit an improbable event some day.

The way you guard against the improbable is to have a way out. Always. Sometimes the way out is as simple as adding extra fuel. Sometimes it's a last-minute check of the weather. Sometimes it's waiting an hour for a storm to pass. Sometimes the only way out is not to go at all.

In this case the pilot wrote his escape clause by checking out the ILS approach at Barrow before he actually needed to fly it and figuring out a way he could safely come in below minima. It's always smart to fly an instrument approach VFR before doing it on the gauges because it can be very educational, but constructing one's own instrument approach procedure or modifying an existing one is frowned upon by the FAA.

Granted, the procedure saved the pilot this time. He didn't have much choice when the fog moved in over Barrow. Experience from the previous three weeks of flying had caused him to become complacent about the fog. He figured it would stay off the coast, even though the weather reports mentioned a chance of it moving over land. What he didn't figure on was the way a change in the wind direction would affect the fog.

On the other hand, the idea of checking out a safe route and altitude between two points you often fly isn't such a bad one. It may save your bacon some day. By devising your own low visibility route for use only in an emergency, you may be able to do safely and legally what the FAA allows you to do legally. (Just because the FAA allows you to do something legally, doesn't necessarily mean it can be done safely.) In uncontrolled airspace, the FAA allows us a good deal of free rope. Just enough rope, some say, to hang ourselves. It's a lot better to fly over a personal route and at an altitude you know is safe than to muck around over uncharted territory trying to stay clear of obstacles you don't know about.

In the final analysis, it's probably better to have some kind of option in your back pocket (even if it does bend the regs a little), than no option at all. At worst, you may end up with your license suspended, but at least you'll still be alive.

Realize, however, that custom-made procedures are really dangerous when they start to become the norm instead of the exception. The attitude, "I did it once, I can do it again," is readily accepted by the macho quirk found in the personalities of most pilots, male or female. Worse, such an attitude easily leads to the even more dangerous "I did it before at 300 feet, I can do it again at 200 feet" attitude. When you find yourself using your emergency route more than once in a blue moon, take a mental step back and figure out why you're getting yourself into such tight spots to begin with. Chances are you'll find you've become a bit too careless or complacent about something and it's time to clean up your act.

20
Tips on How
Not to Get Lost

THE PRIMARY PURPOSE OF ANY CROSS-COUNTRY FLIGHT IS TO ARRIVE AT the desired destination. We look at our charts, draw a more or less straight line from point A to point B, and then try to fly that route with as much precision as possible. Considering that practically every aircraft used for cross-country flying these days is equipped with at least one navigation radio, and with the profusion of electronic nav aids all over the country, it would seem to require considerable genius to get lost. But the fact is that pilots, even experienced pilots, get lost every day, and time and again, FSS specialists and ATC controllers get frantic calls from VFR pilots who haven't the faintest idea where they are.

The most frequent error made by these pilots is to depend on only one indication at a time, without cross-checking to make sure that the indication—be it an OBI reading or a landmark on the ground—is, in fact, correct. For example, I once flew a rented aircraft from Los Angeles to Kerrville, Texas. Unbeknownst to me, both the magnetic compass and the VOR receiver were unreliable, giving readings a considerable number of degrees off the correct direction. After using these instrument readings for some time I suddenly realized that what I was looking at on the ground bore no resemblance to what was indicated on the chart. It took a while to get reoriented and back on course. In that instance, if I had bothered to pay attention to the landscape below, I would immediately have realized what has happening and could have saved myself a lengthy detour.

Even when the nav receiver in the aircraft functions properly and when the compass gives the correct readings, it is possible to tune to a VOR and use it for navigational guidance without realizing we are tuned to a different VOR than we thought we were. We should always listen to the VOR identification—regardless of whether flying VFR or IFR—be it voice or in Morse code, to make sure that the indication we are receiving is derived from the right station.

PROPER CHARTS

Having become used to using the VOR network as our primary means of navigation, most of us have become rather lazy and unaccustomed to flying by pilotage (FIG. 20-1). And many of us, even when flying VFR, will use the low-altitude radio facility charts, either leaving the Sectionals or WACs at home or rarely referring to them. Then comes that inevitable day when the radio decides to give up the ghost or the overcast is so low that we have to fly right down on the deck where reception distances are severely restricted (FIG. 20-2). When that happens, all that is left for us to navigate by is what we can see on the ground. For this we have to have the Sectionals or WACs (preferably Sectionals). The trick here is never to assume that a given road, railroad, or other landmark on the ground is the one we are looking at on the chart (FIG. 20-3). Even two related landmarks—such as a highway crossing a railroad, or some such—are not absolute proof that it's what we think it is. Whenever using the VFR charts in order to fly by pilotage, we should make it a hard and fast rule to look for at least three related features, compare their positions to those indicated on the chart and, if they

Fig. 20-1. *Most of us have become unaccustomed to flying by pilotage.*

Fig. 20-2. *When flying low, all reception capability may be lost.*

match, only then can we be reasonably certain that we actually are where we think we are.

Similarly, if we have been flying above a scattered or broken overcast that appears to be turning solid ahead, we may want to get down below before getting stuck on top with no way down. Having used VORs for navigation we may know that we are somewhere along a given radial or bearing, but unless we've been keeping careful track of our ground speed and the time at which we crossed the last nav aid, (something that is unlikely unless our aircraft is DME equipped), we won't have a clear idea of our position once we get down below the overcast. Also, in order to take advantage of the breaks in the overcast, we probably flew a series of turns while descending, thus further increasing the uncertainty about where we are. If we can spot a group of distinct landmarks, fine. If not, a good practice is to follow a road or highway to the next little town. Most smaller towns and villages have a water tower that is easy to spot and usually has the name of the town or village written on one side. Just fly around it, read the name, and then find the appropriate location on the chart.

One of the most ideal conditions for getting lost is a low overcast combined with

Cessna Aircraft Company

Fig. 20-3. *Never simply assume that a given road is one you are looking at on the chart.*

Fig. 20-4. *A good Loran-C receiver can help make getting lost a thing of the past.*

intermittent rain showers. In order to avoid flying right through the showers, which often severely limit visibility, we tend to turn this way and that, and eventually we haven't got the faintest idea where we are and what exact heading we need to fly in order to get to where we want to go. This is the sort of situation in which it becomes a good idea, if we happen to spot an airport or landing strip, to simply land and ask, "Where am I?" One can end up burning an awful lot of fuel down at that low altitude just scooting around trying to get located without ever picking up a VOR signal or finding a foolproof landmark.

At night the difficulties multiply. More than half the landmarks that can be identified easily during the day disappear completely after dark. What remains are towns and cities, which sometimes, though not always, can be identified by their general shape. And there are highways that can be counted on to carry traffic at all hours. One of the best means of determining location (assuming, of course, you know where *you* are!) is to relate the location of airports to nearby cities or towns. While airports are often hard to spot in the daytime, they suddenly begin to stand out after dark, whether because of the rotating beacon or because of the row of parallel runway lights.

KEEP TRACK

Whether during the day or at night, it is always a good idea to continually keep track of the position of the airplane. Granted, as long as everything continues to work just fine and the weather doesn't hold any unpleasant surprises, simply knowing that one is on course somewhere between here and there would seem to suffice. But the moment something unexpected happens to either the airplane, the pilot, or the weather, then the certain knowledge of the aircraft's exact position at that particular moment can become vitally important.

The fact remains that the only possible way to get lost is to stop paying attention for any length of time. Any pilot who makes it his business to always know where he is can't possibly get lost.

BUY A LORAN-C RECEIVER

For a comparatively small investment, you need never get lost again; $1,000 will buy you a cockpit-mounted or portable Loran-C receiver, and $500 will buy you a hand-held Loran-C receiver. With the geographical coordinates of your location from the Loran and a Sectional chart, you can pinpoint your position with unbelievable accuracy. It's as simple as that. It may not be as macho as map reading and dead reckoning, but it sure beats getting lost, busting airspace, or making an unintentional off-airport landing (FIG. 20-4).

One last piece of advice: When you find that you're lost, don't wait until you're about to run out of fuel before asking for help. Regardless of altitude, there is always someone who can be reached by radio. If high enough, a call in the blind on 122.1 will most likely bring an answer from some FSS. If too low to reach any of the VORs, tune to the center frequency for the approximate sector in which you believe yourself to be. While you may not be able to reach the center itself, you can probably reach an airliner or other IFR traffic flying at higher altitudes and ask them to relay the pertinent information relative to your predicament. The important thing is to ask for help early and not wait until it's too late for anyone to give assistance.

21
Overwater Flying

IF YOU FLY ONLY IN THE CONTINENTAL UNITED STATES, YOU MAY NEVER need to fly overwater for any extended period of time. On the other hand, if you've ever thought of flying to the Bahamas or one of the islands in the Caribbean, you certainly will find yourself over the sea for quite a while (FIG. 21-1). Sometimes even in the Continental United States, the most logical route is along the coast or over a large lake. Whatever the reason for flying overwater, additional precautions should be taken.

First of all, filing a flight plan is always a good idea for extended overwater flights. If your route takes you into the Coastal or Domestic ADIZ/DEWIZ, filing a flight plan—the so-called Defense VFR (DVFR) flight plan—is required for security reasons. If you do have to ditch, a filed flight plan is your best insurance that someone will note your absence, sooner than later, and send out an alert. Search and rescue procedures are started one-half hour after your estimated time of arrival if your flight plan isn't closed or canceled. Because the probability of survival after a ditching decreases rapidly over time, the sooner rescue services start looking for you, the greater your chances of surviving.

A general rule for short overwater flights is to fly high enough to be within gliding distance of land. Obviously, this is not always possible. For one thing, you simply may not be able to fly high enough because of weather or the operating capability of the

Fig. 21-1. *If you fly to the Bahamas or one of the islands in the Caribbean, you'll find yourself overwater for a good part of the flight.*

airplane; for another, the land within gliding distance may be steep, rocky, or otherwise unsuitable for a power-off landing. The only way to mitigate the dangers of a ditching is to carry emergency equipment along with you.

OVERWATER SURVIVAL EQUIPMENT

Strangely, the FARs do not specify any particular requirements for single-engine aircraft operating under Part 91 when flying overwater. Perhaps the Feds don't expect anyone to do it. Paragraph 91.509 "Survival equipment for overwater operations" applies only to large and turbine-powered multiengine airplanes. This can, at least, be used as a guide if you plan to fly overwater often.

For flights that take a multiengine airplane not more than 50 nautical miles from the nearest shore, FAR 91.509 requires that a life preserver or other suitable flotation device (for example, a floatable seat cushion) be carried on board for each occupant.

For overwater flights that last more than 30 minutes or are 100 nautical miles or more from the nearest shore, large and turbine-powered multiengine airplanes are required to carry the following: 1) a life preserver with an approved locator light for each occupant; 2) enough life rafts to accommodate all occupants; 3) at least one pyrotechnic signaling device for each life raft; 4) an independent, floatable, water-resistant emergency radio signaling device; 5) a lifeline; and 6) a survival kit attached to each life raft.

Fifty miles to the nearest shore is a long way to swim—even with a life preserver. So is 25 miles, 10 miles, or even 3 miles. When was the last time you swam a mile? Unless you happen to be a triathalon nut, you probably haven't done it (if ever) since you were a Boy Scout or in the military, and then it was probably in a swimming pool. Swimming in the open sea or a large lake is a lot different.

For anyone contemplating a long flight overwater, life vests *and* a life raft are absolute musts if you want to have any chance at all of surviving a ditching. I consider a long flight one that takes you further from shore than the sum of your airplane's gliding distance and the distance you are able to swim.

Even if you're an excellent swimmer and in superb physical shape, don't forget about hypothermia. No matter the water temperature, your body will lose heat to the sea if you don't get out of the water and into a life raft.

It's a matter of basic physics. The thermal conductivity of water is 240 times greater than that of still air. This means that water, or wet clothing, can extract heat from your body up to 240 times as fast as from dry clothing. The colder the water, the faster you lose body heat.

In 40°F water your effective time is not much more than 30 minutes. After two hours, you have a 99 percent chance of being dead (FIG. 21-2). Even in water warm

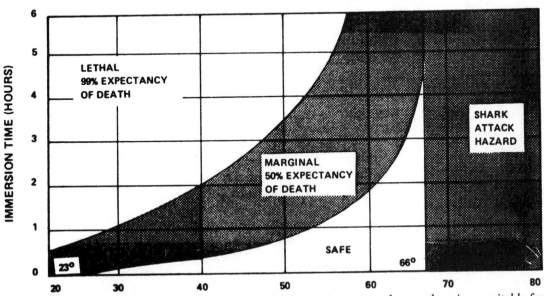

Fig. 21-4. *Ditching may be your only alternative if the coast is steep, rocky, or otherwise unsuitable for a power-off landing.*

enough to comfortably swim in, the average person can't last much longer than 12 to 15 hours before hypothermia sets in. Without a life raft, a life vest only prolongs the agony.

If you have to make a long flight over cold water, seriously consider taking along, or even wearing, a survival suit because wet clothing is almost as bad as being immersed in water. When clothing gets wet, it no longer provides an insulating layer of warm air next to the skin. Instead, it rapidly conducts heat away from the body and dissipates it to the outer environment. Wet clothing is like a wick. If a cold wind is blowing, this "water chill" will dissipate heat much more rapidly than the body can produce it.

Survival suits vary in price and sophistication from relatively inexpensive "rubber balloon" suits that are designed to be carried in a small bag and donned just prior to or after ditching to the more expensive full-fledged flight suits with fire-resistant NOMEX outer layers and breathable, waterproof inner linings. Realize, however, that even the best water survival suits cannot prevent heat loss if a person is immersed in very cold water over an extended period of time. The only sure way to protect against hypothermia is to use both a survival suit and a life raft.

Another important reason for using a life raft is that it is much easier for rescue aircraft to spot a life raft than a person floating in the water with only a life vest. If there are any waves at all, it's nearly impossible to find someone in a life preserver unless you happen to fly right over him.

Which brings up the question of signaling devices. Ninety-nine times out of 100 you will see or hear a boat or aircraft long before the crew in that boat or aircraft see you, even if they are searching for you. Maybe the ratio is closer to 999 times out of 1,000. Whatever. The point is your rescuers will find you much faster if you help them by signaling.

The best way to bring rescue craft to your location, of course, is with an emergency radio. Unfortunately, these are relatively expensive, but one may well be worth the cost and peace of mind if you plan to do extensive overwater flying. They can be tricky to operate, however, so if you can afford to buy one, be sure to read and understand the instructions before you need to use it. And don't forget to buy an extra set of batteries and keep all of them charged.

Less expensive signaling devices include mirrors, flares, and sea dye. Some life rafts come with survival kits that have all three. If yours doesn't, it's worth buying the ones it lacks because all three types are useful in different situations.

Mirrors reflect the light of the sun toward an airplane or boat and are very effective in most daylight conditions, unless the sun is totally obscured. In certain light conditions, a mirror may be more effective than any other signaling device, even a radio. Good signal mirrors are made of rust-free metal and come with a sighting hole that helps aim the reflection. Of course, in a pinch any shiny material can be used to reflect the sun, even a piece of broken glass. For the money, though, a signal mirror is probably the best signaling device you can buy: it never wears out, has no breakable parts, always works when the sun shines, and is very effective (FIG. 21-3).

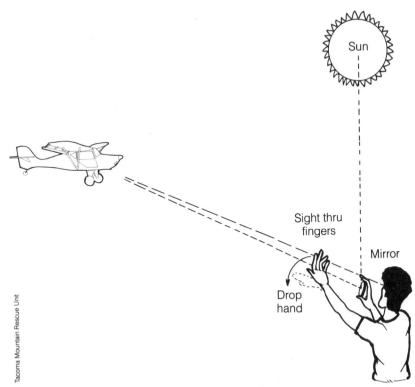

Tacoma Mountain Rescue Unit

Fig. 21-3. *The correct way to use a signaling mirror.*

Flares come in two types, day or night; but each type can be used whenever. The basic difference is that day flares put out more smoke than light, whereas night flares put out more light than smoke. Obviously, if you've used up all your night flares, popping a day flare at night is better than doing nothing at all. It may make the difference between being seen and not being seen because a day flare will produce some light. The reverse is true for night flares during the day.

You can buy hand-held flares and projectile flares. Again, both are worth taking along. Projectile flares obviously permit you to advertise your position to a greater distance, while hand-held flares pinpoint your exact location. Smoke from a hand-held flare also shows the wind direction, which will help the pilots flying the helicopter on its way to rescue you.

Sea dye may not seem like a very effective signaling device, but because it makes such a big "spot" in the water—much bigger than either a life preserver or a life raft—it can really help searching aircraft find your position. Depending on sea conditions, sea dye may last much longer than a flare and has even proven to be a shark repellent in some instances. However, since you have no way of knowing how long the dye will actually hang around your position until you put it in the water, it's best to wait until you actually see an aircraft approaching your vicinity before using it.

Although the danger of shark attack is extremely small, a person in a life raft will be much less attractive to a shark than a person treading water. Shark experts tell us it's the noise a swimmer makes (which sharks mistake for an injured fish) that attracts them—that and the smell of blood. If you're bleeding and treading water, watch out.

Remember, sharks, like people, prefer warm water (FIG. 21-2). The warmer the water, the greater the chance you'll find sharks. On the other hand, the colder the water, the greater the danger of hypothermia. The odds are against you no matter what the water temperature, if you're wearing only a life vest. Do yourself a favor: Buy a life raft . . . and a survival kit.

The contents of a survival kit will depend a great deal on where you'll be flying. Entire books have been written on the subject of survival, one of the best of which is the USAF *AFM 64-5 SURVIVAL* manual. Instead of going into details here, it's recommended that this manual be consulted and the individual decide what he wants to carry. (If you don't want to buy one, you can probably borrow one from your local library.) You may find that ready-made survival kits are sufficient for your needs. Or you may wish to customize a ready-made kit with additional items or make up your own (see Appendix D).

In general, a water survival kit will differ somewhat from a land survival kit. In a nutshell, your main concerns after a ditching will be to stay warm and to signal search aircraft and vessels. Fresh water is an important secondary concern, but you can survive a few days without it. If you filed a flight plan, you'll probably be found and picked up within 24 hours. Food is only a minor concern because you'll probably become sea-sick anyway, unless you happen to be a particularly hardy sailor. The possibility of administering first aid will be limited because everything will be wet. Plan on being uncomfortable. If you have the basics: a life raft, a protective covering, some signaling devices, and perhaps a bottle or two of water, you'll probably survive.

DITCHING

Ditching an airplane, any airplane, under any conditions is going to be tough (FIG. 21-4).

Think of it logically. How long did it take you to learn how to make a decent landing on a normal runway? Then how long did it take you to learn how to land on a short runway? A gravel runway? With a crosswind? How often do you make real "grease-on" landings? How often do you practice power-off landings?

Now think about how many power-off landings you've ever made on water with a landplane. Probably none. It's not a maneuver flight schools normally include in their training curriculum.

If you ever have to ditch, accept the fact that you're going to be a student pilot again. Not only that, you're going to be a test pilot, too, because no manufacturer sends test pilots out to land on water to determine the ditching characteristics of their landplanes. What happens to you after you hit the water is guesswork. Except for two things.

Fig. 21-4. *Ditching may be your only alternative if the coast is steep, rocky, or otherwise unsuitable for a power-off landing.*

One, the airplane will capsize; and two, the airplane will sink.

Bank on it. Bet your life on it. And prepare for it. If you do happen to beat the odds and find yourself right-side-up with the airplane still floating on the sea, you can just sit there smug and happy for a few moments before deploying your life raft. (Don't stretch the odds even further by believing your airplane will stay afloat for long.) But *plan* on being inverted after a ditching.

AIM (para. 462) gives a good deal of advice about how to ditch an airplane. If you have a photographic memory, you might recall some of it in the stress of the moment when your engine quits overwater 100 miles from the nearest land. If you're an average person, you probably won't remember much at all.

To counter brain-lock at such a critical moment, use some time before you take off to prepare a ditching checklist for your airplane and post it where you can find it quickly. Use the information in AIM and the following suggestions when you make your checklist.

In general, prepare as you would for a controlled crash on land.

Attain the lowest speed and rate of descent that permit safe handling, and turn into the wind. Wind direction is a "best guess" thing. If you have a LORAN, RNAV, or other navigation device that determines wind direction, use that. If you don't have such a device, line up with the wind streaks on the sea. It's easy to misinterpret wind streaks by 180°, so always maintain an awareness of the wind direction when flying overwater.

If you have retractable gear, leave it up. If you lower it, it will either shear off when it hits the water or will flip the airplane upside-down sooner than with the gear up. If you have fixed landing gear, you don't have a choice.

Make a quick MAYDAY call on whatever frequency you're monitoring. Don't bother to switch to 121.5 for your first distress call. Your best chance of someone hearing you is on the frequency you last communicated on. Repeat "MAYDAY" three times, give your call sign and position, and say you're ditching. If you have the time (i.e., altitude) to make two calls and no one has acknowledged your first call, then try on 121.5.

Put on your life vest, if you have time, and tighten your seat belt and shoulder harness.

As you descend lower, you'll be able to see the direction of the waves and wind much easier. AIM goes into much detail about oceanographic terminology—swell face, fetch, chop, etc.—and tells us, "It can be extremely dangerous to land into the wind without regard to sea conditions." Unfortunately, taking regard for sea conditions is not always easy.

To the landlubber, a wave is a wave is a wave, but strictly speaking, a wave is "the condition of the surface caused by local winds." A wave that is left over from a storm or is caused by a distant disturbance is called a swell. More than one swell condition can exist in one patch of water, and it's not uncommon for the wind-created waves to be going in one direction, the primary swells in another direction, and the secondary swells in a third. Add to this the fact that there are riverlike currents flowing in the ocean and you can begin to get an idea how complex the situation can become.

The main point to remember is to avoid hitting the face of a swell, which is the side of the swell toward the observer. In other words, don't land going into a wall of water.

This is much easier said than done. With the wind going in one direction and the swell going in another, you'll be making a crosswind landing to a surface that is moving both horizontally and vertically. As you descend just above the water, ground effect will alternately take hold and let go as the waves and swells roll beneath you. You can try, as AIM recommends, to land on a crest or on the backside of a swell, but chances are, even if you manage to do this, you'll meet the face of a swell sooner or later. The nose of the airplane will plow in, the airplane will do a somersault, and you'll find yourself with a fish-eye view of the ocean.

Now your main concern is escape. Unless the force of the ditching has broken the windshield, you'll be in a pocket of air inside the cabin. Release your seat belt and turn yourself right-side up. Grab your life raft and survival kit, and get ready to go swimming.

The force of the water will make it impossible to open the doors until the pressure inside and outside the cabin are equal. Water leaking in may equalize the pressure for you, but you can speed up the process by opening or breaking a side window.

Brace yourself to kick the door open, unlatch the door (or pull the emergency release), take a deep breath, and open the side window. As soon as enough water has entered the cabin to equalize the pressure, kick the door open, swim through the opening, inflate your life vest, and float to the surface. (Never inflate your life vest inside the cabin because it will make it harder for you to get out and may be punctured in the process.)

Most life rafts will float even before they're inflated, but it's a good idea to check this before you have to ditch or you may find yourself being pulled downward as you try to swim upward. If your raft does sink before it's inflated, pull the inflation lanyard after you exit the aircraft (never before, unless you're floating upright on the surface in a calm wind) and hold on tight to the cord. In strong winds, inflated life rafts have a tendency to fly like kites and, if you don't hold onto the lanyard, your raft will scoot away from you faster than you'll ever be able to swim after it.

Climb into the raft, get your signaling devices ready, and wait.

Doing this maneuver right the first time without ever having practiced it is going to take a lot of luck. For pilots who do much overwater flying and want to improve their odds of surviving a ditching, there are schools that specialize in underwater egress training. The courses don't take longer than a day or two, are not overly expensive, and are the closest thing to real ditchings most of us will ever want to experience. Few people enjoy training in a "dunker," but if you ever do have to make a real ditching, a couple of practice ditchings in a swimming pool could well make the difference between being a survivor or becoming a statistic.

POINT OF NO RETURN (PNR)

Point of no return (PNR) is an ominous term often used by pilots on long overwater flights. Its actual meaning is much less dramatic than it sounds.

The point of no return is the point beyond which an aircraft will not have enough fuel to return to its point of origin. In other words, after passing the point of no return one is committed to continuing on to the destination. As a matter of interest, most offshore helicopter operators require their pilots to carry return-to-land fuel when flying to offshore destinations (FIG. 21-5). This means that the point of no return must always be at or past the oil rig or platform they are flying to.

To find the point of no return between two points, you need to calculate your ground speed both ways and your total endurance. The following equation applies:

$$\frac{GS(ab) + GS(ba)}{GS(ba)} = \frac{TE - reserve}{Minutes\ to\ PNR}$$

Fig. 21-5. *Many offshore helicopter operators require their pilots to carry return-to-land fuel and to determine their PNR and PET.*

where:
GS(ab) is ground speed from point A and point B,
GS(ba) is ground speed from point B and point A, and
TE is total endurance in minutes.
Reserve is fuel reserve in minutes.

For an example, let's say that the distance between A and B is 175 nautical miles. Ground speed from A to B is 130 knots and from B to A is 105 knots. Total endurance is 3:40. Reserve is 30 minutes. Therefore,

GS(ab) + GS(ba) = 130 + 105 = 235 knots
TE − reserve = 3:40 − 0:30 = 190 minutes

STEP 1. On a flight computer, set 105 on the inner scale under 235 on the outer scale. This establishes the ratio GS(ab) + GS(ba) over GS(ba) (FIG. 21-6).

STEP 2. Now find 190 on the outer scale. Below it on the inner scale is 85. This is the time in minutes it will take to fly to the PNR on the track A to B. Since the estimated time enroute from A to B is 1:21 (175 nm at 130 knots) and the time to the PNR is 85 minutes, or 1:25, we know that we

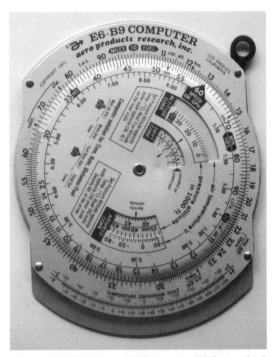

Fig. 21-6. *Establishing the ratio GS(ab) + GS(ba) over GS(ba), which is used for both PNR and PET calculations. In our example, we set 105 under 235.*

can fly all the way to B and still have enough fuel, plus a 30-minute reserve, to return to A.

STEP 3. To find the estimated time of arrival at the PNR simply add 1:25 to the time the aircraft passed over point A.

The calculations can be checked in the following manner. We have found that the PNR is located 1:25 from point A. At 130 knots, we will fly 184 nm in one hour and 25 minutes. If we fly all the way to this point, we should have just enough fuel to fly back to point A and still have our original 30-minute reserve.

One hundred eighty-four nautical miles at 105 knots gives 1:45 from point B to point A. 1:45 (B to A) plus 1:25 (A to B) equals 3:10 (total flight time). 3:10 plus 0:30 (reserve) equals 3:40 (total endurance).

Our PNR calculations are correct.

POINT OF EQUAL TIME (PET)

The point of equal time (PET) is that point between two points from which it will take the same time to fly to either point. If there is no wind, the point of equal time is halfway between the two points. If there is a tail wind between the point of origin and the destination, the PET will be closer to the point of origin. If there is a head wind between the point of origin and the destination, the PET will be closer to the destination.

The PET is useful if you encounter an emergency and want to land as soon as possible. Normally, you don't want to ditch unless you really have to, so the goal is to find the shortest route, in time, to a suitable landing site. Before reaching the PET, returning to your point of origin will get you on the ground sooner than if you flew to your destination. After passing the PET, continuing to your destination is the better course of action, all other things being equal.

To find PET, we use the same ratio on the left side of the equation that we used when figuring the PNR.

$$\frac{GS(ab) + GS(ba)}{GS(ba)} = \frac{\text{Total distance one way}}{\text{Distance to PET}}$$

To illustrate how to find PET, let's use the same conditions as in the PNR example.

STEP 1. Set 130 on the inner scale under 235 on the outer scale (FIG. 21-6).

STEP 2. Find the total distance one way (175 in our example) on the outer scale. Under it, read 78. This is a distance figure. It means that from point A to the point of equal time is 78 nm.

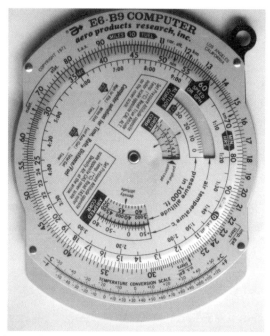

Fig. 21-7. *Calculating the time to PET by setting the black triangle under GS(ab), in our example 130 knots. We then read the time to PET (36 minutes) under the distance figure (78 nm) we found in Step 2.*

STEP 3. Now find the time to PET by setting the black triangle under the ground speed from A to B, 130 knots (FIG. 21-7). Find 78 on the outer scale and under it read 36. From Point A to PET is 36 minutes.

In checking our calculations, we know that from the PET it should take just as much time to fly to point A as it takes to fly to point B.

From the PET to point A the distance is 97 nm (175 nm − 78 nm). At 130 knots, this will take 44.5 minutes. The distance from the PET to point B is 78 nm. At 105 knots, this will take 44.5 minutes.

Therefore, our PET is correct.

22
Flight Number Eight

Date: October 24, 1974.
Pilot: Male, age 56, writer.
License: Private, MEL, instrument.
Pilot-In-Command Time: 4,015 hours.
Aircraft: Piper Cherokee Six.
Flight: From Santa Fe, New Mexico, to Cancun, Mexico, to New Orleans and back.
Purpose of Flight: To research an article about a new Mexican resort.

Technically, the flight started when the pilot received a long-distance phone call from New York from a person of whom he had never heard.

"We are wondering if you might be interested in flying a private airplane to Cancun and spend a few days there as our guest."

"Sounds lovely. What's a Cancun?"

The pilot had never heard of a place called Cancun and, therefore, didn't have the vaguest notion of where it might be. As it turned out he didn't have to feel self-conscious about his ignorance. At that time hardly anyone had heard of Cancun. Cancun, it was explained to him, is a small island off the far eastern tip of the Yucatan Peninsula, a place where the Mexican government had spent, and continues to spend, large amounts of money in an effort to develop it as a new luxury resort. The purpose of the sudden invitation was for the pilot to familiarize himself with the place and then to write about it.

The phone call was followed by a fat envelope in the mail containing information about a new international airport, hotels completed, under construction and planned, mean temperatures, average rainfall, and so on. There was also a map showing Cancun's relation to the mainland.

A date was then agreed upon, and the pilot obtained the charts that he figured he might need: Jeppesen Latin America High/Low Altitude En Route Charts #1, 2, 3, and 4, WAC charts #CH-23 and CH-24; and ONC charts #J-24 and J-25. He spread them all out on the floor in his living room, and it was then that he fully realized for the first time that this flight would require more than the average amount of preplanning. To put it bluntly, Cancun is one hell of a long way from Santa Fe, and much of that distance is covered with huge amounts of water.

Painstakingly measuring the total mileages for different routes of flight, he found that by staying over dry land most of the time, the total one-way distance would be 1,758 nm. In contrast, the shortest route, flying diagonally across the Gulf of Mexico, added up to 1,511 nm—of which 650 would be out of sight of land.

Well, for the roughly 250 nm difference he figured he'd rather take the longer route. Granted, he knew from experience that by throttling back to about 50 percent of power his Cherokee Six would burn about 69 pounds of fuel per hour, giving him a no-reserve range of 953 nm. This was certainly ample, but the idea of spending three-quarters of that time overwater didn't seem too appealing.

On the morning of October 24, the pilot stashed his luggage, the charts, and all necessary papers—such as a passport, a week's worth of Mexican insurance (obtained from Avemco Insurance Company), and documents attesting to the ownership of the aircraft—in the airplane. He then did a thorough preflight and took off toward El Paso and the Mexican border. He landed at El Paso to check with an FBO he had known for some years as to which might be the best place for the initial landing in Mexico. Told that Chihuahua (CUU) was probably as good a place as any, he filed the mandatory DVFR flight plan, took off, and headed south. He had, of course, obtained a weather briefing, which had called for high, thin scattered clouds and ample visibilities all the way to Chihuahua. He didn't bother to ask about the forecast for weather farther to the south, figuring that he would be able to get that once he landed there.

By the time he contacted CUU Tower he was about 10 minutes behind time. Apparently there had been head winds aloft that the fellows at El Paso had not known about. A lightly accented voice cleared him for a straight-in approach and, after touchdown, directed him to the Customs area.

The pilot, though reasonably fluent in three languages, spoke no Spanish and, in a manner typical of most Americans, had assumed that there would always be someone who spoke English. This turned out to be an overly optimistic expectation. Still, Customs itself was a breeze. The fellow at the counter, jabbering away in Spanish and obviously understanding little if anything of what the pilot was trying to say, gave no indication that he or anyone else would be interested in looking at either the airplane or the luggage. He simply handed the pilot a piece of paper, the significance of which he never did figure out, and then waved him on in the direction of some other office where a flight plan would have to be filed.

Having flown in Mexico some years earlier, he remembered that filing a flight plan is mandatory, whether IFR or VFR, and that those flight plans had cost some money. With this in mind prior to departure, he had changed several hundred U.S. dollars into Mexican pesos at the then applicable exchange rate of 12.5 pesos to the dollar.

In the Mexican equivalent of an FSS he was then confronted by two specialists who couldn't have been more friendly and helpful, although their command of the English language (if it can be called that) made communication somewhat inexact.

VFR FLIGHT PLAN

Unaware of the fact that he would be going from Customs directly to the FSS, he had left his charts in the airplane and somehow right at that moment, couldn't remember the distance to Veracruz (VER). But, being early afternoon, he felt certain that he wouldn't be able to get there before dark. He did remember from his previous sojourn into Mexico that flying VFR at night is against the rules and, somehow, the idea of flying IFR in a foreign country didn't appeal to him. He tried to get this across to those two guys as best as he could but, they kept shaking their heads and, as far as he could figure out, seemed to insist that Veracruz was only 450 miles distant. He finally went ahead simply and filed a VFR flight plan to VER, estimating his time en route as three hours. He also came away with the understanding that they had no information about the weather en route or at his destination. Well, he figured he'd find out what weather he'd run into once he did run into it. Once ready to leave, he had expected to be asked for some of those pesos, but nothing was said. Things apparently had changed and flight plans were now free, but the fuel to top off his tanks, 84 litres, came to 194.04 pesos or 81 cents a gallon—which may sound cheap today, but it wasn't then.

Once back in the air he leveled off at 9,500 feet and, with the autopilot locked onto the 130-degree bearing to the Delicias VOR (DEL), he proceeded to take a good look at his charts. Even a quick look reassured him that those fellows in the FSS had been all wet. The distance from CUU to VER was 775 nm, and at his estimated ground speed of 130 knots that would take just about six hours, putting his ETA at about 9 p.m. or so. Furthermore, considering the wild and apparently totally uninhabited landscape along his route of flight with only a few widely separated nav aids to help keep him on course, he felt that would put an unacceptable strain on his fuel reserves. So, what else was there not quite that far away? With all closer cities of any size being way off his course, Tampico seemed to him to be the only sensible destination. The distance to Tampico (TAM) added up to 563 nm or somewhat over four-and-a-quarter hours flying time. Not great, but better.

He had been flying for about an hour when the "hard VFR" weather conditions began to turn soft. The high scattered clouds had slowly coalesced into a solid overcast with occasional rain showers and reduced visibility to a not-too-comfortable degree. He had been locked onto the Torreon VOR (TRC) and now tried to contact TRC radio on a variety of frequencies, but there was no answer. After a while he gave up trying and called Torreon Tower instead. Here someone did answer, so he asked for the latest weather. This elicited information as to the active runway at Torreon. Repeating his request several more times, he finally got the information he was after: "Ten thousand overcast, visibility ten." He would have liked to know more about the expected weather along his route but, considering the difficulty of getting even this much, he gave up trying and flew on.

Looking down at the ground below confirmed what his charts had already told him. The country was not exactly studded with places to land in an emergency. For many miles he would more or less parallel the Sierra Madre Oriental mountain range, some of the peaks of which reached all the way up to over 13,000 feet. Eventually he would have to cross this range in order to get to Tampico and his chart, the ONC J-24, included this encouraging reminder: *Caution—Vertical errors in excess of 2,000 feet have been reported.*

TIME TO CLIMB

By now daylight was fading fast, but the overcast had stayed behind and the sky above was studded with stars but no moon. With apparently no one living or even driving an automobile anywhere around here, there was a near total absence of lights below and, once the sky had lost the last glow of daylight, the tall mountain tops to the left and in the distance straight ahead were barely discernible. Maybe it was time to climb to a higher altitude, one that would keep him safely above even the highest peaks and those 2,000-foot errors.

He leveled off at 13,500. There was no longer any VOR within reception distance and the only instrument offering any kind of reasonably valid position information was the ADF, which was tuned to the San Luis Potosi NDB (SLP). Long ago he had switched the VHF nav receiver to the TAM frequency, and he kept glancing at the OBI to see if, by any chance, the OFF flag started to show any movement. So far, no luck. His com radio was switched to one of the center frequencies on which various U.S. and Mexican airliners made intermittent position reports. Not only did this provide occasional entertainment, he also figured that if he should run into some unexpected problem they'd be able to hear him since he was able to hear them.

By now he knew that the highest part of the mountain range had to be close. He turned down the cabin lights to an absolute minimum and switched off the rotating beacon, which kept lighting up the wings and prop making it difficult to see anything in the blackness outside. And, sure enough, some minutes later he could make out rugged shapes moving below, indicating that he was crossing the ridge. Quite suddenly, things below turned to a kind of dirty gray: clouds. There was no doubt about his being atop a solid undercast and, with the topography from here falling off toward the Gulf of Mexico, it occurred to him that this cloud deck could easily continue all the way to Tampico and make an instrument approach inevitable.

He called the center frequency in hopes of getting some current weather information, but nobody seemed to be home. Again he glanced at the OBI just as the needle shuddered. According to his best guess he was still 100 miles or so from Tampico, but at this altitude some sort of reception just might be possible. He switched the com radio to the TAM tower frequency and turned up the volume on both the nav and com radios, hoping to stretch the reception distance to the maximum. The OFF flag was now dancing in and out of sight and the OBI needle began to react. Another six or seven endless minutes went by before the needle finally settled firmly, and he made a small course correction to point the nose of the airplane straight toward Tampico. Suddenly a voice boomed through the cockpit, forcing him to hurriedly reduce the volume. It was in Spanish and he didn't understand what was said, but he was certain that he was listening to Tampico Tower.

"Tampico Tower, November Three-Three-Zero-Five-Zero, over."

A heavily accented voice said to go ahead. He asked about Tampico weather and was given "Runway One Two." He asked again, and then again, and finally there was a garbled transmission ending in something that sounded like, "Breaks in the overcast." Well, that was all he had wanted to know in the first place.

HAPPY LANDINGS

Shortly after 7 p.m. a faint glow appeared at the horizon. He trimmed the nose down and watched the airspeed climb to just over 150 knots indicated. He was tired now and in no mood to throttle back and save a cupful of fuel. Soon occasional lights below showed that there were indeed breaks in the overcast, and eventually he flew through a great big hole right over the city and landed happily, but wearily, at General Francisco Javiar Mina International.

Having landed VFR at night at an airport other than the one indicated in his flight plan, he expected some static. But there was none. Some friendly fellow, who understood nothing the pilot said, closed his flight plan and then turned him over to the Hertz Rental Car girl who spoke English and, in answer to his question, suggested a taxi to the Holiday Inn.

The dinner was so-so, the room, a typical no-surprise Holiday Inn room, the convention noisy; the breakfast, okay; the service, good; the bill, 414.75 pesos or $33.18 American.

The same friendly fellow from the night before greeted him at the airport.

"To where?"

"Cancun."

"No."

"Why not?"

"Veracruz. No weather Tampico. Weather Veracruz."

"Weather by radio, yes?" The pilot was beginning to talk like the other one.

He hemmed and hawed, mostly in Spanish but, eventually, shrugging his shoulder in obvious despair, he shoved a flight-plan form at the pilot, saying, "Okay, Cancun."

He figured the time en route as five hours and, after he had signed the flight plan, the fellow took a pen and added all sorts of radio frequencies in the margin: *Mexico Radio 126.9; Mexico Center 118.7; Veracruz Radio 112.9; Veracruz Tower 118.5; Cancun Radio 113.4; Cancun Tower 118.6.* The pilot, of course, had most of these on his Jeppesens anyway, but it was nice to know that he apparently cared.

This time the airplane guzzled 232 litres at 535.92 pesos or $42.87, still 81 cents per gallon.

The local weather was scattered to occasionally broken at about 2,500 with no high tops anywhere. He climbed to 7,500 and headed somewhat south of the direct route to Cancun, psychologically compelled to stay within sight of land as long as possible. He also thought that he might be able to pick up Veracruz Radio and get an update on the nonexistent weather information in his possession. Then he changed his mind and climbed another 2,000 feet to 9,500 for better fuel economy and greater reception distance. It took quite a while but eventually he did reach Veracruz Radio and was given the weather for Merida (the reporting station closest to Cancun): 3,000 scattered, visibility eight. Fine. He could relax.

He made a course correction to the left and soon all sign of land retreated into the distance beyond the horizon. Checking his charts he figured that for most of the flight to Merida the northern coast of the Yucatan Peninsula would be some 100 to 150 miles south of his position—not much help in the unlikely event of an emergency—but he figured he might at least be able to pick up an occasional VOR or NDB from down there to give him some continued idea of his rate of progress.

LAND HO!

As best as he could figure, he was still two hours' flight time west of Merida (MID) when the ADF needle locked onto the MID NDB, pointing straight ahead. This being the first time that he had ever been overwater and out of sight of land for such a long time, he had expected to experience that well-known pilot phenomenon known as "automatic rough." He didn't. The engine kept purring smoothly, there was no turbulence and the weather was beautiful. Still, when the first sight of land finally came after all that water, he did feel a kind of warm pleasure in the pit of his stomach.

He passed over Merida; flew on over some long stretches of dense jungle; and, eventually, just about five minutes ahead of his ETA, there, under the nose of the airplane, was a straight tan slash like a just-healing wound in the dense green growth. Cancun International (FIG. 22-1).

"Cleared to land."

He tied his Cherokee Six behind a Cessna and between two Mexican Gulfstream IIs, got his luggage in order and out of the airplane, and closed his flight plan (FIG. 22-2).

Fig. 22-1. *Cancun from the air.*

Fig. 22-2. *On the ground at Cancun International Airport.*

His stay in Cancun was proof of the claims made in that packet of brochures that had preceded his trip. As it turned out he was the first, and at that time only, guest at the just-completed Garza Blanca luxury hotel, where he occupied a bungalow consisting of living room, bedroom, bath, and kitchen and overlooking the ocean (FIG. 22-3). He spent his time roaming the island from one end to the other as part of the research for what he would be writing once he got back home. It was, in fact, a truly beautiful resort even now, with many hotels, streets, and shops still under construction. His only reservation had to do with what it might be like in future years when, like so many such resorts, it might become overbuilt, overcrowded, and overpriced.

But, inevitably, every stay in paradise—even a paradise-under-construction—must come to an end. Back at the airport the inevitable number of Spanish-speaking officials affixed the usual array of signatures and stamps to a variety of mysterious papers, and for the first time since entering Mexico it was suggested that a tip might be in order. And then he filed the last of that never-ending series of flight plans (FIG. 22-4).

NEW ORLEANS

He had decided to return via a different route. The day happened to coincide with the first day of the National Business Aircraft Association's convention and exhibit

Fig. 22-3. *The Garza-Blanca Hotel at Cancun with its circular bar extending into the swimming pool.*

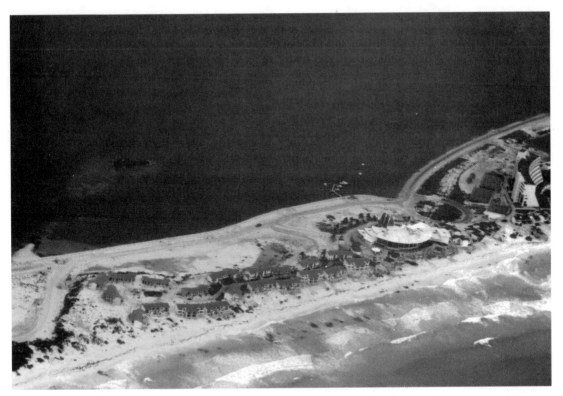

Fig. 22-4. *A last glance at the Garza-Blanca Hotel.*

which, that year, was being held in New Orleans and which he liked to attend whenever possible in order to gather material for his writing.

The straight route from Cancun to New Orleans is 528 nm, all overwater. He had briefly considered flying a detour eastward over Key West, Sarasota, and Tallahassee to New Orleans; but since that is over twice the distance, still includes some three hours of overwater flying, and much is either in or bordering on Cuban airspace, the whole idea seemed unappealing, so he filed his flight plan Cancun to New Orleans direct.

It did bother him a bit that no information about the current or forecast weather for his route or destination was available, especially since a minor tropical storm had been reported some distance west on the previous day and resulted in a fair amount of broken cloudiness in the area. The best he could elicit was that, once aloft, he might be able to contact Merida for weather information.

He leveled off at 10,500 feet after overflying Cancun for one last look and, occasionally looking back, watched the last glimpse of dry land disappear in the distance behind him. When Merida finally did decide to answer one of his often-repeated calls, the best information available was over four hours old but, at that time at least, New Orleans had reported clear and 15.

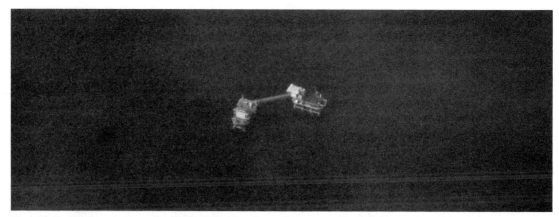

Fig. 22-5. *While crossing the Gulf of Mexico from Cancun to New Orleans, landfall is imminent when you see an off-shore drilling platform.*

The flight turned out to be less harrowing than he had expected. After barely an hour and still some 400 nm south of New Orleans, the Grand Isle NDB glued the ADF needle firmly in place, and within another 20 minutes he was able to read the transcribed weather broadcast through the static. He had to admit that he felt a degree of pleasure at once again hearing complete and detailed weather information and forecasts for dozens of reporting stations, not to mention the fact that New Orleans was still reporting clear and expected to stay that way.

Exactly three hours and 51 minutes after takeoff he spotted an off-shore drilling platform—the first sign that he was getting closer to shore (FIG. 22-5). Then soon, just a minute later than he had expected, there was land.

He called New Orleans only to find that they had no record of his flight plan. He explained where he had come from and that his eventual destination was the New Orleans Lakefront Airport and was told to contact New Orleans Approach Control for vectors to New Orleans International, where he would have to land in order to go through Customs.

Once on the ground he was told to stay by his aircraft until custom officials would come to meet him. He hoped it would be soon because by now his bladder was beginning to voice serious objections. Two men did arrive within minutes and it was a pleasure to be greeted in English.

"Gentlemen, I hope you don't mind. The plane is open for inspection, but I simply must find the nearest john."

They smiled and gave directions. After having heeded the complaints of his bladder, he returned to the airplane and then followed the inspectors to complete the formalities attendant with reentering the United States.

Though, once ready to leave New Orleans, there would still be roughly 1,000 miles of flying to be done before he got back home, the trip itself seemed somehow to have ended.

Appendix A
How to Obtain a Good Weather Briefing

A T THE PRESENT TIME, THE THREE BEST WAYS TO OBTAIN AUTOMATED weather information are the universal toll-free number for Flight Service Stations, 1-800-WX-BRIEF, the IOCS Voice Response System (IVRS), and the Direct User Access Terminal (DUAT) Service.

1-800-WX-BRIEF

WX-BRIEF will automatically connect you to the Flight Service Station serving the area from which you are calling. A Touch Tone phone isn't required, but it will make it possible to access tape-recorded weather messages. With a dial-type phone, you can still get a weather briefing, but you'll have to wait until a briefer is available.

With a Touch Tone phone, you simply punch "pound star" ("# *") followed by the numbers of the services you want. If you don't know what services are available, simply punch in the numbers for the "Main Menu of Services," which is usually "#*200." Be sure to have a pencil and paper ready to write down the menu, so that you don't have to go back to it again.

For example, the menu of services from the Williamsport, Pennsylvania, Automated Flight Service Station is as follows.

    #* 200   Main menu of services.
    #* 301   Harrisburg area weather.
    #* 302   Williamsport area weather.

#* 303	Wilkes-Barre area weather.
#* 304	Allentown area weather.
#* 305	Philadelphia area weather.
#* 306	Eastern Pennsylvania.
#* 325	Recording of special announcements and FAA Aviation Safety Seminars.
#* 401	Fast File of IFR and VFR flight plans with expected departure of less than one hour and cancellation of flight plans.
#* 402	Fast File of IFR and VFR flight plans with expected departures of more than one hour.

The first time you try, WX-BRIEF may take a few minutes longer than talking directly to a briefer, but once you learn how to use the system (and keep a copy of the menu), it goes much faster. Don't wait for a flight to try it. Do it now if you haven't tried it before.

You can also use WX-BRIEF to file and cancel flight plans, both VFR and IFR. "#* 401" is for Fast Filing of Flight plans with an expected takeoff in less than one hour and for canceling of flight plans. "#* 402" is for Fast Filing of flight plans with an expected takeoff time of more than one hour.

With Fast File, you are recording your flight plan on a tape. After you hang up, the Fast File machine signals the controller that there is a flight plan on the tape. He then listens to the tape and logs your flight plan into the computer. If you want to be 100 percent certain the computer has your flight plan, wait a few minutes, call up WX-BRIEF again, wait for a briefer, and ask him if your flight plan is on file. He'll probably confirm it and give you a three-digit number, which is the reference of your flight plan in the computer. You can speed things up when you activate and close your flight plan by telling ATC this number.

One tip: Sometimes a briefer will come on the line even though you have punched in the numbers for an automated weather briefing. This is to your advantage, of course, since he can give you more complete weather information and often you have to wait quite a while when you request a briefer directly. He'll also be able to take your flight plan, so it may be a good idea to have your plan ready to give him before calling up weather. Of course, the weather you receive may cause you to change your route, but it is easier to make a route change on a completed flight plan than on one you haven't started to fill out yet. Don't waste the briefer's and other pilots' time by filling out the flight plan as you talk to the briefer.

IOCS VOICE RESPONSE SYSTEM (IVRS)

Although owned and operated by Input Output Computer Services, the IOCS Voice Response System (IVRS) is based on FAA weather data. This automated weather briefing system is a computer network that continuously receives and stores aviation weather information from the Weather Message Switching Center in Kansas City. Eight weather products are provided by IVRS: Surface Observations (SA), Terminal Forecasts (FT), Winds Aloft Forecasts (GF), TWEB Route Forecasts (TR), Severe Weather Forecast Alerts (AWW), Convective SIGMETs (WST), AIRMETs (WA), and Nonconvective SIGMETs (WS).

You can access IVRS by calling 1-900-370-2424 anywhere in the United States. A call to IVRS costs $1 per minute.

With IVRS, you do need a Touch Tone phone because you must use the push buttons on the phone to respond to questions asked by the automated system. This makes it possible for you to tell the system exactly the information you want. (It is also possible to use a conventional dial-type telephone if you have an acoustically coupled tone signaling device capable of producing standard tones, but this is rather cumbersome. Do yourself a favor and buy a Touch Tone phone.)

IVRS uses the Touch Tone keyboard similar to the way many computer systems use typewriter keyboards. It takes some practice to get used to the IVRS codes and the way letters and numbers are entered into the system, but it's well worth the trouble to learn how to do it. After a few times using the system, it becomes second nature. You can get exactly the same information from IVRS as you can with WX-BRIEF, with the exception that you cannot talk to a weather briefer.

When calling IVRS, the first things you are asked to enter are the location identifiers of the airports for which you want weather information. You can choose up to 10 airports at a time. To enter the identifiers, you use the Touch Tone keyboard (FIG. A-1).

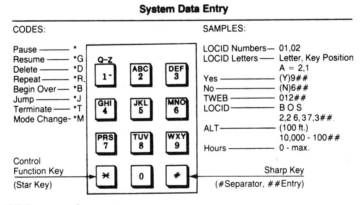

Fig. A-1. *IVRS system data entry.*

A standard Touch Tone keyboard has 12 keys. The keys 2 through 9 also have three letters each, arranged alphabetically. The numbers "1" and "0" have no letters, but for use with IVRS, the number "1" assumes the letters "Q" and "Z" because these letters don't appear elsewhere on the keyboard.

Obviously, since each of the keys (except "1" and "0") represents three letters and one number, a way had to be devised to tell the computer which letter or number you want when you press one key. The system that was selected requires that you depress two keys for each letter or number you want.

To punch in a number when keying in a location identifier, you must first depress "0" (zero) and then the desired number. To obtain a letter, you first press the key that has the letter you want, then you must check the position of that letter on the key to determine the second key you will depress. Since there are three letters on each key and three keys in each row, you depress the key in the row which corresponds to the *position* of the letter on the first key you depressed.

For example, the number "5" key contains the letters "JKL" in that order.

To get a "5" in a station identifier, you press "0" then "5."

To get a letter "J," you press "5" then "4" because "J" is the left letter on the 5-key and the 4-key is the left key in that row of three keys.

To get the letter "K," you press "5" twice.

To get the letter "L," you press "5" then "6."

After you have finished entering the three digits of each identifier, you depress "#" twice and the computer prompter will tell you the letters you entered. If you made a mistake, just try again.

When you are finished keying in the identifiers of all the airports you want, press "#" twice to tell the computer you are finished entering location identifiers.

The computer prompter will tell you if any Selected Weather Warnings exist, and if they do, will ask you if you want to hear them. You must answer yes or no by depressing "9##" for yes (the 9-key holds the letter "Y") or "6##" for no (the 6-key holds the letter "N"). Unfortunately, sometimes the computer has processing difficulties with Selected Weather Warnings and will state, for example, "A severe weather forecast alert exists but cannot be voiced." In this case, you'll have to obtain the severe weather forecast from another source (1-800-WX-BRIEF, ATIS, etc.).

After telling you about the Selected Weather Warnings, the prompter will ask you what kind of weather information you want: Surface Observations, Terminal Forecasts, TWEB Route Forecasts, or Winds Aloft. You answer yes ("9##") or no ("6##") to each of these.

When you respond "yes" to Winds Aloft, the prompter will ask you, "How many hours from now? The maximum is 12." Now when you key in a number, you don't depress the 0-key first, just the number you want followed by "##." For example, if you want the winds aloft in two hours, depress "2##." Next the prompter will ask you for the altitude you want for the winds aloft. Again, you do not depress the 0-key first, but only the numbers of the *Flight Levels* in hundreds of feet. For example, for winds aloft at 7,000 feet, depress "70##."

TWEB (Transcribed Weather Broadcast) Route Forecasts provide a forecast of weather conditions within a 50-mile corridor along a route and within a 50-mile radius for local vicinity forecasts. If you answer "yes" after the prompter asks you if you want TWEB Route Forecasts, it will respond by asking you for a TWEB Route number. These three-digit codes define a number of routes covering the Continental United States (FIG. A-2).

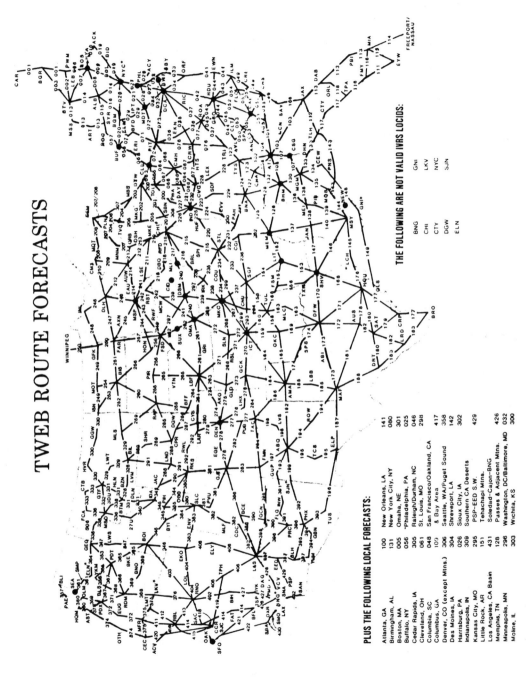

Fig. A-2. *TWEB routes for which IVRS provides forecasts.*

The *—key is used as a system control function key with IVRS as follows:

*   — pause briefing.

*G   — GO, resume briefing.

*D   — DELETE last entry, but only when the system is awaiting a response.

*R   — REPEAT report in progress or last entry.

*B   — BEGIN. Start the session over.

*J   — JUMP to weather for the next location or the next prompt.

*T   — TERMINATE the briefing.

*M   — MODE change. This is used to change the session to *nonprompted* mode, which allows you to enter strings of requests and receive multiple weather products for given locations and TWEB Route Forecasts without having to proceed through the entire prompted mode dialogue. It is about 50% faster than using the prompted mode, but not recommended until you have become comfortable with the system.

This may all seem quite difficult and confusing when you read how to do it, but if you just try it once or twice, you'll get the hang of it quickly.

Information about the system (including complete lists of location identifiers and TWEB Routes) is contained in a brochure entitled "Pilot's Guide to IVRS, An FAA Pilot Weather Information System." To obtain this free brochure or for assistance, call 1-800-for IVRS (In Massachusetts, call 1-800-451-1033) or write to Input Output Computer Services, 400 Totten Pond Road, Waltham, MA 00254.

DIRECT USER ACCESS TERMINAL (DUAT)

The Direct User Access Terminal (DUAT) Service is a service that allows U.S. certified pilots to receive weather briefings and file, amend, and close flight plans via personal computers or terminals free of charge. The service is funded, endorsed, and certified by the FAA as part of the National Airspace modernization program, making it different from other computer weather services that the user must pay for. To provide DUAT to all pilots across the United States, the FAA originally contracted three vendors: Contel Federal Systems, Data Transformation Corporation (DTC), and Lockheed DataPlan. Lockheed DataPlan was sold to Jeppesen in late 1989, became Jeppesen DataPlan, and was dropped from the program by the FAA in March 1990.

DUAT was scheduled to be on-line in the fall of 1989, but bugs in the system that cropped up during operational testing delayed its introduction by the two remaining vendors in February 1990. When fully implemented, the system will allow pilots to use the service at home, in an office, at an FBO, or wherever they have a modem and an IBM, Apple Macintosh, or compatible computer.

Each of the vendors is also tasked with providing user-friendly training packages and software to teach pilots how to use the DUAT Service.

To qualify for DUAT, a person must have at least a private pilot license and a current medical. At initial log-on, a menu leads the user through a registration process, after which an access code is issued.

Like any new system, DUAT has had and is having a few implementation problems. Student pilots, for example, are not able to log onto DUAT since they don't have a private pilot license. Some users have reported minor difficulties getting connected to DUAT. On the other hand, the flight plan filing function of both Contel and DTC have reportedly been working well.

A number of pilots have complained about the requirement to know and use three-letter identifiers for airports and weather stations. Others find it difficult to read the so-called domestic or airway code DUAT uses to report current weather and forecasts. Learning the code is not that difficult (weather questions using the code appear on every written), but if you haven't used it for awhile, it does take effort to decipher. For those pilots who really can't be bothered, there are software programs available that replace abbreviations and code words with more understandable full words.

Any pilot interested in DUAT should contact one of the vendors for their information packets. (Just in case the FAA permits Jeppesen DataPlan back into the program, their address is included, too.)

Data Transformation Corp.
10 Plaza Court
559 Greentree
Turnersville, NJ 08122
1-609-296-3232 (voice)
1-800-245-3828 (data)

Contel Federal Systems
15000 Conference Center
Chantilly, VA 22021-3803
1-800-345-3828 (voice)

Jeppesen DataPlan
90 Albright Way
Los Gatos, CA 95030
1-800-767-3828 (voice)
1-800-767-7000 (data)

Appendix B

How Reliable Are Aviation Weather Forecasts?

PILOTS SHOULD UNDERSTAND THE LIMITATIONS AND THE CAPABILITIES OF present day meteorology. Although meteorologists understand some atmospheric behaviors, they have watched the weather long enough to know that their knowledge of the atmosphere is far from complete.

The wise pilot continually views aviation weather forecasts with an open mind. He knows that weather is always changing and that the older the forecast, the greater the chance some part of it will be wrong. To have complete faith in forecasts is almost as bad as having no faith at all.

Studies of aviation forecasts conducted by the FAA have indicated the following:

1. A forecast of good weather (ceiling 3,000 feet or more and visibility 3 miles or greater) is much more likely to be correct than a forecast of conditions below 1,000 feet or below 1 mile.
2. If poor weather is forecast to occur within 3 to 4 hours, the probability of occurrence is better than 80 percent.
3. Forecasts of poor flying conditions during the first few hours of the forecast period are most reliable when there is a distinct weather system, such as a front, a trough, precipitation, etc. There is a general tendency to forecast too little bad weather in such circumstances.
4. The weather associated with fast-moving cold fronts and squall lines is the most difficult to forecast accurately.

5. Errors occur when attempts are made to forecast a specific time that bad weather will occur. Errors are made less frequently when forecasting that bad weather will occur during some period of time.
6. Surface visibility is more difficult to forecast than ceiling height. On the other hand, actual ceiling height is often more difficult to measure than visibility. According to ICAO regulations (but not FARs), a pilot may start an instrument approach to an airport if the visibility is reported above minimums; reported ceiling height need not be considered.
7. Visibility in snow is the most difficult of all visibility forecasts.

Forecasters *can* predict the following at least 75 percent of the time:

1. The passage of fast-moving cold fronts and squall lines within plus or minus 2 hours with as much as 10 hours in advance.
2. The passage of warm fronts and slow-moving cold fronts within plus or minus 5 hours, up to 12 hours in advance.
3. The rapid lowering of the ceiling below 1,000 feet in pre-warm front conditions within plus or minus 200 feet and within plus or minus 4 hours.
4. The onset of a thunderstorm 1 to 2 hours in advance, if radar is available.
5. The time rain or snow will begin, within plus or minus 5 hours.

Forecasters *cannot* predict the following with accuracy which satisfies present aviation operational requirements:

1. The time freezing rain will begin.
2. The location and occurrence of severe or extreme turbulence.
3. The location and occurrence of heavy icing.
4. The location of the initial occurrence of a tornado.
5. Ceilings of 100 feet or less before they exist.
6. The onset of a thunderstorm that has not yet formed.
7. The position of a hurricane center to nearer than 80 miles for more than 24 hours in advance.

The following story further illustrates the vagaries of weather forecasting.

At an Air Force station in Bodø, Norway, the pilots became disenchanted with the local meteorologist, whose forecasts, they complained, were more often wrong than right. They thought they could do better with their own predictions and devised a simple formula: They predicted that tomorrow's weather would be the same as today's!

Now the climate on the west coast of Norway probably has some of the most changeable weather in the world, so this was a rather risky way to make a forecast. But because most weather systems usually take more than a day to transverse the area, the pilots figured they had a fairly good chance of being correct.

Of course, when the weather did change, their forecast for that particular day was wrong, but then they would simply modify their forecast for the next day. Over a period of several months, the pilots ended up being right better than 50 percent of the time. Compared to the meteorologist, they had a better record.

The point of this story is not to suggest that you ignore the forecasts of meteorologists and blindly believe that tomorrow's weather will be the same as today's. The point is to encourage you to develop your own weather awareness, which you can supplement with the information you obtain from forecasters.

Realize that weather forecasting is fraught with so many variables that it's amazing meteorologists are ever right. Local topographical and man-made features can also create weather in small areas that is completely different from that which is observed and forecast at an airport less than a mile away.

Get a good weather briefing, but don't leave your personal knowledge of the local area, and your common sense, behind.

Appendix C
Airports with Mode-C Exemptions

IN THE SPRING OF 1990, AFTER MONTHS OF LOBBYING BY VARIOUS AVIATION organizations, the FAA granted some relief to the requirement, made effective on July 1, 1989, that all aircraft flying within 30 nautical miles of a terminal control area primary airport must be equipped with a transponder with Mode C capability.

The new rule affects some 299 airports that fall within the terminal control area transponder "veil." Flights must be conducted below specified altitudes and pilots are expected to fly into and out of the Mode C required area as quickly as possible.

The following is a list of airports that were expected to obtain the Mode C exemption from the FAA. Because changes are always possible, pilots should check Class II NOTAMs or telephone the airport to be sure that the exemption has taken effect before flying into the airspace without a Mode C transponder.

Atlanta TCA
   Remain below 1,500 feet agl
Air Acres Airport
B&L Strip Airport
Camfield Airport
Cobb County-McCollum Field Airport
Covington Municipal Airport
Diamond R Ranch Airport
Dresden Airport

Eagles Landing Airport
Fagundes Field Airport
Gable Branch Airport
Georgia Lite Flite Ultralight Airport
Griffin-Spalding County Airport
Howard Private Airport
Newnan Coweta County Airport
Peach State Airport
Poole Farm Airport

Powers Airport
S&S Landing Strip Airport
Shade Tree Airport

Boston TCA
Remain below 2,500 feet agl
Berlin Landing Area Airport
Hopedale Industrial Park Airport
Larson's Seaplane Base
Moore Army Air Field
New England Gliderport
Plum Island Airport
Plymouth Municipal Airport
Taunton Municipal Airport
Unknown Field Airport

Charlotte TCA
Remain below 2,500 feet agl
Arant Airport
Bradley Outernational Airport
Chester Municipal Airport
China Grove Airport
Goodnight's Airport
Knapp Airport
Lake Norman Airport
Lancaster County Airport
Little Mountain Airport
Long Island Airport
Miller Airport
U.S. Heliport
Unity Aerodrome Airport
Wilhelm Airport

Chicago TCA
Remain below 1,200 feet agl
Aurora Municipal Airport
Donald Alfred Gade Airport
Dr. Joseph W. Esser Airport
Flying M Farm Airport
Fox Lake Seaplane Base
Graham Seaplane Base

Herbert C. Mass Airport
Landings Condominium Airport
Lewis University Airport
McHenry Farms Airport
Olson Airport
Redeker Airport
Reid RLA Airport
Shamrock Beef Cattle Farm Airport
Sky Soaring Airport
Waukegan Regional Airport
Wormley Airport

Cleveland TCA
Remain below 1,300 feet agl
Akron Fulton International Airport
Bucks Airport
Derecsky Airport
Hunnum Airport
Kent State University Airport
Lost Nation Airport
Mills Airport
Portage County Airport
Stoney's Airport
Wadsworth Municipal Airport

Dallas-Fort Worth TCA
Remain below 1,800 feet agl
Beggs Ranch/Aledo Airport
Belcher Airport
Bird Dog Field Airport
Boe-Wrinkle Airport
Flying V Airport
Graham Ranch Airport
Haire Airport
Hartlee Field Airport
Hawkin's Ranch Strip Airport
Horsehoe Lake Airport
Ironhead Airport
Kezer Air Ranch Airport
Lane field Airport
Log Cabin Airport
Lone Star Airpark Airport

Rhome Meadows Airport
Richards Airport
Tallows Field Airport
Triple S Airport
Warshun Ranch Airport
Windy Hill Airport
Remain below 1,400 feet agl
Bailey Airport
Branson Farm Airport
Carroll Air Park Airport
Carroll Lake-View Airport
Eagle's Nest Estates Airport
Flying B Ranch Airport
Lancaster Airport
Lewis Farm Airport
Markum Ranch Airport
McKinney Municipal Airport
O'Brien Airpark Airport
Phil L. Hudson Municipal Airport
Plover Heliport
Venus Airport

Denver TCA
Remain below 1,200 feet agl
Athanasiou Valley Airport
Boulder Municipal Airport
Bowen Farms No. 2 Airport
Carrera Airpark Airport
Cartwheel Airport
Colorado Antique Field Airport
Comanche Airfield Airport
Comanche Livestock Airport
Flying J Ranch Airport
Frederick-Firestone Airstrip Airport
Frontier Airstrip Airport
Hoy Airstrip Airport
J&S Airport
Kugel-Strong Airport
Land Airport
Lindys Airpark Airport
Marshdale STOL
Meyer Ranch Airport

Parkland Airport
Pine View Airport
Platte Valley Airport
Rancho De Aereo Airport
Spickard Farm Airport
Vance Brand Airport
Yoder Airstrip Airport

Detroit TCA
Remain below 1,400 feet agl
Al Meyers Airport
Brighton Airport
Cackleberry Airport
Erie Aerodome Airport
Ham-A-Lot Field Airport
Merillat Airport
Rossettie Airport
Tecumesh Products Airport

Honolulu TCA
Remain below 2,500 feet agl
Dillingham Airfield Airport

Houston TCA
Remain below 1,200 feet agl
Ainsworth Airport
Biggin Hill Airport
Cleveland Municipal Airport
Fay Ranch Airport
Freeman Property Airport
Gum Island Airport
Harbican Airpark Airport
Harold Freeman Farm Airport
Hoffpauir Airport
Horn-Katy Hawk International Airport
Houston-Hull Airport
Houston-Southwest Airport
King Air Airport
Lake Bay Gall Airport
Lake Bonanza Airport
RWJ Airpark Airport
Westheimer Airpark Airport

Kansas City TCA
  Remain below 1,000 feet agl
Amelia Earhart Airport
Booze Island Airport
Cedar Airpark Airport
D'Field Airport
Dorei Airport
East Kansas City Airport
Excelsior Springs Memorial Airport
Flying T Airport
Hermon Farm Airport
Hillside Airport
Independence Memorial Airport
Johnson County Executive Airport
Johnson County Industrial Airport
Kimray Airport
Lawrence Municipal Airport
Martins Airport
Mayes Homestead Airport
McComas-Lee's Summit Municipal
  Airport
Mission Road Airport
Northwood Airport
Plattsburg Airpark Airport
Richards-Gebaur Airport
Rosecrans Memorial Airport
Runway Ranch Airport
Sheller's Airport
Shomin Airport
Stonehenge Airport
Threshing Bee Airport

Las Vegas TCA
  Remain below 2,500 feet agl
Sky Ranch Estates Airport

Memphis TCA
  Remain below 2,500 feet agl
Bernard Manor Airport
Holly Springs-Marshall County Airport
McNeely Airport
Price Field Airport
Tucker Field Airport

Tunica Airport
Tunica Municipal Airport

Minneapolis TCA
  Remain below 1,200 feet agl
Belle Plaine Airport
Carleton Airport
Empire Farm Strip Airport
Flying M Ranch Airport
Johnson Airport
River Falls Airport
Rusmar Farms Airport
Waldref Seaplane Base

New Orleans TCA
  Remain below 1,500 feet agl
Bollinger Seaplane Base
Clovelly Airport

New York TCA
  Remain below 2,000 feet agl
Allaire Airport
Cuddihy Landing Strip Airport
Ekdahl Airport
Fla-Net Airport
Forrestal Airport
Greenwood Lake Airport
Greenwood Lake Seaplane Base
Lance Airport
Mar Bar L Farms
Peekskill Seaplane Base
Peters Airport
Princeton Airport
Solberg-Hunterdon Airport

Philadelphia TCA
  Remain below 1,000 feet agl
Ginns Airport
Hammonton Municipal Airport
Li Calzi Airport
New London Airport
Wide Sky Airpark Airport

Phoenix TCA
> *Remain below 2,500 feet agl*

Ak Chin Community Airfield Airport
Boulais Ranch Airport
Estrella Sailport
Hidden Valley Ranch Airport
Millar Airport
Pleasant Valley Airport
Serene Field Airport
Sky Ranch Carefree Airport
Sycamore Creek Airport
University of Arizona, Maricopa
  Agricultural Center Airport

St. Louis TCA
> *Remain below 1,000 feet agl*

Blackhawk Airport
Lebert Flying L Airport
Shafer Metro East Airport
Sloan's Airport
Wentzville Airport
Woodliff Airpark Airport

Salt Lake City TCA
> *Remain below 2,500 feet agl*

Bolinder Field-Tooele Valley Airport
Cedar Valley Airport
Morgan County Airport
Tooele Municipal Airport

Seattle TCA
> *Remain below 1,500 feet agl*

Firstair Field Airport
Gower Field Airport
Harvey Field Airport

Tampa TCA
> *Remain below 1,500 feet agl*

Hernando County Airport
Lakeland Municipal Airport
Zephyrhills Municipal Airport

Washington TCA
> *Remain below 2,000 feet agl*

Barnes Airport
Davis Airport
Fremont Airport
Montgomery County Airpark Airport
Waredaca Farm Airport
> *Remain below 1,000 feet agl*

Aqua-Land/Cliffton Skypark Airport
Buds Ferry Airport
Burgess Field Airport
Chimney View Airport
Holly Springs Farms Airport
Lanseair Farms Airport
Nyce Airport
Parks Airpark Airport
Pilots Cove Airport
Quantico Marine Corps Air Field
Stewart Airport
U.S. Naval Weapons Center,
  Dahlgren Lab Airport

Washington Tri-area
> *Pending adoption: remain below*
> *2,000 feet agl*

Albrecht Airstrip Airport
Armacost Farms Airport
Barnes Airport
Carroll County Airport
Clearview Airpark Airport
Davis Airport
Fallston Airport
Faux-Burhans Airport
Forest Hill Airport
Fort Detrick Helipad Heliport
Frederick Municipal Airport
Fremont Airport
Good Neighbor Farm Airport
Happy Landings Farm Airport
Harris Airport
Hybarc Farm Airport
Kennersley Airport
Montgomery County Airpark Airport

Phillips Army Air Field
Pond View Private Airport
Reservoir Airport
Scheeler Field Airport
Stolcrest STOL
Tinsley Airstrip Airport
Walters Airport
Waredaca Farm Airport
Weide Army Air Field
Woodbine Gliderport
Wright Field Airport
Remain below 1,500 feet agl
Aviacres Airport
Birch Hollow Airport
Flying Circus Aerodrome Airport
Fox Acres Airport
Hartwood Airport
Horse Feathers Airport
Krens Farm Airport
Scott Airpark Airport

The Grass Patch Airport
Walnut Hill Airport
Warrenton Airpark Airport
Warrenton-Fauquier Airport
Whitman Strip Airport
Remain below 1,000 feet agl
Aqua-Land/Cliffton Skypark Airport
Buds Ferry Airport
Burgess Field Airport
Chimney View Airport
Holly Springs Farms Airport
Lanseair Farms Airport
Nyce Airport
Parks Airpark Airport
Pilots Cove Airport
Quantico Marine Corps Air Field
Stewart Airport
U.S. Naval Weapons Center,
   Dahlgren Lab Airport

Appendix D
Private Aircraft Survival Kit—Land

(Components of this vital kit may be found in most homes and garages.)

Container—Any lightweight metal container with lid, suitable to heat and store water.

Life Support Tools:
- Hack saw - Single handle with wood blade and metal blade
- Plier - vise grip
- Plier - slip joint
- Screwdriver set (multiple)

First-Aid Kit - Personal:
- Sealable Plastic Container
- 2 - Compress bandages
- 1 - Triangle bandage
- Small roll 2″ tape
- 6 - 3 × 3 gauze pads
- 25 - Aspirin
- 10 - Bandaids
- Razor blade or scissors
- Hotel size soap
- Kotex - purse size
- Kleenex - purse size, or toilet paper
- 6 - Safety pins
- 1 - Small tube of Unguentine or Foile

Shelters (minimum of 2):
- Large plastic sheets - 9′ × 12′ - Heavy gauge (one for each person) colored red or yellow preferred for signal panels

Food and Energy Package - 1 man 5-day rations

    2 or 3 cans of Sego, Nutriment or
        Metrecal for liquid and energy

    30 - sugar cubes - wrapped

    10 - pilot bread or 25 crackers

    10 - packets of salt

     3 - tea bags

    12 - rock candy

     5 - gum

    10 - bouillon cubes

    20 - protein wafers (if available)

Use poly bags for water storage.

Put each item in small plastic bag
    and seal. Put everything in
    small metal can (cook pot),
    seal with poly bag and tape.

Requirements for Life:

    Air

    Body shelter

    Water

    Food

    Will to live

You can live without it approximately

    3 minutes

    6 hours in severe weather

    3 − 6 days

    3 weeks

    ?

Life Support Kit:

    Waterproofed matches

    Candle or fire starter

    Signal mirror

    Compass - small

    Knife - Boy Scout style

    Insect repellent

    Mosquito net

    50′ 1/8″ nylon rope or shroud line

    Whistle

    Smoke flares or red day-nite flares

Courtesy of the Tacoma Mountain Rescue Unit

Glossary

ADF—Automatic direction finder.

AFB—Air Force Base.

agl—Above ground level.

Ambiguity meter—The TO/FROM indication in an omni-bearing indicator.

AOA—Angle of attack.

AOPA—Aircraft Owners and Pilots Association.

ARSA—Airport Radar Service Area.

ATC—Air traffic control.

ATIS—Automatic terminal information service.

ATL—Atlanta.

Avionics—Aviation radios.

BOS—Boston.

CAVU—Ceiling and visibility unlimited.

CDI—Course deviation indicator.

Cessna—Any aircraft manufactured by Cessna Aircraft Company.

Cherokee Six—A six-place, single-engine, fixed-gear aircraft manufactured by Piper Aircraft Corporation.

CLC—Course line computer.

Collins—Manufacturers of avionics. Collins Radio Division of Rockwell International.

Com—Communication radio.

Comanche—A high-performance, retractable-gear, single-engine airplane manufactured by Piper Aircraft Corporation. No longer in production.

Controlled airport—Airport with an operating control tower.

CUU—Chihuahua, Mexico.

Directional gyro—Gyroscopic compass.

DME—Distance measuring equipment.

Downwind (leg)—The portion of the landing pattern parallel to the runway opposite to the direction of intended landing.

DUAT—Direct User Access Terminal.

DVFR—Defense visual flight rules.

EAA—Experimental Aircraft Association.

EGT—Exhaust gas temperature (gauge).

ELT—Emergency locator transmitter.

Encoding altimeter—A means of automatically transmitting the aircraft altitude to ATC.

ETA—Estimated time of arrival.

ETD—Estimated time of departure.

ETE—Estimated time en route.

EWR—Newark.

F—Fahrenheit.

FAA—Federal Aviation Administration.

FAR—Federal Aviation Regulations.

FBO—Fixed base operator.

Foxtrot—In aviation-radio phraseology, the term used for the letter F.

FPM—Feet per minute.

FSS—Flight Service Station.

FTY—Fulton County Airport, renamed Charlie Brown Airport.

gph—Gallons per hour.

"Glass cockpit"—A cockpit equipped with flat, cathode-ray video screens instead of electromechanical flight and system instruments.

Ground speed—The speed with which an aircraft is moving across the surface of the earth.

Gulfstream II—A twin-jet corporate aircraft manufactured by Gulfstream American Corporation.

Gyro compass—Directional gyro.

Gyro horizon—Artificial horizon.

Hand-held transceiver—A portable, battery-operated VHF navcom.

HF—High frequency.

hg—Mercury.

Hood—A contraption worn by student pilots when practicing instrument flying. It blocks out the view through all windows but permits sight of only the instrument panel.

HSI—Horizontal situation indicator.

IAS—Indicated airspeed.

IFR—Instrument flight rules.

IFR conditions—Weather conditions that in terms of ceiling and/or visibility are below the minimums at which VFR flight is permitted.

ILS—Instrument landing system consisting of a combination of localizer and glide slope.

IMC—Instrument Meteorological Conditions.

in hg—Inches of mercury.

INS—Inertial guidance system.

Integrated flight control system—A combination of flight director and autopilot with one coupled to the other.

IVRS—IOCS Voice Response System.

JAX—Jacksonville.

JFK—Kennedy International Airport.

kHz—Kilohertz.

km— Kilometer.

Knots—Nautical miles per hour.

KNS 80—A combination RNAV and DME manufactured by King Radio Corporation.

kph—Kilometers per hour.

LA—Los Angeles.

LAX—Los Angeles International Airport.

lbs—Pounds.

LGA—La Guardia Airport (New York).

LOC—Localizer.

Loran-C—An area navigation system that computes position based on signals received from a primary and at least two secondary transmitting stations.

MCN—Macon.

MDW—Midway Airport (Chicago).

MEA—Minimum en route altitude.

MID—Merida, Mexico.

MLB—Melbourne.

Moving map—A type of navigational equipment that presents a picture of the landscape as the aircraft flies over it.

MP—Manifold pressure.

mph—Statute miles per hour.

msl—Height above mean sea level.

Narco Superhomer—A primitive navcom radio manufactured by Narco Avionics. No longer in production.

Nautical mile—6,076 feet, or 1.15 statute miles; equal to one minute of latitude.

Nav—Navigation radio.

Nav aid—A ground-based station used for navigation.

Navcom—A radio used for navigation and communication.

NDB—Nondirectional beacon.

Needle and Ball—A turn-and-bank indicator.

nm—Nautical mile.

Nonprecision approach—An instrument approach lacking vertical guidance.

OAK—Oakland.

OBI—Omni-bearing indicator.

OBS—Omni-bearing selector.

Omega—A system of long-range navigation using very low frequency radio transmitters for guidance.

OMN—Ormond Beach.

ONC—Operational navigation charts, scale 1:1,000,000.

ORD—O'Hare International Airport (Chicago).

Piper Cub—A single-engine, fixed-gear, steel-tube-and-fabric tail-dragger manufactured by Piper Aircraft Corporation.

pph—Pounds of fuel per hour.

Precision approach—An instrument approach that includes vertical guidance.

RMI—Radio magnetic indicator.

RNAV—Random Navigation systems. A generic term that originally applied to any navigation system that permitted point-to-point navigation, but which is now generally accepted to apply only to those systems that use VOR and DME signals.

RON—Rest overnight or remain overnight.

rpm—Revolutions per minute.

SEA—Seattle.

Sectionals—Sectional aviation charts; scale 1:1,500,000.

Service ceiling—The altitude at which an aircraft, at gross, will still climb 100 fpm.

SFO—San Francisco International Airport.

Sierra—In aviation-radio phraseology, the term used for the letter S.

Single-engine ceiling—The highest altitude at which a twin-engine aircraft can maintain level flight on one engine.

Skyhawk—A single-engine, fixed-gear aircraft manufactured by Cessna Aircraft Company.

SLP—San Luis Potosi, Mexico.

sm—Statute mile: 5,280 feet or .87 nautical mile.

SMO—Santa Monica Municipal Airport.

SST—Supersonic transport.

STOL—Short takeoff and landing (aircraft).

Super Puma—A large, twin-engine helicopter built by Aerospatiale of France.

Super Viking—A high-performance, retractable-gear, single-engine aircraft manufactured by Bellanca Aircraft Corporation.

Squall line—Solid line of thunderstorms.

S/VFR—Special VFR.

Tach—Tachometer.

TAM—Tampico, Mexico.

TAS—True airspeed.

TBO—Time between major overhauls.

TCA—Terminal control area.

TO/FROM Indicator—Ambiguity meter.

Transceiver—Aviation radio capable of transmitting and receiving.

Transponder—A cockpit instrument that responds when interrogated by a radar beam, causing the blip of the aircraft on the radarscope to stand out more clearly.

TRC—Torreon, Mexico.

Tripacer—A single-engine, fixed-gear aircraft manufactured by Piper Aircraft Corporation. No longer in production.

TRSA—Terminal Radar Service Area.

Uncontrolled airport—An airport without an operating control tower.

Unicom—A two-way radio operated by an FBO or airport manager, used to transmit advisory information to pilots.

UTC—Universal Coordinated Time, formerly GMT.

VER—Verarcuz, Mexico.

VFR—Visual flight rules.

VFR minimums—Weather conditions in terms of ceiling and/or visibility below which flight by visual flight rules is not permitted.

VHF—Very high frequency.

VLF—Very low frequency.

VMC—Visual Meteorological Conditions.

VNY—Van Nuys.

VOR—Very high frequency omnidirectional radio range.

VOT—Terminal VOR.

VRB—Vero Beach.

WAC—World Aeronautical Charts; scale 1:1,000,000.

Wing leveler—A simple autopilot capable of keeping the wings level.

Zulu—In aviation-radio phraseology, the term used for the letter Z.

Zulu time—UTC, formerly Greenwich Mean Time.

Index